D1736299

YOUNG ABOLITIONISTS

Young Abolitionists

Children of the Antislavery Movement

Michaël Roy

NEW YORK UNIVERSITY PRESS

New York

NEW YORK UNIVERSITY PRESS
New York
www.nyupress.org

Please contact the Library of Congress for Cataloging-in-Publication data.

ISBN: 9781479830091 (hardback)
ISBN: 9781479830121 (library ebook)
ISBN: 9781479830107 (consumer ebook)

This book is printed on acid-free paper, and its binding materials are chosen for strength and durability. We strive to use environmentally responsible suppliers and materials to the greatest extent possible in publishing our books.

Manufactured in the United States of America

10 9 8 7 6 5 4 3 2 1

Also available as an ebook

For Judith and Anna

CONTENTS

ILLUSTRATIONS

ABBREVIATIONS

AASS American Anti-Slavery Society

ASSU American Sunday School Union

GLBA Garrison Literary and Benevolent Association

JASSP Junior Anti-Slavery Society of the City and County of
Philadelphia

JGIS Juvenile Garrison Independent Society

MASS Massachusetts Anti-Slavery Society

NAACP National Association for the Advancement of Colored People

NYAFS New York African Free School

NYMS New York Manumission Society

SFASS Salem Female Anti-Slavery Society

Introduction

The hearts of those who are very young are often inclined to serious concerns.
—Susan Paul

Hal woke up early that day. It was the first of August, a date he knew was a holiday, though he was not exactly sure what it was for. Hal, his younger brother George, and their uncle and aunt set out for Dedham, Massachusetts, soon after seven and got there a little after nine. There were a great many people assembled before the town hall, some just arrived from Boston. Soon they formed into a procession and started to march to the music of a band made up entirely of children.

Hal watched from the sidelines, taking note of the banners and their inscriptions. "One had on it a fine figure of a black man," he later wrote his mother, "with his arms thrown up, exultingly, and his broken chains falling to the ground, and his foot upon a whip, the words over him were, 'This is the Lord's doing,' and underneath, 'Slavery abolished in the West Indies, August 1st, 1834, Laus Deo.'" Another asked, "Shall a republic which could not bear the bonds of a King, cradle a bondage which a King has abolished?" It was borne by a boy about Hal's age—thirteen-year-old Charles Christopher Follen, son of the German American abolitionist Charles Follen and the author of antislavery children's literature Eliza Lee Follen. The procession walked to a large pine grove half a mile off, where a platform had been raised and seats arranged as an amphitheater. There followed a succession of antislavery hymns and speeches, some of which Hal did not fully understand. Still, what he saw and heard had a strong effect on the boy. An account of enslaved people being sold to the highest bidder made his blood "run cold." An address given by "a man who had been a slave"—Lewis Clarke, a fugitive from Kentucky who in 1845 would publish the *Narrative of the Sufferings of Lewis Clarke*—was just as chilling: "Oh, dear mother, I never felt so slavery before." Yet perhaps there was something Hal could do against slavery, in spite of his young age. The presence of young Charles Christopher Follen on the platform, reciting lines from the antislavery poet John Greenleaf Whittier, suggested as much. "I think that if the men don't all do something about slavery soon, we boys had better see what we can do, for it is too wicked," he mused.

The celebrations lasted all day. A collation was provided by the organizers, much to everyone's delight. Before it was time to go, the company, which must have numbered around fifteen hundred, united in singing a final hymn. To Hal, it felt like a spiritual experience. He confided candidly, "I never had such a feeling of awe in my life." On the way home, Hal told his uncle what a beautiful time he had had. His uncle responded that the First of August was a glorious day to him—more glorious than the Fourth of July, because it celebrated a "bloodless victory," and it was won "by persevering love and justice, against selfishness and tyranny." "It is such a victory as this," he added, "that we abolitionists strive for, pray for, and are willing to suffer for."[1]

* * *

Hal never existed. Most of what precedes is taken from an epistolary short story by Eliza Lee Follen, "Pic Nic at Dedham," published in Follen's own juvenile magazine, the *Child's Friend*.[2] Hal's letter to his mother, dated August 3, 1843, was not pure fiction, however.

Known as Emancipation Day or West India Day, the First of August was widely celebrated among antebellum abolitionists, from 1834 onward, as the date when slavery in the British Empire legally ended. It was originally an African American celebration, but in the early 1840s, it was adopted by white abolitionists, who started organizing "antislavery picnics" on that day.[3] "Pic Nic at Dedham" was based on a two-part report of the Dedham festivities written by the abolitionist Maria Weston Chapman and published in the nation's leading antislavery newspaper, the *Liberator*; Eliza Lee Follen herself probably participated in the event.[4] The day unfolded exactly as narrated in the letter. The report also makes it clear that children attended the picnic with their parents or other family members. They included not only young Follen and the youths of the juvenile band, "with drum, trumpet and fife, cymbals and bugle," but also countless children like Hal and his brother who, during lunch, were allowed to mingle under the watchful eye of adults. The antislavery picnic was initially conceived as an event in which all—adults and children—could participate. Its instigator, John A. Collins, insisted that parents and teachers involve children in the preparations and the celebration itself. "Our enterprise is a school for the young," he wrote in the preface to The Anti-Slavery Picknick (1842), a volume directed at children. "It calls out the sympathies of their souls, and gives energy and life to all their faculties. It is pre-eminently adapted to their humane feelings and ardent temperament. There is no reason why the cause of perishing millions in our midst should not have their sympathies, their prayers, and their hearty co-operation."[5]

Collins was hardly alone in calling for children's participation in the abolition movement. Throughout the antebellum period, a number of abolitionists—the Liberator's editor, William Lloyd Garrison, and the African American primary school teacher Susan Paul, the white reformer Henry Clarke Wright and the internationally renowned activist Frederick Douglass—made similar appeals to children's antislavery sympathies. Children, they argued, had a natural detestation of violence and oppression. Presented with the facts of slavery, they would instinctively perceive the iniquity of such a system and might be persuaded to do something against it. "Should not all abolitionists take advantage of this peculiar tenderness of little children, to give them a just horror of slavery and the sin of slaveholding?" Wright suggested.[6] Likewise, children had a role to play in the fight against racial prejudice. Young children, abolitionists reasoned, did not "see" color. They did not identify as either Black or white, and white children did not consider Black children to be their inferiors. "Children are abolitionists in many important respects," wrote Wright. "They have no prejudices against color. To the artificial distinctions of society they are strangers."[7] Yet children would soon enough be apprised of these "artificial distinctions," with white children imbibing white supremacist ideas and Black children growing aware of their second-class social status. Abolitionists thus had to act quickly. They needed to expose even the youngest of children to antislavery and antiracist arguments so as to "fix in them an everlasting abhorrence of all cruelty and injustice."[8] Children embodied the promise of a US society refounded on anti-

rinciples. They were a canvas on which more mature activists
vision an abolitionist future. "If . . . we desire to see our land
uciivered from the curse of PREJUDICE and SLAVERY," Garrison declared in 1835, "we must direct our efforts chiefly to the rising generation."[9] His call did not go unheeded.

Antebellum abolitionists drew on modern notions of the child that
had emerged in the middle of the eighteenth century. John Locke and
Jean-Jacques Rousseau are commonly regarded as two of the most important theoretical influences in changing attitudes toward childhood.
As Steven Mintz explains in his authoritative history of childhood in
the United States, the child was increasingly viewed as an individual
distinct from the adult, and childhood, as a separate, formative stage of
life—a "highly plastic period when character and habits were shaped for
good or ill."[10] Americans became more attuned to children's needs and
potentialities. Opportunities for schooling expanded—a robust public
school system was established in the Northeast between the Revolution
and the Civil War, leading to rising literacy rates—as did a body of literature intended specifically for children. The new conception of childhood led to a changing social landscape in which northern middle-class
children spent more time at home or in school, reading, studying, and
playing.[11]

Abolitionists both benefited from and contributed to these developments. They paid significant attention to children, whom they realized
needed to be addressed in specific ways. Most discussions of abolition, Collins observed, were "too complicated" for them and "above
their comprehension."[12] US abolitionists, following in the footsteps of
their British counterparts, published antislavery magazines and books
adapted to the capacities of children. Literary scholars have examined
publications such as the *Slave's Friend*, an abolitionist monthly for children published by the American Anti-Slavery Society in the 1830s, and
Hannah and Mary Townsend's *Anti-Slavery Alphabet* (1846).[13] The juvenile dimensions of Harriet Beecher Stowe's antislavery best seller *Uncle
Tom's Cabin* (1852) have likewise been explored in depth. It is common
knowledge that Stowe read completed installments of the novel to her
own children. In her farewell to the readers of the *National Era*, in
which *Uncle Tom* was first serialized in 1851–52, Stowe addressed child
readers: "Dear children, you will one day be men and women; and

[I hope] that you will learn from this story always to remember and pity the poor and oppressed, and, when you grow up, show your pity by doing all you can for them. Never, if you can help it, let a colored child be shut out of school, or treated with neglect and contempt, because of his color."[14] Little Eva has been called by one critic "the first girl to articulate abolitionist principles."[15] Another has shown how adaptations for children transformed the meaning of *Uncle Tom's Cabin*.[16]

Historians have been slower to consider how historical children—as opposed to imagined child abolitionists like Follen's Hal and Stowe's Eva—took part in antebellum struggles for racial justice. *Young Abolitionists* is the first book-length examination of juvenile abolitionism as it happened on the ground. Juvenile abolitionism, I contend, encompassed much more than simply reading the *Slave's Friend* and the *Anti-Slavery Alphabet*. Children read a broad selection of antislavery texts, some explicitly designed for them but others written for a wider audience: slave narratives, for instance, have rarely been studied as "children's literature," yet children constituted a significant part of their readership. A real-life Hal would probably have been gifted a copy of the *Narrative of the Sufferings of Lewis Clarke*. Most importantly, antislavery literature was only one avenue through which children encountered abolition. Children recited antislavery speeches at school; they joined juvenile antislavery societies; they assisted in the editing of antislavery newspapers and in aiding fugitive slaves; they attended antislavery fairs and participated in programs to honor the memory of John Brown; they raised money to finance antislavery lecturers' international travels; they even signed antislavery petitions, testing the limits of their citizenship. This book attempts to document the varied and sometimes unexpected ways in which children were involved in the abolition movement. Children's "hearty co-operation," it shows, helped bring about the abolition of slavery itself.

Studying children's participation in the abolition movement inevitably raises questions of agency. How aware were children of the meaning of their actions? Did they join antislavery societies and sign petitions of their own free will, or did they do so under the influence of parents? Juvenile abolitionism almost sounds like a contradiction in terms. Abolitionism connotes action and determination, while children have generally been regarded as, at best, passive recipients of antislavery content provided by adults. Hal, for one, did not ask to be taken to an antislavery picnic. As he writes to his mother, "Uncle told us the day before yesterday that he was going to take us the next day, to the Pic-nic at Dedham, for they were going to celebrate the first of August, and he must be there."[17] Yet the antislavery sentiments that historical children experienced at antislavery events like this one were very much their own. This is why I call Hal and children like him who expressed disapproval of slavery in however inchoate a form "abolitionists." Most of the children discussed in this book first heard about abolition as a result of adult-led initiatives: a teacher brought up slavery in class; a grandfather forbade the use of slave-produced sugar in his house; a mother took her daughters to an antislavery meeting. Children, however, soon came to develop their own understandings of abolition, deploying surprising degrees of agency in the process.

Young Abolitionists provides a child's-eye view of abolition, revisiting familiar sources such as antislavery newspapers, convention proceedings, correspondence, and autobiographies from a new angle and using juvenile antislavery fiction to fill in archival gaps. A literal history of abolition "from the bottom up," it attends to children's perspectives on slavery while recognizing the role that adults may have played in shaping them and the role they most certainly played in preserving them. The voices of historical children often come to us mediated by adults. This does not mean that these voices should be ignored or deemed inauthentic. Throughout this book, I have taken care to relay the words of juvenile abolitionists, which I have submitted to the same kind of analysis that we usually reserve for older, more articulate activists. Responding to recent calls for bridging the gap between childhood studies and intellectual history, I have considered children as producers of antislavery ideas—as "intellectuals in their own right."[18] Children were vocal in condemning slavery. Their words deserve to be heard, and their "serious concerns" (Susan Paul's term) should be taken seriously.[19]

I have paid particular attention to the perspectives of African American children. Most discussions of juvenile abolitionism have derived from the partial view of juvenile antislavery literature outlined earlier. This has had the result of erasing African American children from histories of abolition. Indeed, there are few Black child abolitionists in the *Slave's Friend*: Black children are more often victims of slavery than agents of abolition. As decades of scholarship have shown, free and enslaved African Americans were at the vanguard of antislavery.[20] African American children, no less than adults, were responsible for keeping the antislavery fire going. Abolition, in fact, was a more vital goal for them than it ever was for their white counterparts. Free Black children often had relatives who were still enslaved; they themselves were susceptible to being kidnapped and sold into slavery. Southern slavery, they realized, was connected to northern racism, the effects of which they could feel in their daily lives. Many free African Americans first experienced the sting of racial prejudice as children. Sarah Parker Remond's abolitionism crystallized on the day she was removed from her Salem, Massachusetts, school because of her race; Remond, who was eight years old, later became a renowned antislavery lecturer. "Black children," James Oliver Horton and Lois Horton rightly note, "were engaged in the struggle for equality partly because they could not be sheltered from it."[21] Slavery had northern ramifications that simply could not escape free African American children and that survived abolition.

African American abolitionism was wide in scope. African American abolitionists "did fight fiercely for the end of slavery," Jim Casey argues, "but they cared about far more."[22] For them, the fight to abolish slavery was systematically intertwined with a broader struggle against segregation, disfranchisement, and violence and for education, civil rights, and social reform. Racial uplift was another key aspect of the Black freedom struggle in which children had a special role to play. As scholars such as Patrick Rael and Erica Ball have demonstrated, middle-class African Americans embraced notions of morality, virtue, and self-improvement not out of a desire to look respectable in the eyes of whites but as a defining feature of their personal identity, one that tied with their radical antislavery principles. Children and youth, even more so than adults, could come to embody the benefits of education and the possibility of Black self-improvement.[23] Educated Black children *were* abolitionists to the extent that they disproved the racist logic that buttressed slavery. As they grew up, they appropriated their parents' discourse and formed juvenile associations focused as much on economy, industry, and the acquirement of "useful knowledge" as on antislavery. Conversely, Black children whose parents neglected their schooling and left them "to wander from street to street [and] to indulge in every species of juvenile dissipation" unwittingly confirmed the prejudices of racist whites; they were, in the words of an African American educational activist, "the means of binding together the fetters of our enslaved brethren."[24] Juvenile abolitionism took different forms depending on the age and race of the children being considered. I have taken the broadest view possible.

Young Abolitionists joins a growing body of scholarship on the history of children and youth in the nineteenth-century United States. Age has recently emerged as a "useful category" of analysis in historical scholarship. Children and youth have attracted particular attention among historians of the antebellum and Civil War era. James Marten has edited several essay collections on the subject, notably *Children and Youth during the Civil War Era* (2012), and he has shed light on the experiences of children during the Civil War in his own *The Children's Civil War* (1998). Jon Grinspan has explored young people's involvement in electoral politics in *The Virgin Vote* (2016). Corinne Field and Nicholas Syrett have noted "the often overlooked significance of numerical age before the later nineteenth century." More generally, they have encouraged scholars of American culture "to incorporate age into their analyses as a key axis of identity for Americans."[25] Scholars of slavery and race have proved willing to do so. As early as 1995, Wilma King published a foundational study of enslaved children in the United States, *Stolen Childhood*. Over the past few years, a younger generation of scholars, including Crystal Lynn Webster, Vanessa Holden, and Kabria Baumgartner, have explored topics such as the lives of African American children after northern emancipation, the role of children in Nat Turner's slave rebellion of 1831, and the campaign for the desegregation of schools led by African American girls and women in the Northeast before the Civil War.[26] Nineteenth-century children and youth are now regarded as historical agents whose political resistance mattered.

While historians of abolition have long explored the intersections of race, gender, and class within abolitionist ranks, age has rarely featured in the equation. Manisha Sinha, in her magisterial *The Slave's Cause* (2016), has observed that "abolition was a young people's movement."[27]

Indeed, Garrison was twenty-five years old when he started the *Liberator*; Douglass was twenty-three when he gave his first lecture before an interracial audience in Nantucket, Massachusetts; Sarah Forten was seventeen when she published her first poem, the much-reprinted "The Grave of the Slave" (1831), in Garrison's paper. A number of antislavery societies were formed by "young men," as their names indicate (the Boston Young Men's Anti-Slavery Society and New York Young Men's Anti-Slavery Society are two examples). As Michael Jirik has shown, institutions of higher learning such as universities and theological seminaries were breeding grounds for antislavery activism: students, too, were abolitionists.[28] This book focuses on an even younger group of people. I have taken just as broad a view of childhood as I have of abolitionism. In the following pages, I discuss children as young as two and some in their late teens. Most, however, are between seven and fifteen. A child, for the purpose of this study, is anyone who was regarded as such by their contemporaries or who self-identified as a child. I was not able to ascertain, for instance, how old William Henry Webb—probably the son of Douglass's Dublin printer, Richard D. Webb—was when he wrote to Henry Clarke Wright to tell him about two lectures by Douglass he had recently attended. Yet the young Webb wrote of Douglass, "I think he is a pleasant man & able to interest children very much for I know he interested me greatly about slavery and other things too."[29] Whatever his exact age at the time, Webb thought of himself as a child, which makes him relevant to this book. Similarly, I discuss the children and youth who participated in "juvenile" and "junior" antislavery societies even though some of them were nearing or even past the age of majority. My main focus, of course, is on younger children—those whom we do not spontaneously think of as abolitionists and who therefore have escaped the attention of historians.

Though this book sheds light on the activism of both young men and women, gender does not feature prominently in it. When it came to juvenile abolitionism, the category of age outweighed that of gender: young people were addressed as children rather than as men- or women-to-be. Juvenile antislavery meetings were attended by children of both genders; juvenile antislavery literature did not differentiate between boys and girls. Children did turn to different kinds of activism as they grew up. While young women sold handmade holders and pincushions at antislavery fairs, young men practiced their oratorical skills on the assumption that they, rather than women, would lecture on the antislavery stage. Yet gender was not as rigid a category for children as it was for their elders, and abolitionists did not usually treat boys and girls in gender-specific ways. Juvenile abolitionism was all the more subversive for not being hampered by strict hierarchies of gender.

Young Abolitionists attempts to do for the antebellum abolition movement what other books have done for the twentieth-century civil rights movement. Children and teenagers, V. P. Franklin has argued, "often took the lead in challenging the disparities in educational resources between rich and poor, Black and white public schools; opposing Jim Crow practices in public accommodations; and protesting the unprovoked violence carried out by law enforcement officials."[30] Claudette Colvin, one of Rosa Parks's lesser-known predecessors, was fifteen when she refused to give up her seat on a public bus in Montgomery, Alabama, in 1955. In accounting for her gesture, Colvin invoked the Black women abolitionists whom she had been studying at school. "It felt like Sojourner Truth's hands were pushing me down on one shoulder and Harriet Tubman's hands were pushing me down on another shoulder," she recalled.[31] What Colvin did not know was that women as young as herself had protested slavery and fought against segregation in Tubman's and Truth's times. Rather than looking toward the twentieth century, however, this book reaches back into the late eighteenth century—or the "first wave" of abolition—and situates antebellum ("second-wave") juvenile abolitionism within longer histories of abolition in both the United States and Great Britain.[32] Antebellum abolitionists did not exactly innovate. Rather, they systematized what opponents of slavery on both sides of the Atlantic had always been doing: they sensitized children to a system that they, in turn, would have to combat. Abolition was a long-term project, Henry Clarke Wright predicted in 1837. "We are engaged in a work not to be done in a day," he wrote to William Goodell, the editor of the *Friend of Man*. "You, and I, and all engaged in this fearful struggle, will soon pass away. Let us, then, prepare our children for the part they must take in it when we are dead."[33] Some children responded well and turned into full-blown abolitionists; others did not. Parents and teachers did not indoctrinate children, as proslavery apologists would have it. They did not force abolition on the children under their care. Quite the contrary, they encouraged children to challenge the racial status quo, thereby enabling them to hone their critical faculties. It is a testament to the abolitionists' progressive vision that they were able to regard children as political actors who could and should speak out against slavery and racism.

Young Abolitionists is organized in five chapters. Chapter 1 traces the "origins" of juvenile abolitionism, looking at early efforts to promote an antislavery stance among children. It shows how the idea of involving children in the abolition movement emerged in the late eighteenth and early nineteenth centuries and fully bloomed in the United States during the antebellum period, to the dismay of proslavery apologists and even some abolitionists. Chapter 2 makes the case for an expanded understanding of juvenile antislavery literature. It looks at familiar sources such as the *Slave's Friend* but also at lesser-known juvenile texts written, among others, by the African American activist Sarah Mapps Douglass and the white abolitionist Jonathan Walker. It emphasizes the radical nature of this literature and pays attention to texts not specifically written for, yet read by, children. Chapter 3 explores the activities of juvenile antislavery societies and Black-led literary associations that fought for abolition. Very young children were organized into antislavery societies, while their older brothers and sisters formed their own organizations. There they received or made their antislavery education, learning about the concrete ways in which slavery could be resisted. Chapter 4 follows Susan Paul and other abolitionist teachers into their classrooms. It examines how educators discussed slavery and racial prejudice with their pupils and recovers the words of children who wrote antislavery compositions and delivered antislavery orations. Black education, it shows, was intertwined with the project of abolition. Antiabolitionists denounced all attempts at providing children with an antislavery education: racist northerners attacked Black schools, while white southerners led a campaign against what they claimed were "abolition" textbooks. Finally, chapter 5 moves from the classroom to the family unit. Juvenile abolitionism often developed in the home, where children absorbed some of their parents' antislavery sentiments and contributed to their antislavery endeavors. Children of abolitionists from Francis Jackson Garrison and Charles Remond Douglass to Sarah Parker Remond and Lillie Chace entered the world of abolition at an early age. They never really left it. They carried the ideals they inherited from their parents into and beyond the Civil War and fought for a host of social justice causes—racial justice, women's suffrage, and workers' rights—until their deaths.

1

"What Can Children Do for the Slaves?"

The Origins of Juvenile Abolitionism

"What can children do for the slaves?" was a recurring question in juvenile antislavery literature, to which abolitionists provided no single answer.[1] Some believed that children could do much, indeed, that they represented a key constituency of the abolition movement; others were dubious that children could make a meaningful contribution to—or even had a place in—a struggle of such magnitude. A majority probably never gave much thought to the question. Admittedly, the involvement of children and youth in organized abolition was less of an issue than, say, the involvement of women. The "woman question," as it came to be known, was so contentious that it famously led to a schism within abolitionist ranks in 1840, with followers of William Lloyd Garrison favoring women's full participation in antislavery societies, including in leadership roles, and conservative evangelical abolitionists denying them the right to vote, hold office, or speak publicly.[2] There was no "child question" bitterly dividing abolitionists. Still, children's participation in the movement was far from self-evident, and advocates of juvenile abolitionism needed to account for their views. They were vocal enough that they attracted criticism from apologists of slavery. Slaveholding politicians as prominent as John Tyler of Virginia and James Henry Hammond of South Carolina thundered against the *Slave's Friend* in Congress—an indication that they, at least, took juvenile abolitionism seriously. In this chapter, I outline the stakes of this debate, explaining how some abolitionists came to see children as potential allies in the antislavery cause. Antebellum juvenile abolitionism, I argue, traced its roots to juvenile acts of slave resistance and the first wave of abolition. The involvement of children in other, less radical reform movements such as temperance also served as a source of inspiration. Abolitionists of

the second wave, unlike their predecessors, theorized juvenile abolitionism. I look at the rationale they deployed and the objections with
which they were met.

Juvenile Slave Resistance and the First Wave of Abolition

Enslaved children were the first juvenile abolitionists. Perhaps the most
well-known example of a youth actively resisting slavery is provided by
Frederick Douglass in his *Narrative of the Life of Frederick Douglass, an
American Slave* (1845)—"a narrative not only of slavery or emancipation,
but of childhood," as Brigitte Fielder observes, written by a young man
not far removed from either slavery or childhood.[3] Douglass was twelve
when he clandestinely procured a copy of *The Columbian Orator*, sixteen
when he fought back against the slave breaker Edward Covey, eighteen
when he plotted his first (failed) escape. His detestation of slavery preceded these youthful acts of resistance. "I was just as well aware of the
unjust, unnatural, and murderous character of slavery, when nine years
old, as I am now," a more mature Douglass wrote in *Life and Times of
Frederick Douglass* (1881).[4] Wilma King, in her study of enslaved childhood, has shed light on the many ways, both subtle and overt, in which
enslaved children, once they reached a level of understanding about
their enslavement, resisted being held in bondage. They ran away and
remained in hiding; they fought against sexual exploitation; they joined
the Union army during the Civil War.[5] More recently, Vanessa Holden
has explored the role of children and youth in slave rebellion, focusing on the Southampton Rebellion of 1831. Children, she argues, were
"participants in, witnesses to, and survivors of" the rebellion, yet they
have been largely overlooked by historians (including King). A whole
community of enslaved people rebelled in Southampton, not just a small
group of men led by Nat Turner.[6] Juvenile acts of resistance in the South
proved that children could play a role in the demise of slavery. They
paved the way for juvenile abolitionism in the North.

Though slavery was abolished in the North during the revolutionary
era, it cast a long shadow over the lives of northern Black children. Gradual emancipation laws such as those adopted in New York in 1799 and
1817 led to a protracted emancipation process that lasted well into the
nineteenth century and left many Black children somewhere between

freedom and enslavement. New York's 1799 Act for the Gradual Abolition of Slavery granted only partial freedom to the children of enslaved
mothers: they were to serve lengthy indentures to their mothers' enslavers and would not obtain complete freedom until their midtwenties.
The 1817 Act Relative to Slaves and Servants set July 4, 1827, as the date
when all remaining enslaved people would be free. As Sarah Levine-
Gronningsater has argued, Black abolitionists of the antebellum period
were "children of gradual emancipation." Their commitment to immediatism from the late 1820s owed much to their youthful experience of
a painfully slow and precarious gradual emancipation regime. Aided by
the white-led New York Manumission Society (NYMS), young Black
New Yorkers and their parents appealed to the law to reduce indenture
terms, resist kidnapping and illegal sales, and challenge violent enslavers. The legal and political consciousness they gained in the process later
guided their antislavery efforts on the national stage. "The generations
of black children who grew up within the legal and social structures
of gradual emancipation," Levine-Gronningsater writes, "would become particularly vital figures in the longer story of nineteenth-century
American freedom."[7]

Free (and partially free) Black children occupied an essential place in
early abolitionist strategies. Abolition could only be attained, activists
reasoned, by first disproving racist claims that African Americans were
inherently inferior and therefore unfit for freedom. First-wave abolitionists embraced an agenda of "societal environmentalism," in Paul
Polgar's terms, which posited African Americans' ability to improve
themselves, given equal opportunities.[8] As the Black ministers Absalom Jones and Richard Allen put it in 1794, "We believe if you would
try the experiment of taking a few black children, and cultivate their
minds with the same care . . . as you would wish for your own children,
you would find upon the trial, they were not inferior in mental endow-
ments."[9] Black children, if adequately educated, would become knowl-
edgeable, virtuous citizens worthy of being incorporated into the body
politic. This, in turn, would lead to a weakening of racial prejudice and
a gradual end to slavery.

Accordingly, abolitionists set to providing children with a positive
educational environment. In 1787, the NYMS established the New York
African Free School (NYAFS), which in the following decades educated

thousands of children of both sexes, a number of them sons and daughters of enslaved people. The NYAFS did more than just teach its students lessons in reading and writing: like other schools founded by antislavery societies or run independently by African Americans, it "became a vehicle for the production of black reformers," as Leslie Harris notes.[10] Abolition was woven into its curriculum; students already familiar with the impact of gradual emancipation over their lives received a thorough antislavery education, as I show in chapter 4. The NYAFS graduates James McCune Smith and Henry Highland Garnet, for instance, later assumed leadership in New York's radical abolition movement.[11] William Hamilton, father of two NYAFS students, made an early case for juvenile abolitionism when, in an oration delivered on July 4, 1827, he told fellow parents that "the names of WASHINGTON and JEFFERSON should not be pronounced *in the hearing of your children*, until they could clearly and distinctly pronounce the names" of the men who had formed the NYMS and NYAFS.[12] This was a bold recommendation at a time when parents were routinely enjoined to teach their children reverence for the Founding Fathers: the preservation of the nation depended on it.[13] The nation's preservation, Hamilton would have argued, depended on the intergenerational transmission of the antislavery principles that had existed at its commencement but had been lost from view. Hamilton's two sons—Robert and Thomas Hamilton, respectively eight and four years old when their father pronounced his 1827 oration—understood the lesson well. In the years just before the Civil War, they published the *Anglo-African Magazine* and the *Weekly Anglo-African*, two influential newspapers advocating for abolition and Black rights.[14] The juvenile abolitionists of the first wave of abolition were the adult abolitionists of its second wave.

Though juvenile abolitionism as a concerted, deliberate tactic took off during the antebellum period, first-wave abolitionists denounced slavery in works intended for children and youth. Two of the new nation's foremost educators, Noah Webster and Caleb Bingham, joined the ranks of the abolition movement early on.[15] The textbooks they produced left no doubt as to their disapproval of slavery. Webster's *Little Reader's Assistant* (1790), which Paula Connolly calls "one of the earliest examples of radical abolitionism in U.S. children's literature," includes "Story of the Treatment of African Slaves," which describes the Middle Passage

Figure 1.1. A slave coffle. Noah Webster Jr., *The Little Reader's Assistant*, 4th ed. (Northampton, MA: William Butler, 1798), 39. Courtesy of the American Antiquarian Society.

in graphic terms.[16] It discusses the branding of the enslaved after they are captured, suicide and rebellions aboard slave ships, and the separation of enslaved families in America; its woodcut of a white man with a whip behind a coffle of slaves may well be the first visual representation of slavery in a US children's book (figure 1.1). Another piece in the same reader, "Lamentation of an Old Female Slave," is the fictional recollection of an aged woman who has been cast off by her enslavers after she has become unable to labor. "Wretched before in bondage; now still more wretched in freedom—Of what use is life to me?" she asks.[17] Bingham's *American Preceptor* (1794) includes an anti-slave-trade speech by the British prime minister William Pitt; "The African Chief" (1792), a popular antislavery poem by Sarah Wentworth Apthorp Morton; and an elegy on British slavery conjuring up gory images that must have struck the young reader's imagination.[18] *The Columbian Orator* (1797) famously includes "Dialogue between a Master and Slave," in which an enslaved man wins his freedom through his own argumentation. Young Frederick Douglass read it again and again during his Baltimore days. "The moral which I gained from the dialogue," he recounts in his *Narra-*

tive, "was the power of truth over the conscience of even a slaveholder."[19] Less famously, the *Orator* reprints part of a 1797 speech delivered by the white abolitionist Samuel Miller before the NYMS. A searing critique of the slave trade, it lambastes those "who claim the title, and enjoy the privileges of American citizens" yet "employ themselves in the odious traffic of human flesh."[20] Jedidiah Morse's and Susanna Rowson's early geography textbooks, meant to be used in schools and academies, were no less direct in denouncing the slave system. In Morse's *American Geography* (1789), he called the slave trade an "infernal commerce . . . carried on by the humane and polished, the christian inhabitants of Europe," while Rowson, in her *Abridgment of Universal Geography* (1806), wrote, "The negro on the burning sands of Africa was born as free, as he who drew his first breath in America or Britain."[21] In a nation still reverberating with revolutionary calls for liberty and equality, children were likely to come across antislavery statements in their schoolbooks.

Antebellum advocates of juvenile abolitionism also followed in the footsteps of British abolitionists. "Have we children?" the English Dissenter Robert Robinson asked in a 1788 sermon attacking the slave trade. "Let us call them to our knee, and early inspire them with the love of virtuous freedom. . . . Let us set before their eyes the sad but instructive histories of consciences oppressed, property plundered, [and] families divided."[22] Robinson's call did not go unheard. As the antislavery campaigner Thomas Clarkson reminisced about his travels around British slave ports in the early 1790s, he noted that many families had adopted the new abolitionist strategy of abstaining from slave-grown sugar. He observed, "even children, who were capable of understanding the history of the sufferings of the Africans, excluded, with the most virtuous resolution, the sweets, to which they had been accustomed, from their lips."[23] Another early historian of British abolition, Esther Copley, granted children even more agency, affirming that in some instances they "introduced into whole families the system of abstinence."[24] Kathryn Gleadle and Ryan Hanley have examined the dynamics behind juvenile sugar abstention in British middle-class families, arguing that parents were keen to present their offspring's abolitionism as spontaneous when in fact it was often the result of adults' expectations and demands. Juvenile anti-saccharism emerged in a family environment conducive to such engagement, which did not prevent children from exercising agency. Panton,

Josepha, and Jane Plymley, children of the Shropshire abolitionist Joseph Plymley, grew up in a home where Clarkson was a frequent guest. When Clarkson recommended that Panton "read on the [slave trade] that he may grow up with a just detestation of it," the seven-year-old was eager to please. On the very next day, he could be found engrossed in Clarkson's *Essay on the Slavery and Commerce of the Human Species* (1786). Yet it was on his own initiative that Panton asked the servants to stop polishing his shoes when he heard that shoe polish contained sugar—an idiosyncratic form of abstention that demonstrated Panton's ability to form judgments and take decisions independently of adults.[25] Olaudah Equiano was another eminent visitor of the Plymleys. In 1793, he gave Panton one of his "little pamphlets against the use of sugar" and an autographed copy of his autobiographical narrative.[26] These early encounters with the leading lights of British abolitionism made a mark on Panton Plymley: three decades later, he supported the campaign against colonial slavery as a member of Parliament.[27]

Though British children under the age of fourteen were discouraged from signing antislavery petitions, they seem to have done so on occasion.[28] They also contributed financially to the cause, with or without the mediation of parents and teachers.[29] As I show in chapter 2, juvenile antislavery literature developed in Britain before it bloomed in the United States. By 1825, a booklet on abstention titled *Pity the Negro; or, An Address to Children on the Subject of Slavery*, authored by the Birmingham abolitionist Charlotte Townsend, was going through its third edition; seven editions of two thousand copies each were published.[30] US abolitionists were in contact with their British counterparts and knew of these developments.

Children of the Temperance Movement

Juvenile participation in the temperance movement offered a more immediate blueprint for antebellum juvenile abolitionism. The involvement of children and youth in temperance reform was perhaps less surprising than their involvement in antislavery reform. Middle-class African Americans strongly believed in temperance, along with education and economy, as a way of "uplifting" the race and undermining racism in the North. They taught their offspring the virtues of abstaining from alcohol. White temperance discourse frequently centered children as the main victims of intemperate parents. As John Frick notes in his study of nineteenth-century temperance plays, "Invariably, the drunkard's child was shown, emaciated and dressed in rags, waiting in a squalid apartment for his or her drunkard father to return home . . . or quaking in fear and anticipation of the beating and verbal abuse that would certainly be forthcoming upon the drunkard's return."[31] One of the most popular temperance stories in the 1850s, first published by Solon Robinson in the *New York Tribune* and then turned into a successful play, was that of Little Katy, a hot-corn seller on the street who is beaten to death by her alcoholic mother for failing to sell all of her corn supply. On her deathbed, Little Katy becomes a temperance advocate of sorts, begging her mother to stop drinking.[32] While northern white children were not directly concerned by slavery, intemperance was a social evil with potentially grave consequences for them. Temperance may have felt like a more pressing social issue than abolition for reform-inclined children and their parents. It was generally regarded as a less subversive cause, which also made it more suited to the younger generation.

The temperance movement gained traction at a time—the mid-1820s—when the abolition movement had not yet turned to immediatism. The American Temperance Society was formed in 1826, seven years before the American Anti-Slavery Society (AASS); organized Black efforts against intemperance began in 1829 with the formation of the New Haven Temperance Society of the People of Color.[33] Likewise, juvenile temperance societies preceded juvenile antislavery societies, a product of the mid-1830s. Antebellum abolitionists who made the case for juvenile abolitionism often acknowledged the preexisting participation of children in the temperance movement. "In the cause of Temperance the aid of Juvenile societies has been hailed with delight," the AASS noted in 1835.[34] Lewis Tappan, one of the society's leading members, observed two years later that "the late Temperance Convention at Saratoga Springs resolved that it was proper to invite . . . children to join Temperance Societies." He then asked, rhetorically, "Is not slavery as bad as intemperance?"[35] The Juvenile Temperance Society of Amherst, Massachusetts, was organized spontaneously in 1829 "at a social party for young people [who had] met together for amusement. Wine being offered and no one accepting it, it was proposed to form a Temperance

Society, which was immediately agreed to by all present of both sexes."
Formed in 1830, the Juvenile Temperance Society of Newport, New
Hampshire, proudly numbered 150 members between the ages of eight
and sixteen at its first anniversary. In Napoli, New York, some members
of the local juvenile temperance society, formed in 1831, were as young
as five.[36] African American children organized their own "colored" societies, as was the case in Hartford, Connecticut, in December 1833; the
group soon numbered thirty-five members. A decade later, Cincinnati,
Ohio, boasted an African American juvenile temperance society of ten
times that number.[37] "Let the lessons be improved which the experience
of that enterprise has given us," the abolitionist John A. Collins wrote in
1842 in reference to temperance.[38]

The early 1840s saw the emergence of the Cold Water Army. "THE
COLD WATER ARMY! What is that?" asked the white reformer Charles
J. Warren. "It is an attempt to enrol the names of all the children and
youth in the country on the pledge of Total Abstinence from the use
of all intoxicating drinks."[39] The phrase was coined by a Virginia-born
minister, Thomas P. Hunt, who also happened to be an antislavery colonizationist; in 1827, he had emancipated his own slaves and sent them
to Liberia. Hunt used it metaphorically to refer to people who refrained
from drinking alcohol but also, more specifically, as the name of a children's temperance organization he founded in Boston in 1839. Parents
played a key role in enrolling their children in the Cold Water Army. In
Hunt's words, it was they who judged of their children's "fitness" to join
its ranks. Another advocate of juvenile temperance made it clear that
the "consent of parents" was a precondition for enrollment.[40] Aspiring
members took the Cold Water Army pledge:

> We, Cold Water Girls and Boys,
> Freely renounce the treacherous joys
> Of Brandy, Whiskey, Rum, and Gin;
> The Serpent's lure to death and sin:
>
> Wine, Beer, and Cider, we detest,
> And thus we'll make our parents blest;
> *"So here we pledge perpetual hate*
> *To all that can intoxicate."*[41]

The Cold Water Army soon spread to other northern cities. A native of Rocky Hill, Connecticut, young James A. Williams took the pledge in the early 1840s, at the age of nine or ten. His signature appears at the bottom of a sheet published by the Connecticut Temperance Society, with the pledge and a certificate of membership on the front and the lyrics of Cold Water Army songs at the back. The president of the Connecticut Temperance Society, Thomas S. Williams, was probably James's father.[42]

The Cold Water Army was meant to be seen and heard. Its youthful soldiers often took part in public processions organized on given days of the year. On July 4, 1841, in Hartford, the local arm of the Cold Water Army joined adults of the Connecticut Temperance Society and paraded through the streets with music and banners. Temperance advocates presented themselves as patriots, and Fourth of July celebrations accordingly provided an opportunity for temperance children to show themselves and affirm or renew their commitment to the cause. That same day, the children of the Boston arm of the Cold Water Army also joined in their local procession. They could be seen holding a banner representing two boys, "one with a mallet beating in the head of a cask of rum, and the other emptying the contents of a demijohn, with 'Go a head!' in large letters underneath." Later, one boy "addressed a spirited ode to a bottle of liquor, and emptied its contents on the ground," while two "lads" acted out a temperance dialogue. (Charles J. Warren published a selection of such dialogues, with titles like "The Beer Trial" and "Root Beer and Temperance Bitters," the following year.) Like most temperance processions, the Boston procession was a masculine affair. Women and their daughters watched from the windows and balconies as men and their sons marched through the streets. In the words of one reporter, their "happy faces gave evidence of the joy which filled their bosoms in seeing husbands and fathers, sons and brothers, enrolled in a mighty army, marching with firm step and firmer resolution to exterminate from our beloved country, the great cause of misery and crime."[43] The Cold Water Army was an army after all and, as such, was mostly geared toward boys, as illustrations attest (figure 1.2).

It might be thought that the martial, patriotic spirit of such events alienated abolitionists, a number of whom, like William Lloyd Garrison, advocated nonresistance and peace principles and called for penitent silence on the country's birthday rather than noisy theatrics.[44]

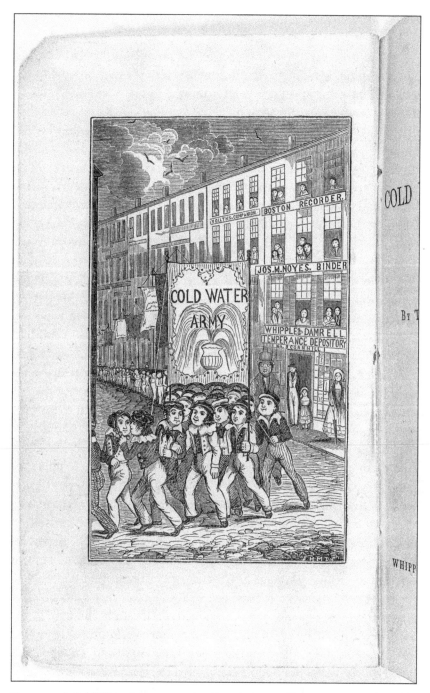

Figure 1.2. A Cold Water Army procession. Frontispiece to Thomas P. Hunt, *The Cold Water Army* (Boston: Whipple and Damrell, 1840). Courtesy of the American Antiquarian Society.

Garrison, however, did not object to the procession he witnessed in Northampton, Massachusetts, in July 1843. On the contrary, he found it "a very pleasing spectacle." Garrison was in truth less interested in juvenile temperance per se than in the fact that Black and white children mingled freely at this particular event. "Colored children were not only allowed to walk in the procession," he noted in the *Liberator*, "but in some instances were coupled with white ones; and I saw no token of contempt or disapprobation among the numerous spectators."[45] The interracial dimension of the event trumped its military undertones. Children, because they mingled more willingly than adults, could help radicalize temperance, a movement whose leading white advocates seldom came out in favor of racial equality.

Children likewise participated in the Temperance Jubilee, a day of celebration organized in both England and the United States on the last Thursday (then Tuesday) of February from 1833 onward. On February 28, 1837, no fewer than three thousand New York City schoolchildren gathered for a meeting. "Such an assembly of children . . . was probably never before witnessed in this city," a reporter noted. Temperance speeches were delivered by professional speakers, temperance medals distributed. "The little auditors seemed to enter with spirit into the proceedings of the occasion. They made the house ring with plaudits."[46] Another "*great* meeting of *little* folks" held in Boston in early 1841 drew an even more impressive crowd of four thousand children. Temperance publications were given away after the meeting.[47] Children were the lifeblood of the antebellum temperance movement.

Like the abolition movement, the temperance movement capitalized on print culture to convey its message to the young. Both movements embraced new print technologies and produced massive amounts of print directed to various segments of US society, including children.[48] "Of all reform efforts," Anne Scott MacLeod writes, "temperance probably generated the largest quantity of writing aimed specifically at children."[49] The 1840s saw a proliferation of juvenile temperance periodicals such as the *Youth's Temperance Enterprise*, the *Cold Water Army and Youth's Picnic*, and the *Cold Water Boy* and its companion the *Cold Water Girl*. Charles Jewett—brother of the Boston book publisher John P. Jewett, famous for publishing Harriet Beecher Stowe's *Uncle Tom's Cabin* (1852)—authored several temperance publications for children. *The Temperance Toy* (1840) was aimed at the very young. In the preface, Jewett lamented that "among the various efforts which have been put forth with a view to rid the earth of the evil of intemperance, so little has been done to guard CHILDREN and YOUTH against the influence of temptations which surround them on every side."⁵⁰ Loosely modeled on the nursery rhyme "The House That Jack Built," and complete with pictures of drunkards, distilleries, and dangerous decoctions, *The Temperance Toy* told a simple tale of a man led "to perdition" by the "bottle and can" despite warnings from his teetotal physician. The following year, Jewett published another heavily illustrated book for older children, *The Youth's Temperance Lecturer*, which mingled lessons in chemistry (how distilled spirits, wine, and beer are made) and ethnography (who patronizes the "tavern-bar" and the "grog-shop") with a more didactic message on the effects of drunkenness on the drunkard's family. Children were shown begging for food, forced to work at the factory to pay for their father's rum, and killed in a house fire in the absence of their intemperate mother. "Let a youth's or juvenile temperance society be formed in every town and village in the country," Jewett recommended, "and get all the children to sign the total abstinence pledge, if possible."⁵¹ Fiction, of course, also served as a vehicle for temperance. Popular temperance stories for children included Aunt Julia's *The Brandy Drops: A Temperance Story* (1858) and its sequel, *The Temperance Boys* (1858). The temperance message, John Crandall argues, was "clear, uncomplicated and repetitious" and, as such, was "tailor-made for the writers for the young."⁵²

Antebellum Americans lived in a world where children were commonly associated with reform movements that we tend to imagine as the exclusive province of adults. Young age was not seen as an obstacle to participation, as Hannah and Mary Townsend made clear in the *Anti-Slavery Alphabet* (1846): "Y is for Youth—the time for all / Bravely to war with sin; / And think not it can ever be / Too early to begin."⁵³ Seeking to regenerate US society, reformers turned toward children as the promise of a better future—one without alcohol and the social disorder resulting from its consumption, as far as proponents of temperance were concerned. It was one thing, however, to involve eight- or ten-year-olds in fairly consensual temperance activities; it was quite another to have them support the radical project of immediate abolition. Yet abolitionists found good reasons for doing so.

Juvenile Abolitionism in the Age of Immediatism

Immediatist abolitionists often meditated on childhood, age, and the passage of time. "Time has perfected my twenty-fifth year," Garrison mused in the *Genius of Universal Emancipation* in January 1830. "TWENTY-FIVE!—brief as it now seems, it was once too long for admeasurement—an unwasting immortality, shoreless, boundless, inconceivable."[54] Four months earlier, Garrison had publicly recanted his former gradualist-colonizationist views in favor of immediatism. Though his conversion is generally—and correctly—explained as a result of his contact with Black Baltimoreans who led him to embrace more radical views, Garrison may also have been prompted by a more intimate sense of urgency. There was no time for gradualism: slavery must be abolished *now*. "How is it that time has borne me along so swiftly?" Garrison wondered in an 1834 letter to Helen Benson, the woman he would soon marry. "How is it that I have been so imperceptibly carried over the threshold of manhood?" Though now close to thirty, and gaining in maturity, Garrison had not entirely divested himself of the attributes of childhood. "I love to be a child," he continued, perhaps aware that this would endear him to his future wife. "I weep as easily as a babe, am as sensitive as a flower, and as aerial as a bird."[55] The latter phrase formed an interesting contrast to his reputation as a man "all on fire."[56] A lover of poetry, Garrison wrote sonnets on the occasion of the birth of his first son in 1836 as well as to mark some of his most important birthdays—his thirtieth in 1835, his thirty-fifth in 1840.[57] Contemporaries commented on his "interest in children," his "love of their society," and his "aptitude to win their gentle and tender hearts and their unsuspicious confidence."[58] "The little ones were drawn to him as if by a magnet," his daughter, Fanny Garrison Villard, later reminisced.[59] Throughout the 1830s, Garrison was also an ardent promoter of juvenile abolitionism. Notably, he edited a volume titled *Juvenile Poems, for the Use of Free American Children, of Every Complexion* (1835) and included a column for children called the Juvenile Department in the *Liberator* (figure 1.3).

Abolitionists viewed children as morally pure and therefore as naturally opposed to slavery. Perhaps the most consistent theorizer of children's abolitionism in the antebellum era was the white activist Henry

JUVENILE POEMS,

FOR THE USE OF

FREE AMERICAN CHILDREN

OF EVERY COMPLEXION.

BOSTON:
PUBLISHED BY GARRISON & KNAPP.

1835.

Figure 1.3. Title page of William Lloyd Garrison, *Juvenile Poems, for the Use of Free American Children, of Every Complexion* (Boston: Garrison and Knapp, 1835). Courtesy of the American Antiquarian Society.

Clarke Wright, who, in the mid-1830s, was appointed as the AASS's children's antislavery agent. "Children shrink back instinctively from all cruelty, till taught it by examples of violence in others," Wright wrote in a letter to Garrison. "They are by birthright abolitionists. When a child once understands what slavery is, it fills his heart with unutterable horror."[60] Likewise, Wright affirmed that children were naturally color-blind. "White children play with colored children, they walk together, eat together, and kiss each other, and never think that the color of the skin makes one better than the other."[61] Wright's positive image of the child was in line with nineteenth-century conceptions of childhood inherited from the Enlightenment. Historians of childhood have traced the changing attitudes toward children in North America, from Puritans' belief in infant depravity to Romantic notions of childhood innocence. References to children's sinful nature were not absent from religious literature in the 1820s and 1830s. Yet, for the most part, antebellum Americans no longer believed that the infant's soul was tainted with original sin. The Transcendentalist Bronson Alcott, a careful observer of the intellectual development of his own children, called this doctrine "debasing." "Happy is it for the world . . . that nobler views are gaining currency. Infancy is beginning to be respected."[62] Children, as Steven Mintz writes, came to be seen instead as "symbols of purity, spontaneity, and emotional expressiveness."[63]

The change owed largely to the philosophy of John Locke and Jean-Jacques Rousseau. In *Some Thoughts Concerning Education* (1693), Locke had emphasized children's malleability through his theory of the child as *tabula rasa*, or blank slate, waiting to be shaped by experience and education. Similar metaphors appeared in antislavery print culture, showing the popularity of Lockean discourse among Black and white abolitionists. An 1855 editorial in the *Christian Recorder*, the official organ of the African Methodist Episcopal Church, compared the minds of children to "a clean, white sheet of paper, which is ready to receive and will show any impression made upon it. It may be filled with intelligible writing, containing great and good ideas, or with bad writing, and wicked thoughts expressed."[64] Rousseau insisted that children were born innocent but risked being stifled by "prejudices, authority, necessity, example, all the social institutions in which we find ourselves submerged."[65] Slavery was one such institution, mentioned in the very first lines of his educational treatise, *Émile* (1762). Abolitionists, in Rousseauist fashion, claimed that children would do good—that is, reject slavery—if left to respond to their natural instincts. As Wright neatly put it, "Every child's heart is an Anti-Slavery heart."[66]

Frederick Douglass claimed to know of children's antislavery disposition from personal experience. In his 1855 autobiography *My Bondage and My Freedom*, he tells how, as a child in Baltimore, he would discuss slavery with his white playmates, lamenting that he was enslaved for life while they would enjoy complete freedom once they reached the age of majority. "Words like these," Douglass writes, "always troubled them; and I had no small satisfaction in wringing from the boys, occasionally, that fresh and bitter condemnation of slavery, that springs from nature, unseared and unperverted." He adds, "I do not remember ever to have met with a *boy*, while I was in slavery, who defended the slave system."[67] Central to Douglass's political philosophy was the belief that human beings are endowed with a natural affection for one another, as Nicholas Buccola has argued. Because children are closest to a state of nature, they provide evidence of original goodness.[68] Douglass also maintained that racial distinctions are meaningless to children. "Aside from the curious contrast to himself, the white child feels nothing on the first sight of a colored man," he wrote in his 1881 examination of the color line.[69]

Yet how were human goodness and indifference to race to survive in a country where slavery reigned supreme? Douglass's young Baltimore friends lived in its midst and would soon be perverted by its corrupting influence. Northern white children had little chance of escaping it either. As abolitionists reiterated in speech after speech, slavery was not simply a southern institution: its spirit could be felt in the free states too—in politics, at the pulpit, and in the press. Even juvenile literature was full of it. "Look . . . at the children's books which swarm in the bookstores," exclaimed Nathaniel Southard, the editor of the antislavery *Youth's Cabinet*. "You find some of them ingeniously devised to reconcile the young mind to slavery, but which of them utters a word of sympathy for the slave?"[70] Members of the AASS executive committee worried "lest the children growing up around them, and soon to come into possession of our country with all her mental, moral, political, and physical power, should imbibe the spirit of *slaveholding*, which now pervades the land."[71] Perhaps the most insidious manifestation of the spirit of slavery in the

North was racial prejudice. White children "scarcely learn to speak before they are taught to despise a colored man," Southard wrote.[72] Echoed
another abolitionist, "It is in our childhood that this prejudice is imbibed, of which we are so tenacious in after-life."[73] The most elaborate
version of this argument was made by the Black intellectual Hosea
Easton in his 1837 *Treatise on the Intellectual Character, and Civil and
Political Condition of the Colored People of the U. States.* Easton blamed
white parents and teachers for instilling in children the idea that Black
people were deficient. Most shocking was their constant use of the n-
word as a way to frighten children into obedience: "The universality of
this kind of education is well known to the observing. Children in infancy receive oral instruction from the nurse. The first lessons given are,
Johnny, Billy, Mary, Sally, (or whatever the name may be,) go to sleep,
if you don't the old *nigger* will care [*sic*] you off; don't you cry—Hark;
the old *niggers'* [*sic*] coming—how ugly you are, you are worse than a
little *nigger*. This is a specimen of the first lessons given."[74] Unless some
effort was made to counteract these nefarious influences, antislavery,
color-blind white children would inevitably turn into proslavery, racist
adults who would transmit their prejudiced views of African Americans to their offspring—and the nation would remain forever tainted
with the sin of slavery. "Children are born abolitionists," Henry Clarke
Wright insisted, and grown-up activists should strive "to keep them so."
The peaceful abolition of slavery could be easily effected if only antislavery adults managed to prevent white children "from imbibing the spirit
of violence and oppression that is so rife around them in this land of
boasted liberty."[75]

Black children, on the other hand, should receive proper intellectual,
moral, and religious training, as the African American activist and educator Maria W. Stewart argued in her 1860 lecture "The Proper Training
of Children." Given the harmful effects of racial prejudice and limited
opportunities for African Americans, Stewart feared that Black children,
as they moved into adulthood, might succumb to idleness and intemperance, which in turn would reinforce the prejudices against them. She
emphasized the necessity of a rigorous home education: it belonged to
parents to "lay the platform of piety and intelligence for our children to
walk upon."[76] The images of children presented in African American
public discourse and print culture did not significantly differ from those

that prevailed among white abolitionists. In the pages of *Freedom's Journal*, the first African American newspaper, childhood and youth were situated as "periods of cherished innocence and virtue that must be defended from corruption," as Michael Hines notes.[77] Though the effects of the spirit of slavery on Black and white children were of a different nature, it was damaging to both.

Abolitionists thus subscribed to modern notions of childhood innocence. As Robin Bernstein has shown, childhood innocence was a contested terrain in the nineteenth-century United States. The concept came to be weaponized by proponents of white supremacy, who pitted angelic, vulnerable white children against devilish pickaninnies impervious to pain. Innocence became the "exclusive property" of the white child, while Black children were "exiled from innocence and with it, from childhood—and humanity."[78] Abolitionists bucked the trend, insisting, in Douglass's succinct formulation, that "SLAVE-children *are* children."[79] Slave narratives written by young people shed light on the condition of the enslaved child, while white-authored abolitionist literature presented children as helpless victims of slavery: "Think of an infant, only FOUR WEEKS old, and another eighteen months old, seized for debt, and sold to the highest bidder!!!" Garrison wrote in the *Liberator*, commenting on an advertisement for a public auction published in a Georgia newspaper.[80] Abolitionists, however, did not just reclaim innocence for enslaved children. They turned free children's innocence into a weapon against slavery. At a time when childhood innocence came to be equated with "obliviousness to politics," they made innocence—understood as a spontaneous abhorrence of slavery and an indifference to race—a springboard for juvenile activism.[81] They recognized the "political power of childhood."[82]

On at least two occasions, abolitionists penned tributes to antislavery children—one Black, the other white—whose exemplary lives were cut short before they could reach adulthood. Stories of pious children who died prematurely, or "joyful death narratives," as Ivy Linton Stabell calls them, had long been popular with American audiences.[83] Abolitionists politicized the genre. In *Memoir of James Jackson* (1835), discussed at greater length in chapter 4, Susan Paul memorialized the life of one of her pupils, James Jackson, who had expressed concern about the plight of the enslaved. Likewise, the anonymous author of the little-known

Tribute to the Memory of Fitzhugh Smith, the Son of Gerrit Smith (1840) emphasized the "readiness" with which young Fitzhugh Smith, who died a few months before his twelfth birthday, "took his stand—firmly, and not to be shaken—on the doctrine of man's inalienable rights; as involved in the question of emancipating the enslaved." Fitzhugh, the author claims, "did not arrive at his abolitionism by the persuasions of others, or by the discussions he daily heard, so much as by his own reasoning." He developed an interest in the subject of slavery before his father, later an organizer of the Liberty Party, "had seen fit to become what is called an abolitionist." This account of a child's unprompted espousal of abolitionism is perhaps not entirely believable: the author themselves mentions the formative influence of the white abolitionist Charles Stuart, who "saw the plastic state of the lad's mind and . . . plied it with . . . arguments; though these were clothed in the simple drapery which boyhood could understand."[84] Children's abolitionism, though rooted in their natural instincts, needed to be nurtured. If James Jackson and Fitzhugh Smith differed from other children, it was because they had met with an early death and therefore their antislavery sentiments could never fade. *Memoir of James Jackson* and *Tribute to the Memory of Fitzhugh Smith* served as mementoes of their untainted commitment to the slave's cause.

Abolitionists went further than affirming young people's innate sympathy for the enslaved: they portrayed children as torchbearers in the fight for abolition. Children, they argued, knew better. They could see moral truths to which most adults had become blind. "It is not in the old, hardened with predjudices [sic] and follies and sins but in the growing generation of which you and I are a part that the hopes of the crushed slave and of the race rest," twenty-two-year-old Robert Bartlett wrote to the young women of the Plymouth, Massachusetts, Juvenile Anti-Slavery Society.[85] The more mature Benjamin Lundy, founder of the *Genius of Universal Emancipation*, one of the first abolitionist newspapers in the United States, concurred: "Of the old, or even of the middle aged, whose habits of thinking and acting are settled, and whose prejudices are confirmed, much cannot be expected in the way of reform."[86] Abolitionists could help children actualize their antislavery potential and protect them from the twin spirits of slavery and racism. Children, in turn, could be the means of converting adults. In a sonnet published in the 1841 edition of the antislavery gift book *The Liberty Bell*, which she edited, Maria Weston Chapman eulogized an imagined "LITTLE child" who "spake as one / Having authority of God to pour / The living words of liberty before / The wise and prudent," whose "aged eyes are sealed."[87] Chapman's depiction of the child as a divinely inspired oracle of freedom harked back to the Bible, where God is said to have ordained strength "out of the mouth of babes and sucklings" (Psalms 8:2)—a now common phrase used when children make remarkably insightful statements. An illustration placed before the sonnet shows a child in conversation with three bearded men: the boy has his hand raised and seems to be explaining something to the men, who are knitting their brows. The illustration brings to mind an oft-depicted episode from the New Testament in which twelve-year-old Jesus, who has gone missing for several days, is found in the temple "sitting in the midst of the doctors, both hearing them, and asking them questions"; the elders are "astonished at his understanding and answers" (Luke 2:46–47). The engraving used by Chapman had first appeared in an earlier publication, Bronson Alcott's *Conversations with Children on the Gospels* (1836–37), where a caption made the biblical subtext explicit (figure 1.4). Chapman thus drew on a repertoire of familiar images to make the radically new proposition that adults pay attention to what children had to say on the subject of slavery and perhaps even follow their lead.

Another concept that advocates of juvenile abolitionism drew on was "female influence," which under their pen coexisted with what I term "juvenile influence." Garrison himself had authored a series of articles on female influence early in his career, calling for the support of women in promoting temperance.[88] The notion posited women's natural ability to influence people around them—family and friends—through gentle persuasion. As I document more fully in chapter 5, this included children, for whose education mothers were assumed to be responsible. The question of what women could do for the slaves was an even more pressing one than how children might contribute to the cause. One answer was that women could cultivate their children's antislavery sentiments. "As mothers—impress upon the minds of your children the principles of Anti-Slavery," H.E.C.F. recommended in the *Advocate of Freedom*.[89] "Let [our nation's] juvenile population be effectually taught by your instilling precepts and convincing examples, that the enslaving of human beings

Jesus conversing with the Doctors.

Figure 1.4. Jesus among the doctors. Bronson Alcott, *Conversations with Children on the Gospels*, vol. 1 (Boston: James Munroe, 1836), 186. Courtesy of the American Antiquarian Society.

is the worst of crimes," T.H. concurred in the *Liberator*.[90] Though partly excluded from public culture, women could exercise a positive influence in the home and its immediate surroundings—"around your own fireside, in the domestic circles of your friends, sitting in the house, and walking by the way."[91] As Martha Jones has pointed out, the scope and limits of female influence was a commonly debated issue among African American activists in particular.[92]

Abolitionists argued that children themselves could act as conduits for antislavery, among fellow children but also among adults. "You may have some influence with your parents, and persons who are older than you," the *Slave's Friend* assured.[93] Whereas abolitionists faced bitter and sometimes violent opposition to their arguments, children were less likely to be resisted, especially by their (presumably loving) parents. Their perceived innocence made simple expressions of antislavery sentiments on their part more convincing than lengthy harangues by mature abolitionists. The Townsend sisters suggested as much in their preface to the "little readers" of the *Anti-Slavery Alphabet* when they wrote about men who buy slaves, "They may hearken what *you* say, / Though from *us* they turn away."[94]

Juvenile influence was a widespread notion in antebellum reform and religious culture. Religious journals and Sunday-school reports insisted that children could be the means whereby irreligious parents were led to church. In "A Father Converted through the Influence of His Own Child," published in the *Sunday-School Journal*, an eight-year-old gently reproved his father for spending his Sundays at the tavern rather than going to meeting with him. The father, mortified by his son's remark, determined to "abandon the drunkard's bowl" and "consecrate himself to God."[95] Such articles were commonly reprinted in the Black press, for instance in the *Colored American*, where they presented the "gentle admonishments" of Black children as "salvific influences" that could rescue their parents.[96] Abolitionists applied juvenile influence to the more controversial topics of slavery and racism. The *Slave's Friend* printed a brief story of a boy who had heard his father call a man of color the n-word. The boy's comment on his father's behavior was unwittingly sharp: "Where were you brought up, father?"[97] Reporting on a January 1837 meeting for children held in Newark, New Jersey, Henry Clarke Wright wrote that he had "let the children preach abolition to the parents. One person who was a colonizationist, said, 'the children have given me such an awful view of the sin of slavery, as I never had before.'"[98] In June of the same year, Wright enthused about the "mighty influence" of the young girls of the Providence, Rhode Island, Female Juvenile Anti-Slavery Society: "They . . . will do more to make the whole city Anti-slavery, than any others can do."[99] A decade later, Jane Elizabeth Jones noted in her children's book *The Young Abolitionists; or, Conversations on Slavery* (1848) that "benevolent enterprises have received great advantage from the moral influence of children." Through the character of Mrs. Selden, an abolitionist mother, she returned to by-then-common motifs of children's "freedom from guile" and "clearness of vision," which made them "effective preachers of righteousness."[100] Frederick Douglass praised the book in his newspaper, the *North Star*. "We have reason to believe that to the young of this day the slave and this country are to be indebted for emancipation," he predicted.[101]

Garrison, Douglass, Wright, Chapman, and Jones did not believe that children alone could defeat slavery. They were aware of the limitations of childhood and acknowledged children's specific needs—hence the development of a youth-oriented antislavery literature. Yet they also acknowledged children's agency. "Children sometimes think they can do nothing for others, while they are children," wrote a contributor to the antislavery *Juvenile Instructor*. "This is a sad mistake. The sooner children begin to do good, the better. Let them begin when they are little, and do more and more as they grow older."[102] The *Slave's Friend* put it in more metaphorical terms, comparing children to drops of rain on the leaves of trees: "When they are older and can do more good, they may be likened to springs, rivulets, or rivers; and at last their united efforts may roll in a flood of benevolence."[103] What mattered, in the end, was not so much the extent of children's participation in antislavery activism but that children be recognized as intelligent beings capable of comprehending the plight of the enslaved. Once familiarized with the tenets of abolitionism, children would grow up into responsible citizens committed to abolition and with real power to effect change. Most importantly, childhood, with its associations of innocence, purity, and virtue, served as a powerful rhetorical engine for critics of slavery. If five-year-olds could spontaneously differentiate right from wrong, just from unjust, how was it that so many adult white Americans failed to see the horror of slavery, let alone act against its perpetuation? Abolitionists did not believe that an army of child prophets would rise and redeem the country from its sins. But they realized how potent such an image could be.

Contesting Juvenile Abolitionism

Children's involvement in the abolition movement, like the involvement of women, did not go unchallenged. For some abolitionists, there were limits to what children could do for the slaves. One source of disagreement in the latter half of the 1830s concerned the signing of antislavery petitions by minors. Petitioning, as Kate Masur writes, was understood

in the early United States as "an act of supplication available to even
the most marginalized individuals."[104] It had long been used by various categories of disenfranchised Americans to demand the abolition
of slavery. From the earliest days of the republic, enslaved people in
Massachusetts, Connecticut, and New Hampshire petitioned state
legislatures for individual freedom and the adoption of emancipation
laws. Starting in the mid-1830s, white and free Black women "defied the
long-standing custom of females limiting their petitioning of Congress
to individual prayers regarding personal grievances," in Susan Zaeske's
words, and petitioned Congress for the abolition of slavery, asserting
"substantial political authority" in the process.[105] Children, on the other
hand, did not enjoy any of the rights commonly associated with citizenship. Political rights such as the right to vote and hold office were—and
still are—defined as privileges of adulthood; minors may not have been
explicitly deprived of the right to petition, but they were not assumed
to possess it either. In fact, white women and African American men
and women in the antebellum United States were often denied civil and
political rights on the basis of their being considered "perpetual children." Their struggle was a struggle for what Corinne Field has termed
"equal adulthood."[106]

Yet some reformers imagined an expanded civic role for children, one
that involved the signing of petitions as a way to influence public policy.
An 1847 issue of the *Youth's Temperance Advocate* featured a (perhaps
imagined) petition signed by children "between the age of four and sixteen," urging New York legislators not to repeal a recently passed law re-
straining the sale of intoxicating drinks. A half-page illustration showed
a band of boys and girls, some of them quite young, writing their names
on a sheet of paper twice their size (figure 1.5). Abolitionists likewise
encouraged children to sign petitions for the abolition of slavery in the
District of Columbia and the prohibition of the interstate slave trade.
Nathaniel Southard was an active promoter of the plan. At an 1837 meeting of the Massachusetts Anti-Slavery Society, he suggested that "those
engaged in circulating petitions" have "one copy for minors."[107] In a dialogue for the *Liberator*'s Juvenile Department, he educated the young
on what petitioning meant and how it worked. "The people can send
on written or printed petitions to Congress, with their names signed to
them, to let them know what they want done," he explained. "May I sign

THE MERRY SIGNING.

Figure 1.5. Children signing a temperance petition. "The Children's Petition," *Youth's Temperance Advocate*, March 1847. Courtesy of the American Antiquarian Society.

such a petition?" asked little Martha. "Yes," Southard answered. "There is one on purpose for children. You must put your age at the end of your name, so that folks may know you are a little girl."[108] Abolitionists did not try to pass off children as adults so as to artificially inflate the number of signers. They made sure that children's signatures would be immediately recognized as such by lawmakers, who might thus be shamed into acting against slavery. "You will all undoubtedly have an opportunity to sign petitions against the annexation of Texas to the Union," a pseudonymous contributor wrote in the *Herald of Freedom.* "Avail yourselves of the opportunity, not that your names may pass for men and women, but as *children,* that Congress may know . . . that children in New-Hampshire are opposed to the continuance of the oppressive system of slavery."[109] Forms of petitions for minors were circulated in the antislavery press. All that remained was for juvenile abolitionists to collect signatures among friends and neighbors. Members of the Boston Juvenile Anti-Slavery Society did so in the summer of 1837, as reported in the *Liberator.* "Abolitionists should aid and encourage their children in this good work," Garrison recommended.[110] Evidence reveals that not unsignificant numbers of children signed antislavery petitions. A petition by inhabitants of Westford, Vermont, was signed by "seventy-four minors, between the ages of 14 and 18 years," in January 1837; in December of that same year, a "memorial of 78 minors" of Attleboro, Massachusetts, was sent to Congress.[111] A historian of petitioning estimates that children from eight to nineteen signed antislavery petitions, "surg[ing] collectively into politics."[112]

Not all abolitionists looked kindly on juvenile antislavery petitioning. The white activist Lydia Maria Child, a writer of juvenile fiction, denounced it in no uncertain words. "I consider it an error of judgment, because the inevitable tendency will be to throw contempt on *all* our petitions," she wrote, "and it seems to me improper, because children are of necessity guided by others, and because this step is involved with questions evidently above juvenile capacities." Child did not dispute the fact that children should be informed about the evils of slavery. Her own *Juvenile Miscellany* included antislavery stories, as noted in chapter 2, and she acknowledged that "abolition parents ought thoroughly to prepare the hearts and minds of their children for the conscientious discharge of duties that will come with their riper years." What she challenged was the method of having them sign antislavery petitions, which she felt amounted to a manipulation of their still-rudimentary notions about slavery and the legal system protecting it. Children simply were not mature enough to understand the stakes of both the antislavery campaign and the act of petitioning the government. "This haste to invest them with the attributes of citizenship appears premature, and almost ridiculous," she went on. "I have not as yet conversed with an abolitionist, who did not view the subject in the same light."[113] The volatile political context of the latter half of the 1830s helps account for Child's visceral reaction. Only the year before, the House of Representatives had instituted its infamous "gag rule" providing that all antislavery petitions should be automatically tabled. Minors' petitions would bring discredit on abolitionism as a whole and seem to justify the curtailment of civil liberties by Congress. The children's petition campaign was too short-lived to create significant tensions within the abolition movement; it did not last much beyond 1837. Yet it reveals internal dissension about the role of children in the struggle for abolition and the limits of their citizenship, which some activists—and, arguably, children themselves—tested to an unprecedented degree.

Resistance to juvenile abolitionism came mostly from outside abolitionist ranks. In 1840, the white abolitionist Nathaniel Peabody Rogers recalled in the *National Anti-Slavery Standard* "the ridicule which the leading politicians, in Congress and out, and the newspapers generally, attempted to cast upon the anti-slavery enterprise, a few years ago, because . . . *minors* and *children* were allowed to sign petitions, and in other ways to manifest their sympathy for the slaves. . . . It was thought to be very improper for any person, who had not arrived at the grave age of twenty-one, to meddle with a matter so closely connected with the politics of the country."[114] Indeed, figures from various backgrounds came to criticize juvenile abolitionism in the late 1830s. The New England Democratic editor Orestes Brownson commented disparagingly on the abolitionists' "thousands of Petitions to Congress, with their seven hundred thousand signers, a large portion of whom are women and children."[115] Only legal voters, he seemed to say, could legitimately exercise the right to petition. Reviewing antislavery literature before the House of Representatives, the South Carolina planter-politician James Henry Hammond, who had first proposed the gag rule in 1835, brandished copies of the *Slave's Friend*. "On the covers, and within each of these are . . . pictures calculated to excite the feelings, and to nurture the incendiary spark in the tender bosom of the child," he fumed, unintentionally drawing attention to a publication that most Americans had never heard about. Garrison's *Juvenile Poems*, he went on, "contains, besides a great number of doggerel articles of the most inflammatory character, some nine or ten disgusting prints."[116] Senator John Tyler of Virginia—soon to become president of the United States—likewise denounced the gross misrepresentation of slavery to be found in abolitionist publications for children. "I am told that they [the abolitionists] are also addressing themselves to the growing generation through horn-books and primers—that the youthful imagination is filled with horror against us and our children by images and pictures exhibited in the nursery," he observed in a virulently antiabolition speech.[117] Juvenile abolitionism was caricatured in popular culture as well as politics. On the eve of the Civil War, at a time when the *Slave's Friend* had long been discontinued, the pseudonymous author of *The Devil in America: A Dramatic Satire* (1860) mocked the "pedagogues with knowledge overcharged" who

> In figures, spelling-books, and grammars skill'd,
> Descanted freely on the rights of man,
> And frightful pictures to the children show'd,
> Of monsters holding lashes in their hands,
> Of darkies tied or chain'd to whipping-posts,
> Till infant tears were trickling down their cheeks.[118]

Abolitionists, these critics claimed, were fanatics who would indoctrinate children to the point of traumatizing them. They had no regard for children's tender feelings—no qualms about destroying their sacred innocence.

Abolitionists countered these attacks by pointing out that enslavers, not opponents of slavery, had been ruining children's innocence for generations—enslaved children's innocence, as noted earlier, but also that of their own children. According to the *Slave's Friend*, children of enslavers who grew up on southern plantations were "tyrants in miniature": they grew accustomed to exploitation and violence, which they themselves soon visited on the enslaved, as a cartoon by David Claypoole Johnston (known for designing the first masthead of Garrison's *Liberator*) also disturbingly suggested (figure 1.6).[119] This view was first expressed not by second-wave abolitionists, however, but by a first-wave critic of slavery—albeit an enslaver himself—Thomas Jefferson. "The whole commerce between master and slave is a perpetual exercise of the

Figure 1.6. Tyrants in miniature. David Claypoole Johnston, "The Early Development of Southern Chivalry," ca. 1864. Courtesy of the American Antiquarian Society.

most boisterous passions, the most unremitting despotism on the one part, and degrading submissions on the other," Jefferson wrote in his 1785 *Notes on the State of Virginia*.

> Our children see this, and learn to imitate it; for man is an imitative animal. This quality is the germ of all education in him. From his cradle to his grave he is learning to do what he sees others do. If a parent could find no motive either in his philanthropy or his self-love, for restraining the intemperance of passion towards his slave, it should always be a sufficient one that his child is present. But generally it is not sufficient. The parent storms, the child looks on, catches the lineaments of wrath, puts on the same airs in the circle of smaller slaves, gives a loose to his worst of passions, and thus nursed, educated, and daily exercised in tyranny, cannot but be stamped by it with odious peculiarities.[120]

In a world where slavery was the norm, there was no need to actively raise a proslavery child. The child would naturally imbibe their parents' prejudices and, at a later age, realize that their own economic security depended on inheriting the people enslaved by their family. The slave system contained the seeds of its own perpetuation through generations.

Jefferson's foundational critique became a commonplace of abolitionist discourse. It cropped up in an 1820 essay on slavery by Charles J. Fox, later reprinted in Benjamin Lundy's *Genius of Universal Emancipation*: "Where Slavery exists, the child is not merely a *passive* spectator of the inconsistency subsisting between professed freedom and practical tyranny—He becomes, himself, an actor in the scene—and frequently, ere he learns our boasted political creed, begins to play the part of a despot."[121] In *Biographical Sketches and Interesting Anecdotes of Persons of Colour* (1826), the white abolitionist Abigail Mott pitied those "who, being trained up in the midst of Slavery, are inured from their infancy to see the sufferings of the poor slaves, and to hear their cries." Such people "become almost insensible to . . . the enormity of the evils they are committing."[122] Jefferson's words were paraphrased in the *Slave's Friend* and quoted in the *Liberator*'s Juvenile Department.[123] They were anthologized in John A. Collins's antislavery compendium for youth, *The Anti-Slavery Picknick* (1842).[124]

Slave narratives provided concrete examples of enslavers' children acting in abusive ways toward their enslaved peers. James W. C. Pennington wrote of "the tyranny of the master's children" in his 1849 autobiography *The Fugitive Blacksmith*. "My master had two sons, about the ages and sizes of my older brother and myself," he explained. "We were not only required to recognise these young sirs as our young masters, but *they* felt themselves to be such; and, in consequence of this feeling, they sought to treat us with the same air of authority that their father did the older slaves."[125] Another leitmotif of slave narratives was the transformation of the kind, generous white child who would share their bread with enslaved children into a callous adult who flogged or sold their former playmates. As James Curry put it in 1840,

> From my childhood until I was sixteen years old, I was brought up a domestic servant. I played with my master's children, and we loved one another like brothers. This is often the case in childhood, but when the

young masters and misses get older, they are generally sent away from home to school, and they soon learn that slaves are not companions for them. When they return, the love of power is cultivated in their hearts by their parents, the whip is put into their hands, and they soon regard the negro in no other light than as a slave.[126]

Historians have shed light on the process through which children were acculturated into the slave system. Stephanie Jones-Rogers has characterized daughters of enslavers as "mistresses in the making." Mary, Sarah, and Catherine Martin of Georgia, for instance, witnessed the brutal beating—and eventual murder—of twelve- or thirteen-year-old Alfred by their father and brother. Testifying before court after their father was convicted, the three sisters showed no sign of distress. They had done nothing to prevent the beating either. They were wholly desensitized to the violence of slavery.[127]

Juvenile literature played a role in southern white children's acculturation to slavery, though there was no proslavery counterpart to the *Slave's Friend* strictly speaking. There was little in common between the social contexts of southern and northern white children. Public education developed much more slowly in the South than it did in the North, as the dispersed population made the creation of a viable school system difficult. As a result, the South trailed behind the rest of the United States with regard to literacy rates, and its publishing industry was likewise underdeveloped.[128] Still, the 1830s saw the birth of the first US children's magazine published in the South, the proslavery *Rose Bud* (later the *Southern Rose Bud* and the *Southern Rose*), edited by Caroline Howard Gilman of Charleston, South Carolina. Child readers of the *Rose Bud* "acquired extraordinary insight into the daily practice of slave ownership," learning about proper slave management, forms of religious instruction for enslaved people, and the pass system.[129] Again, Gilman did not need to make an emphatic case for slavery but simply to make slavery an unproblematic part of her poems and plantation stories. As Paula Connolly notes in her study of proslavery children's literature, the *Rose Bud*'s stories, like proslavery novels, presented the plantation as "an arcadian idyll seemingly insulated from outside chaos"—a "liminal place" peopled with loyal, happy slaves and firm yet kind-hearted mistresses.[130] Slavery did not necessarily feature prominently in such literature: it served as a background, its existence unquestioned, its horrors nowhere to be seen. Proslavery authors contested that slavery had deleterious effects on children, contending instead that early association between free white and enslaved Black children led to reciprocal affection between the grown-up master or mistress and their slaves. As Elizabeth Kuebler-Wolf sums up, "Antislavery forces typically depicted naturally innocent children who were irrevocably corrupted, damaged, and destroyed by slavery, while proslavery advocates represented childhood acculturation to slavery, for enslaved and free alike, as a necessary ingredient of a benevolent, hierarchical, organic plantation society."[131]

Abolitionists and proponents of slavery alike understood that children had a place in their vision of the United States' future. They used a variety of resources to ensure that their offspring would come to espouse their views. Enslavers and antiabolitionists, however, fought to maintain a status quo. The white supremacist and proslavery values they cherished were shared by a majority of white Americans, notably those in power; their children would be exposed to them in one way or another. Abolitionists, on the other hand, hoped to radically transform US society. They educated children in ways that ran counter to the proslavery consensus. Print culture, as I have pointed out, was one of their most important resources for talking to children about slavery. In chapter 2, I map out the terrain of juvenile abolitionist literature.

2

"Anti-Slavery Publications Adapted to the Capacity of Children"

What Was Juvenile Antislavery Literature?

The abolition movement invested heavily in print culture throughout the antebellum period. The American Anti-Slavery Society published books, newspapers, and tracts in the tens of thousands before its breakup in 1840, distributing them widely across the North and South. The 1840s saw a number of formerly enslaved people publish autobiographical narratives, which were sold at antislavery book depositories and meetings on both sides of the Atlantic. After Harriet Beecher Stowe's *Uncle Tom's Cabin* became a best seller in 1852, mainstream trade publishers—once wary of alienating southern white readers—proved more willing to publish antislavery literature.[1]

Print culture was an essential tool for enlisting children and youth in the antislavery cause. In *Domestic Abolitionism and Juvenile Literature, 1830–1865* (2003), Deborah De Rosa has recovered and examined a wealth of juvenile antislavery stories and poems authored by white women, later collected in the anthology *Into the Mouths of Babes* (2005).[2] Yet the vast territory of juvenile antislavery literature remains largely uncharted, I argue, and our sense of what counts as antislavery literature for children much too restricted. Juvenile antislavery literature as I understand it comprised a variety of genres and formats. It was authored by men and women, African American as well as white—and not unfrequently by children themselves. It included not just stories and poems by the white abolitionists Elizabeth Margaret Chandler and Eliza Lee Follen but graphic accounts of slavery by the white slave rescuer Jonathan Walker, stories about racial prejudice by the Black activist Sarah Mapps Douglass, and antislavery orations by students of the African Free Schools. At a time when distinctions between children's literature and literature for adults were less sharply drawn than today, the body of antislavery writings deemed suitable for children also included works not written especially for them. Slave narratives are a case in point.

In the spirit of Katharine Capshaw and Anna Mae Duane's essay collection *Who Writes for Black Children?* (2017), I seek to approach juvenile antislavery literature "capaciously," adopting the point of view of young Black and white readers (and producers) of antislavery literature rather than the narrower perspective of women who, in De Rosa's terms, used the "nonthreatening" genre of children's literature to critique slavery.[3] What emerges is an expanded canon of antislavery literature for children with truly radical—indeed, threatening— potentialities. Juvenile antislavery literature went beyond metaphors of caged birds and prayers for the slaves. It discussed the imperialistic dimensions of the slave system, the moral necessity of assisting fugitives, and the workings of systemic racism. It armed children with the intellectual tools to combat slavery.

The British Origins of Juvenile Antislavery Literature

Juvenile literature as a distinct cultural and commercial phenomenon first took hold in Britain in the mid-eighteenth century.[4] "Giving, as it did, direct access to young and impressionable minds, children's literature . . . provided the perfect vehicle for the dissemination of humanitarian ideas," J. R. Oldfield argues. It played "a vital role in creating an anti-slavery consensus" across the Atlantic.[5] Many early US children's books were British reprints. Any account of the development of juvenile antislavery literature in the United States must therefore start in Britain.

Antislavery sentiment first cropped up in children's books not ostensibly about slavery. Geographies and travelogues were two of the genres most suited to discussions of slavery and the slave trade, as the examples of Susanna Rowson and Jedidiah Morse in chapter 1 have suggested. *Geography Made Familiar and Easy to Young Gentlemen and Ladies* (1748), written by John Newbery, a prolific author and pioneering publisher of instructional books for children, includes a chapter on Africa with a section on "Guinea." The "chief Commodities" of Guinea, Newbery explains, are gold, ivory, hides, wax, pepper, several drugs, and "Negro Slaves." A description of the slave trade soon turns into reproof of the system. "Many thousands of these unhappy Creatures are annually transported by the *Europeans* to *America*, either to work in the Plantations there, or in the Mines of *Mexico* and *Peru*: A Sort of Commerce scarce to be defended either upon the Foot of Religion or Humanity!"[6] The morality of the slave trade was also questioned in children's books dealing with science and natural philosophy. A later volume by Newbery, *The Newtonian System of Philosophy Adapted to the Capacities of Young Gentlemen and Ladies* (1761), presents itself as a series of lectures read to the "Lilliputian Society" by a young philosopher named Tom Telescope. In one of his lectures, Tom decries the behavior of a neighbor who "will not sell a horse, that is declining, for fear he should fall into the hands of a master who might treat him with cruelty; but . . . is largely concerned in the slave trade . . . and makes no difficulty of separating the husband from the wife, the parents from the children, and all of them . . . from their native country, to be sold in a foreign market, like so many horses, and often to the most merciless of the human race."[7] Juvenile literature was never just a means to entertain or educate youthful readers. From its very origins, it was also used to politicize them.

Condemnations of slavery in juvenile literature became more common after the British campaign against the slave trade took off in the late 1780s. The British Quaker William Darton's first publication as author and publisher, *Little Truths Better than Great Fables* (1787–88), contains strong anti-slave-trade sentiment. A parent's conversation with their child about the evils of tobacco gradually leads into a denunciation of the traffic in enslaved people. Why are some Africans called slaves? the child asks. Answers the parent, "On account of their being made so by great numbers of people, who go from England, Holland, and France, to several parts on the Coast of Africa, and encourage the strong and wicked people of the land to make war, and steal away the inland natives, whom the Europeans purchase by hundreds, and carry to America and the West-India islands, where these poor creatures must work so long as they live!" The parent then provides a graphic description of the Middle Passage, quoting from a 1666 account of a voyage to Brazil by the Capuchin priest Denis de Carli. The passage, however, ends on a more hopeful note: when the child points out that there are many good people in England and asks why they do not strive to stop such cruelties, the parent reassures them that "a great number of tender-minded people, both in America and England" have been trying "to abolish a trade so big with numberless evils."[8] Historians of education have shown the role of conversation in the intellectual training and development of children in eighteenth- and nineteenth-century England. Middle-class parents came to see conversation as a method of cultivating the child's mind, while authors and their publishers popularized the instructional dialogue as a subgenre of children's literature.[9] Abolitionists participated in making domestic conversation into a pedagogical tool, as it provided a familiar, reassuring setting in which to impart potentially distressing information about slavery. The family dialogue became a staple of juvenile antislavery literature.

Darton was largely responsible, along with his partner, Joseph Harvey, also a Quaker, for keeping antislavery before young British readers in the decades that followed.[10] Not only were Quakers key actors in the emergence of the Anglo-American abolition movement, but their "traditionally intense concentration on the rearing of children" also made them early advocates of juvenile abolitionism.[11] A leading purveyor of juvenile literature, Darton (and his successors) issued a number of children's books that dealt frankly with slavery.[12] *Mental Improvement* (1794), a two-volume work by the Quaker feminist and abolitionist Priscilla Wakefield, consists in a "series of instructive conversations" between Mr. and Mrs. Harcourt and their children. Conversation 9 has nine-year-old Henry asking about the cultivation of sugar, which allows for a lengthy discussion of the slave trade. "Negro slaves" are "natives of Africa," Mr. Harcourt explains, "but snatched from their own country, friends, and connections, by the hand of violence, and power." They are "crouded [*sic*] together in the hold" of slave ships, Mrs. Harcourt goes on, "where many of them mostly die from want of air and room," while others throw themselves into the sea. The Harcourts provide a detailed account of the slave system, from enslavement in Africa to exploitation in the West Indies, before praising the efforts of abolitionists like William Wilberforce to obtain an act for the abolition of the trade. Most importantly, *Mental Improvement* suggests that children themselves have a role to play in the struggle for abolition. Hopeful that "the rising generation will prefer justice and mercy, to interest and policy," Mr. Harcourt asks twelve-year-old Cecilia if she would be "willing to debar [her]self of . . . sugar, coffee, rice, calico, rum, and many other things"—in other words, to abstain from the products of enslaved labor. Cecilia firmly answers that she would, while her sixteen-year-old sister, Sophia, later discusses maple sugar as a substitute for cane.[13] The pages of juvenile antislavery books and magazines would soon be filled with poems about children abstaining from sweets, petitions by sugar-making slaves, and short pieces about the promises of beet and butternut sugar.

The Dartons pioneered many of the genres that came to be popular among US juvenile abolitionists and their parents. Over three decades before the Townsend sisters published the *Anti-Slavery Alphabet* (1846), Darton's eldest son, William Darton Jr., issued *New and Entertaining Alphabet, for Young Children* (1811). Though the alphabet has no overarching theme—*C* is for "Countess," *G* for "Geese," and (unsurprisingly) *Q* for "Quaker"—two of its letters directly reference slavery (figures 2.1 and 2.2). The letter *N* is illustrated by "Negro," with an engraving of a man seated with a rake and the following verse:

> N stands for a Negro, far from his home,
> To work as a slave in West India his doom,
> Laboriously toiling beneath the hot sun,
> Among sugar-canes working till day-light is done;
> Oh! think he may say, when you sweeten your tea,
> Oh! think of some method to set Negro free.[14]

Such clearly expressed antislavery sentiment is unexpected in a book—let alone one for children—published in the early 1810s. After the British Parliament outlawed the slave trade in 1807, the abolition movement experienced a lull in its activities. Abolitionists believed that the ending of the trade would compel planters to treat their workforce more humanely. They advocated gradual abolition, maintaining that the enslaved needed to be prepared for freedom. A renewed struggle to eradicate slavery immediately did not happen until a decade later.[15] Yet Darton's *New and Entertaining Alphabet* urged its young readers, in the voice of a Black man, to "think of some method to set Negro free." Letter

Y also conveys an antislavery message by referencing the well-known story of Yarico, a woman sold into slavery by a shipwrecked English sailor, Thomas Inkle, whom she has rescued from death. Though Yarico was usually portrayed as an Indian, her pathetic figure helped stimulate sympathy for American slaves; the tale was appropriated by antislavery writers such as the Abbé Raynal.[16] In Darton's alphabet, Yarico's skin tone matches that of the unnamed "Negro," and her position exactly mirrors his: they are both sitting, their heads lowered—only the "Negro" seems to be cautiously looking up, as if toward the "poor simple maid . . . by Incle [*sic*] betray'd."[17] Taken together, the enslaved man and woman form two parts of an antislavery diptych.

The revival of British abolitionism in the 1820s led Harvey and Darton, as their publishing firm was then known, to issue children's books entirely focused on slavery. In particular, the firm published several pamphlet-length poems, two by Amelia Opie, one by William Cowper. Opie's *The Negro Boy's Tale, a Poem, Addressed to Children* (1824) had first been published in 1802, in the context of a conservative backlash against anti-slave-trade campaigning following the French and Haitian Revolutions.[18] "The Negro Boy's Tale" did not originally identify children as its primary audience, yet it featured two child characters: Zambo, an enslaved youth who pleads for passage from Jamaica to England, and Anna, the daughter of a British gentleman on his way to England and the sympathetic (though ultimately powerless) auditor of Zambo's plea.[19] This made the poem particularly adapted for the juvenile audience Harvey and Darton were trying to cultivate. Opie prefaced this new, separately published edition of "The Negro Boy's Tale" with an address to children in which she urged "the rising generation" to "never lose sight of the wrongs of the Negroes."[20] Opie, unlike Elizabeth Heyrick, who in 1824 famously called for "immediate, not gradual abolition" in a pamphlet of the same name, took a gradualist stance in her preface.[21] Two years later, Harvey and Darton issued *The Negro's Complaint: A Poem* (1826), another reprint of a popular antislavery ballad by William Cowper, first written at the onset of the anti-slave-trade campaign, in 1788, and repurposed as a children's book—as its format and illustrations suggest—on the eve of the campaign for immediate slave emancipation.[22] Though not initially written for a juvenile audience, these two poems were incorporated into the print culture of juvenile abolitionism.

Figure 2.1. N for "Negro." *New and Entertaining Alphabet, for Young Children, Where Some Instruction May Be Gained, and Much Amusement* (London: W. Darton Jr., 1813), 16. Courtesy of the Lilly Library, Indiana University.

Also in 1826, Amelia Opie, who by then had converted to Quakerism, published another pamphlet-length antislavery poem with Harvey and Darton. *The Black Man's Lament; or, How to Make Sugar* differed from both *The Negro Boy's Tale* and *The Negro's Complaint* in that it was expressly written for juveniles, as the first stanza points out: "COME, listen to my plaintive ditty, / Ye tender hearts, and children dear!"[23] A

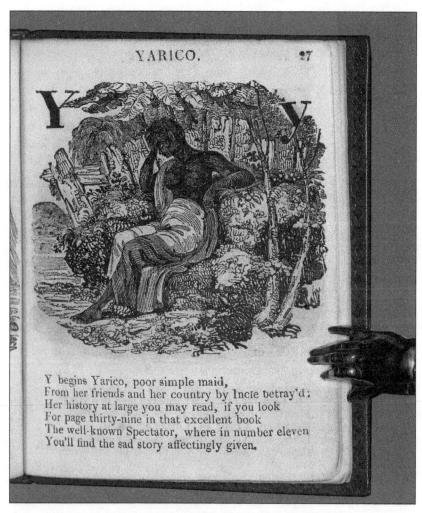

YARICO. 27

Y begins Yarico, poor simple maid,
From her friends and her country by Incie betray'd;
Her history at large you may read, if you look
For page thirty-nine in that excellent book
The well-known Spectator, where in number eleven
You'll find the sad story affectingly given.

Figure 2.2. *Y* for "Yarico." *New and Entertaining Alphabet, for Young Children, Where Some Instruction May Be Gained, and Much Amusement* (London: W. Darton Jr., 1813), 27. Courtesy of the Lilly Library, Indiana University.

"ditty" rather than a long-form narrative poem, *The Black Man's Lament* is written in more accessible language than Cowper's ballad is. Contrary to Zambo in Opie's previous work, the eponymous Black man speaks in plain English rather than in dialect. The poem's structure is also much more straightforward. *The Black Man's Lament* has no characters or plot to speak of: it follows the journey of a generic "Negro slave" captured by "the cruel White man" in Africa, transported to the West Indies, sold to the highest bidder, and made to toil in the cane fields. Its most original aspect, as the title indicates, is its detailed examination of the cultivation and production of sugar. Opie makes it clear that violence and exploitation are embedded in each and every step of the sugar-making process: clearing away the weeds, holing the fields ("the whip our strength must aid, / And lash us when we pause or drop!"), planting, manuring, hoeing, cutting down the sugarcane ("'Tis then begin our saddest pain"), bringing the canes to the bruising mill ("And if we faint, the cart-whip's power, / Gives force which *nature's* powers *deny*"), boiling and cooling the sugar, filling and heading casks, shipping the casks.[24] Though Opie does not explicitly call on her readers to abstain from sugar, she does envision an active political role for them.[25] This is evident not only from the first stanza, where children are encouraged to act against slavery— "And, should [my plaintive ditty] move your souls to pity, / Oh! try to *end* the griefs you hear"—but also from the illustration above the text, depicting children signing a petition for abolishing the slave trade (figure 2.3).[26] *The Black Man's Lament*, like *The Negro's Complaint*, is notable for its eighteen hand-colored copperplate engravings, which make it a visually striking volume and doubtless one that captivated young readers at a time when even black-and-white illustrations in printed books were few and far between (*The Negro Boy's Tale* only has one as its frontispiece). Martha Cutter calls Opie's 1826 volume "one of the earliest and most elaborate graphic illustrated books for children exclusively devoted to an antislavery topic." Counterbalancing the generic voice, the illustrator "takes care to depict distinctive (rather than stereotypical) persons" and mainly "eschews the use of voyeuristic scenes of sadomasochistic torment," foregrounding instead the laboring skills of the enslaved.[27] The image of the slave ship, recalling the well-known diagram of the *Brookes*, introduces its young viewer to the visual culture of transatlantic abolitionism.

The Black Man's Lament's front matter includes a list of children's books published by Harvey and Darton that usefully groups together the publishers' antislavery titles. To Opie's and Cowper's volumes are added *Samboe; or, The African Boy* (1823) and *Radama; or, The Enlightened African* (1824) by Mary Anne Hedge; *Prejudice Reproved; or, The History of the Negro Toy-Seller* (1826) by Catherine Parr Traill; and the

THE

BLACK MAN'S LAMENT.

THE PETITION FOR ABOLISHING THE SLAVE-TRADE.

———

COME, listen to my plaintive ditty,
　Ye tender hearts, and children dear!
And, should it move your souls to pity,
　Oh! try to *end* the griefs you hear.

Figure 2.3. Children signing an anti-slave-trade petition. Amelia Opie, *The Black Man's Lament; or, How to Make Sugar* (London: Harvey and Darton, 1826), 2. Courtesy of the Lilly Library, Indiana University.

1825 slave narrative of Solomon Bayley. These books belonged to a variety of genres—poetry, narrative, life-writing—but they all contained strong denunciations of slavery and the slave trade as well as racial prejudice. *Prejudice Reproved*, for instance, features youths harboring antislavery and antiracist sentiments: Richard Herbert "reproves" his young cousin Edward Greville for insulting a Black man, whom we learn was enslaved in St. Domingo. These works also frequently referenced "adult" antislavery works by Thomas Clarkson or John Newton in their footnotes, paving the way for more robust reading on the subject.[28] Harvey and Darton, together with the mostly female antislavery authors whom they published, thus helped invent the literary figure of the juvenile abolitionist. They likewise contributed to the development of juvenile antislavery literature as a genre in and of itself, one that drew on the manifold literary, linguistic, and visual resources of children's literature to convey an explicitly antislavery message. As J. R. Oldfield notes, the 1830s witnessed a sharp decline in antislavery sentiment in British children's literature, particularly after the abolition of slavery in the West Indies in 1834.[29] US abolitionists picked up where their British counterparts had left off and made sure that children would have plenty of reading material suited to their needs. It was in the United States that juvenile antislavery literature came of age.

The Golden Age of Juvenile Antislavery Literature

Juvenile antislavery literature entered its heyday in the 1830s, with the rise of immediatism. The press proved its most fertile breeding ground. On January 1, 1831, William Lloyd Garrison founded the famed *Liberator*, read by both white and Black abolitionists. Within a month of its creation, the paper had a Juvenile Department. For Garrison, slavery was a "national crime" in which every white American was an abettor; no one should feel innocent of it, and everyone should aid in its extermination, including children. As he put it in an early prospectus for the newspaper, "The people, the whole people, must engage in the work; every man, and every woman, and every child."[30] Though he was not yet a father when he launched the *Liberator*, Garrison already felt that the young generation might have a role to play in the fight for abolition. He created the Juvenile Department at the suggestion of a reader known only by his initials. "It has occurred to me that it would greatly extend the usefulness of your paper," U.I.E. wrote Garrison, "if a small portion of it were regularly appropriated to the use of the young." Children, whose minds are "easily accessible to the force of truth," would prove receptive auditors to tales of oppression and might be turned into "future co-operators." "Every body writes now for children," U.I.E. added, pointing to the rapid development of children's literature in the first decades of the nineteenth century.[31]

U.I.E. contributed much of the material to the early iterations of the Juvenile Department. His story "The Family Circle" was serialized over a period of nine months, from January 22 to October 22. Like Wakefield's *Mental Improvement*, it took the form of a family conversation between Helen, George, Lucy, and their parents. The story starts with Lucy reciting a famous antislavery passage from Cowper's meditative poem *The Task* (1785), a favorite among British and US abolitionists.[32] This leads her younger sister, Helen, to inquire about the meaning of the word "slave." "Is it any body that works very hard?" she asks, to which her father provides a thoughtful answer:

> "No," said her father; "I have been working very hard at my office to-day, and John Wilson has worked very hard sawing wood for us, and he works very hard every day; but we are neither of us slaves. But if I were forced to work for some other person, and to do whatever he told me to do, without my having agreed with him to work for him, and if this man could beat me and punish me if I did not do what he liked, and could sell me to somebody else, and could do almost any thing he chose to me, then I should be his slave. Do you understand me, Helen?"

The father and mother then discuss the treatment of the enslaved at great length—how they are made to work beyond their strength, how their food and clothing are often inadequate, how they are deprived of an education—each of their answer prompting more questions from the two older children. Though the father's opinion on slavery is obvious, he makes a point of not giving it outright, wishing his children "to think, and judge for [them]selves." George and Lucy, in fact, come out as more radical than their father in their heartfelt denunciations of slaveholders as "the wickedest people in the world," to which the father replies that some slaveholders simply do not realize "how wrong [slavery] is." The conversation then takes a more political turn as the father evokes the compromises over slavery that were made between North and South at the 1787 Constitutional Convention, in particular the fugitive slave clause of the US Constitution, causing Lucy to wonder why the free states entered into "such a wicked agreement"—words that foreshadow Garrison's own description of the Constitution as "an agreement with hell" a decade later. Predictably, the following installment deals with antislavery activism, especially in the form of abstinence from slave-labor goods, and has Lucy exclaim, "Let us never wear any thing more, or eat any thing more, that the poor slaves have to suffer so much for."[33] "The Family Circle" ends with a frank discussion of northern racism. The mother points to its systemic nature, explaining, for instance, how segregation in schools and exclusion from the workplace lead to poverty among African Americans.

"The Family Circle" promotes not just abolitionist principles but an idea of the child as a rational being who can understand the social and political stakes of issues such as slavery and racism. Far from being disconnected from the public sphere of politics, the private sphere of the home is depicted as "a kind of school for citizenship"—a place where children can become informed citizens able to form independent judgments.[34] Installments of "The Family Circle" were interspersed with a variety of other writings designed to appeal to both the head and the heart of young readers. Garrison gave a prominent place to poetry in the Juvenile Department, reprinting Opie's "The Negro Boy's Tale" thirty years after its initial publication as well as poems by Elizabeth Margaret Chandler. Many of the poems appearing in the Juvenile Department, such as "Letter from an Infant Slave to the Child of Its Mistress" and its companion piece, "The White Infant's Reply to the Little Slave," were written in the voice of children, enslaved and free. Black and white children also populated stories such as Mary Russell Mitford's "The Two Dolls," in which young Fanny Elvington is taught a lesson about racial prejudice. In Chandler's "Edward and Mary," young Edward Middleton, who at first cares little for the enslaved, commits to abolitionism thanks to the joint influence of his mother and sister. Besides dialogues, poems, and stories, the Juvenile Department presented factual information about slavery drawn from travel narratives and other kinds of eyewitness testimonies. Garrison reprinted a description of a slave market from Robert Walsh's *Notices of Brazil in 1828 and 1829* (1830)—"we think [it] is calculated to make a deep impression upon the minds of our juvenile readers," he commented—and an account of an enslaved youth being auctioned off from Basil Hall's *Travels in North America, in the Years 1827 and 1828* (1829). Nor did he shrink from including graphic descriptions of slave torture, reprinting for instance a "PARTICULAR ACCOUNT OF THE MURDER OF FIVE NEGROES; SHEWING HOW ONE HAD HER NOSE, EARS AND BREASTS CUT OFF, AND OTHERS WERE FLOGGED TO DEATH." Some parents probably thought twice before placing such accounts in their children's hands, and at least one mother of two who had discussed the slave trade with her three-year-old son after her slightly older daughter had read about it in the *Liberator* "was almost sorry she had told him so much about the sufferings of the slave."[35]

The Juvenile Department was a space for the development and circulation of Black writing. At a time when most US slave narratives had yet to appear, Garrison reprinted excerpts from more or less recently published British slave narratives. A passage from Ottobah Cugoano's *Thoughts and Sentiments on the Evil and Wicked Traffic of the Slavery and Commerce of the Human Species* (1787) focused on the kidnapping, enslavement, and transportation to Grenada of young Cugoano. The brief "Narrative of Louis Asa-Asa, a Captured African," originally appended to *The History of Mary Prince, a West Indian Slave* (1831), was presented in full. This little-known narrative was particularly adapted for a juvenile audience as it was given by a young person: Asa-Asa was enslaved around the age of thirteen, and he must have been around eighteen when Thomas Pringle, the editor of Prince's *History*, took down his account, rendering it "as nearly as possible in the narrator's words." Told in short, simple sentences by a young man who still had vivid memories of his experience as an enslaved child, Asa-Asa's narrative was sure to engage the younger readers of the *Liberator*. Garrison also published several antislavery essays and speeches by Black children and youth, discussed at greater length in chapter 4. Aged twelve to sixteen, Isaiah G. De Grasse, John E. Burr, and William H. Matthews eloquently attacked slavery, showing, in Garrison's words, "how deeply the spirit of liberty is pervading the breasts of the rising generation." These youths may have been readers of the *Liberator* themselves. Garrison envisaged an interracial audience for the Juvenile Department, as was made clear by the title of the compilation of poems he published in 1835, most of which had first appeared in the *Liberator*: *Juvenile Poems, for the Use of Free American Children, of Every Complexion*. A (perhaps Black-authored) piece titled "A Good Plan for Colored Boys" features two African American youths, John and Lucas, who plan to excel at school so as to defeat prejudices against them.[36]

The Juvenile Department also provided an outlet for the young African American women of the Philadelphia-based Female Literary Association, in particular for Sarah Mapps Douglass, one of its leaders. In mid-1832, the twenty-five-year-old Douglass, writing under the pen name Zillah, contributed several pieces for children to the *Liberator*. Her stories all centered young Black characters. Two of them discussed racial prejudice, though in a more subtle way than most white-authored juvenile antislavery stories: prejudice against children of color was linked to other themes such as education and disability. One story, headed "For the Children Who Read the Liberator," is about an African American girl named Elizabeth, a character modeled on Douglass's older sister. Despite constant pain caused by a hip disorder, Elizabeth manages to reach the head of her class, leading her schoolmates to complain "that a negro stood above them." The young girl is expelled from school. The homeschooled Elizabeth not only proves just as bright as before but she now takes care of some of her mother's domestic duties, watching over her younger siblings, at least until her premature death at the age of fourteen. In "A Dialogue between a Mother and Her Children," little Henry is scolded for throwing away his bread. His mother tells him about a "poor old slave man" who was "turned off" to provide for himself. Nothing is said about the family's race until the end of the story, when Henry, feeling sorry, says that he will buy some bread to send the old man. The mother answers that the man has long been dead and advises her son to save his money instead. "Uncle will put it into the funds now preparing to build a College for our youth," she says, connecting antislavery with the Black-led struggle for education. Though Douglass's role as an educator and activist has been well documented, she is often left out from discussions of juvenile antislavery literature, despite her significant contributions to the genre.[37]

Children who read the Juvenile Department got acquainted with the *Liberator* as a whole, moving from one section to the other as they grew up—from family dialogues such as "An Evening at Home" to articles titled "Blood! Blood!! Blood!!! Another Insurrection!" (both appeared on the same page of the September 24, 1831, issue). By December 1831, Garrison believed that the Juvenile Department had been "eminently successful in awakening the sympathies of youthful readers in behalf of the suffering slaves."[38] Despite this assessment, the Juvenile Department did not become a permanent feature of the *Liberator*. From 1833 onward, the column became more and more sporadic. It appeared one last time in April 1837. The dialogue between "Mr. S." (the white abolitionist Nathaniel Southard) and little Martha tackled the perennial question, "What can children do for the slaves?" Whereas earlier pieces had focused on explaining slavery and showing its evil character to young readers, Southard recommended that Martha actively work for the abolition of slavery by signing petitions—a controversial proposition even among abolitionists, as has been discussed in chapter 1.[39] Such practical advice as to what children could "do for the slaves" also abounded in the *Slave's Friend*.

The founding of the *Slave's Friend* in 1835–36 marked a milestone in the history of juvenile abolitionism.[40] Whereas Garrison had introduced articles for children in a publication otherwise directed at adults, the *Slave's Friend* was conceived as a magazine wholly for children, as its contents but also its format make clear: the sixteen-page magazine was "small in size to accommodate youthful hands," Christopher Geist writes, assuming a six- to twelve-year-old readership.[41] The *Slave's Friend* was one of four periodicals created by the AASS, alongside *Human Rights*, the *Anti-Slavery Record*, and the *Emancipator*, each published in a different week of the month.[42] As Teresa Goddu and Trish Loughran have explained, the AASS was "at the height of its organizational powers" in the mid-1830s. From its headquarters in New York, it churned out massive amounts of print designed to reach "a densely differentiated field of readers" across the nation, including children.[43] The *Slave's Friend* was sold at the "unusually low" price of one cent per copy, but like all AASS-sponsored publications, it was meant to be purchased in bulk (the initial print run was twenty thousand copies) and distributed far and wide rather than sold individually; it cost "10 cents a dozen, 80 cents per hundred, and $6.50 per thousand."[44] The magazine was sold to abolitionists or distributed for free to people who might be gained to the antislavery cause. This included people in the South. During the AASS's Great Postal Campaign of 1835, hundreds of thousands of antislavery publications were mailed below the Mason-Dixon line, provoking the ire of white southerners: "The Mail brought by the Steam Packet Columbia" on July 29, 1835, the editor of the Charleston, South Carolina, *Southern Patriot* reported, "has come . . . literally overburthened, with the newspaper, called 'The Emancipator,' and two tracts entitled 'The Anti-Slavery Record,' and 'The Slave's Friend,' destined for circulation all over the Southern and Western Country."[45] A lithograph of the raid on the Charleston post office that took place later that day shows, among other publications, a copy of the *Slave's Friend* being burned (figure 2.4). A few weeks later, the *Emancipator* estimated that "the publications destroyed in Charleston, amount to about 1000 copies of the Emancipator, A.S. Record, and Slave's Friend."[46] Elsewhere in the South, copies of the *Slave's Friend* may have ended up in the hands of children.

A sign reading "$20000 Reward for TAPPAN" hangs on the wall of the post office in the lithograph, referring to the bounty placed on the head of Arthur Tappan, AASS president and brother of Lewis Tappan—the man behind the Great Postal Campaign and editor of the *Slave's Friend*. The Tappan brothers belonged to the evangelical wing of the abolition movement, which explains the markedly religious tone of the magazine edited by Lewis. Indeed, the pages of the *Slave's Friend* are filled with scriptural references, hymns, and prayers. The May 1836 issue, for instance, contains an "Anti-Slavery Catechism" reminding young readers that God "hath made of one blood all nations of men, for to dwell on the face of the earth" (Acts 17:26), a verse from the Bible frequently quoted by abolitionists; an essay explaining the abstract notion of faith to children ("*It means believing just what God says*"); a follow-up article about little Sophia, a child abolitionist who likes to "pray for the poor slaves" ("Sophia had *faith*"); and an address to an enslaved child promising him freedom in the afterlife. With pieces titled "The Weasel and Chicken," "The Butterfly," and "The Worm," the issue is also characteristic for its focus on animals. Stories and poems about caged birds and trapped insects abound in the *Slave's Friend*, an obvious though effective metaphor for the condition of enslaved people, who "like the butterfly . . . love

NEW METHOD OF ASSORTING THE MAIL, AS PRACTISED BY SOUTHERN SLAVE-HOLDERS, OR

ATTACK ON THE POST OFFICE, CHARLESTON, S.C.

Figure 2.4. Burning the *Slave's Friend*. "New Method of Assorting the Mail, as Practised by Southern Slave-Holders; or, Attack on the Post Office, Charleston, S.C." (1835). Courtesy of the American Antiquarian Society.

freedom."[47] Some scholars have pointed to the paternalistic dimension of such comparisons. While "creating sympathetic identification with both the suffering slave and the suffering animal," one of them argues, the "ethical equation" between slavery and animal cruelty "dehumanized slaves by placing them metaphorically in the same status as animals."[48] Yet animal imagery is not restricted to the enslaved in the magazine. The slave system as a whole is captured through metaphors drawn from the animal world: slavers "are MEN-WEASELS," stealing babies from enslaved mothers like the weasel, which snatches away chickens from the hen.[49] Such images could also be found under the pen of Black abolitionists. Frederick Douglass, in his third autobiography, relates about his childhood, "I used to contrast my condition with that of the black-birds, in whose wild and sweet songs I fancied them so happy."[50] More importantly, the humanity of the enslaved is repeatedly affirmed in the Slave's Friend, and racial hierarchies are systematically challenged.

Attention to religious rhetoric and animal imagery should not detract from the radical political message articulated in the Slave's Friend. As Manisha Sinha points out, "The journal afforded children a serious education in abolition," providing substantial essays on a variety of subjects linked to slavery, abolition, and race in the United States but also in the British West Indies, Canada, and Haiti.[51] The Slave's Friend did not shield its readers from the violence of slavery. It reprinted extracts from slave narratives such as Charles Ball's Slavery in the United States (1836) illustrating the plight of enslaved children; conversely, it published letters by James A. Thome, coauthor of Emancipation in the West Indies (1838), highlighting the benefits of emancipation.[52] It kept children abreast of current events: the journal reported on the 1834 abduction of seven-year-old Henry Scott by a New York kidnapping ring, on the 1835 wave of proslavery mobs against the British abolitionist George Thompson, on the 1836 Commonwealth v. Aves case, and on the 1837 murder of the antislavery editor Elijah P. Lovejoy. Of course, it did so in a manner adapted to its readership. The abduction of Henry Scott is told as a brief dialogue between two sisters, while the Aves case, in which a Massachusetts judge denied a Louisiana enslaver the right of transit with her six-year-old slave Mary (or Med) and set the child free, is presented in a way that centers its young protagonist.[53] In another article, what starts as a geography lesson about Texas soon turns into a conversation about the hotly contested issue of annexation and its relation to capitalism and slavery. "A great many land speculators in the United States have bought lands in Texas at a very low price," Mr. Bourne explains to his son, James. "If Texas continues to be a part of Mexico there will be no slavery there; but if it is separated they will join this country and we shall have several more slave states."[54]

The *Slave's Friend* strikes a very modern note at times. The journal came out in favor of reparations for formerly enslaved people before the term even existed: "Compensation! Who deserves it most, the master or the slave? The slave, undoubtedly." Several articles foreshadow twenty-first-century debates about "reparative semantics," or what vocabulary we should use for describing slavery. "Do not ever say slave-*owner*, but slave-*holder*," Tappan recommended. "No man *owns* a man." Likewise, no Black person should be said to "belong" to a white person. "That is slaveholders' language," Tappan declared, suggesting instead that enslaved people "*are held* by white people." Over the course of several issues, the *Slave's Friend* offered a sustained examination of language as a vehicle for racism. The n-word is a "brutal, vulgar word" that no white reader of the magazine should ever use; nor should they "call a person A NEGRO," for Black people "*do not like to be called so.*" "The word negro . . . has been made a term of reproach," and therefore "it is better to say colored people, or people of color." Better even, "instead of saying that *man of color*, say that *colored American*," Tappan wrote in an article on the newly created Black-owned paper of the same name.[55]

The *Slave's Friend* advised children to take action against slavery, encouraging them to "believe in their own creative agency," in Barbara Hochman's terms.[56] It enthusiastically reported on the meetings of juvenile antislavery societies. The whole May 1837 issue was devoted to the formation of the Chatham Street Chapel Juvenile Anti-Slavery Society in New York. The journal reprinted the society's constitution as well as two speeches, one by Tappan, given at its inaugural meeting. A recurring (textual and visual) motif in the *Slave's Friend* is the antislavery collection box: two-year-old Anna asks her father for a coin to put in the family's collection box, displayed in the living room, while a "little fellow" two and a half years old is said to have "collected 120 cents, and had it put into the anti-slavery treasury!" Patrick, an African American child, proves a more thorough abolitionist than his white schoolfellow Edward when he commits to giving all of his money to the antislavery cause: "If I spend my money for candy, or sugar-plums, I am no better for it. It is gone then. Now I had rather think when I awake, up in the morning, it is safe in the anti-slavery collection-box." Candy, moreover, was usually made of slave-produced sugar. "We will not eat nor wear slave products, if we can help it, will we, mother?" asks Peter, one of many children in the magazine willing to abstain from slave-labor goods. In the same issue, Charles and Theodore (perhaps an uncle and his nephew) discuss the French production of beet sugar as a substitute for cane, mingling arithmetic with antislavery. Children in the *Slave's Friend* sometimes assume unexpected roles, for instance, that of distributing abolitionist literature: a "little boy" on board a steamboat "took anti-slavery tracts from his father . . . and gave them to the passengers." More commonly, they are represented reading abolitionist literature themselves. One "little girl" who "was . . . very anxious that her playmate should be as much of an abolitionist as she was" insists on reading the *Slave's Friend* to her friend, while seven-year-old Sarah, a pious child with an incurable disease, reads it on her deathbed. In "The Emancipated Family," a formerly enslaved father reads the Bible to his children, and the children in turn read "the Slave's Friend, and other pretty books" (figure 2.5). These forms of juvenile activism aligned with the moral-suasionist orientation of the abolition movement in the 1830s. Yet children were also prepared for more controversial forms of activism such as assistance to fugitives. When Mr. Adams's son, George, asks him, "[Do] we have a right to take a fugitive into our houses, to give him bread to eat, to give him clothes, to give him money, lend him a horse to carry him on his journey[?]" Mr. Adams's answer is unambiguous: "Yes, my son, and for one I do not wish to be in better business."[57]

No other publication than the *Slave's Friend* was as systematic in picturing children as abolitionists in their own right. These "little abolitionists" may seem like a figment of Tappan's imagination—young people too mature and too wholly dedicated to antislavery to be credible. There may never have been "a young lady, who read Clarkson's History of the slave-trade, when she was *seven years old*," if only because Thomas Clarkson's *History of the Rise, Progress, and Accomplishment of the Abolition of the African Slave-Trade by the British Parliament* (1808) was a multivolume work of about one thousand pages.[58] (There did exist a

THE

SLAVE'S FRIEND.

VOL. II. No. VIII.   **WHOLE No. 20**

THE EMANCIPATED FAMILY.

The above picture has been in the
Slave's Friend before, but there was no
story with it.   As my little readers

Figure 2.5. A father reading to his children. "The Emancipated Family," *Slave's Friend* 2, no. 8 (1837): 1. Courtesy of the Schomburg Center for Research in Black Culture, Manuscripts, Archives and Rare Books Division.

US abridgement of Clarkson's *History* whose publisher sought to "bring the most of it within the comprehension of children.")[59] Rather than reflecting reality, the *Slave's Friend* strove to shape it—to inspire young people to take on political roles that they or their parents may not have thought of as children's roles. Still, not all juvenile abolitionists in the *Slave's Friend* were fictional. Like Garrison's Juvenile Department, the magazine recorded the voices of real Black and white children espousing abolitionist views. It featured articles on children of famous abolitionists such as Edward Payson Lovejoy (son of Elijah P. Lovejoy) and Fitzhugh Smith (son of Gerrit Smith).[60] The *Slave's Friend* attended to children's perspectives on slavery and deemed their words worthy of being preserved in its pages.

Tappan's magazine was the only children's periodical with such a clear focus on slavery in the 1830s, but other children's periodicals leaned more or less openly toward abolitionism. Lydia Maria Child's *Juvenile Miscellany*, created in 1826, is a well-known example. Child converted from gradualism to immediatism soon after meeting Garrison in June 1830. From September 1830 on, as her biographer notes, nearly every issue of the *Juvenile Miscellany* carried some item aimed at denouncing slavery or countering antiblack prejudice.[61] In "The Prisoners Set Free," an 1831 story by Hannah Flagg Gould, three siblings liberate their caged pets after their mother has told them that they "[long] for freedom as much as the poor Africans do, who have to live and die in bondage to white men."[62] Child's own "Jumbo and Zairee," published the same year, tells the story of two children who are abducted by traders in Africa, transported aboard a US slave ship, put up for auction, and made to work on a Georgia plantation, until they are reunited with their father several years later. Child's 1834 story of interracial friendship "Mary French and Susan Easton" first appeared in the *Juvenile Miscellany* before it was reprinted in the explicitly abolitionist context of the *Slave's Friend*; so did her 1833 "The Little White Lamb and the Little Black Lamb."[63] Less well known than the *Juvenile Miscellany*, Nathaniel Southard's *Youth's Cabinet*, founded in 1837, was energetically promoted in the *Liberator*. It was "devoted to Liberty, Peace, Temperance, Purity, [and] Truth," thus covering a wider array of reform subjects than the *Slave's Friend*. After the *Friend* was discontinued in early 1839, Southard presented the *Youth's Cabinet* as "the only

juvenile periodical designed to educate the young to be THE LIBERA-
TORS OF THE SLAVE."[64] Among other antislavery topics, the magazine
covered the much-publicized *Amistad* case, keeping its readers informed
of new developments and the eventual release of the slave rebels.

Besides Garrison, other early antislavery newspaper editors included
an occasional column for young readers in their publications. Charles
B. Ray did so in the *Colored American*, founded in 1837. Ray's emphasis in the Youth's/Children's Department was less on slavery and racial
prejudice than on the benefits of education, tidiness, obedience, and
morality—middle-class values that were integral to the African American freedom struggle. If the *Slave's Friend*'s favorite animal was the bird
freed from its cage, the *Colored American*'s was the squirrel, a creature
"remarkable for its agility, industry, cleanliness and liveliness." Birds are
rather vain animals in the *Colored American*, boasting of their song and
plumage, while the squirrel is busy "furnishing [its] nest with necessar-
ies and comforts."[65] In the words of Nazera Sadiq Wright, articles in the
Youth's/Children's Department were intended "to teach black children
to grow into responsible, law-abiding citizens through edifying tales
and moral lessons." Ray viewed them as "political actors whose litera-
cies contributed to early African American activism."[66] Slavery did not
go unmentioned either. One piece advised young readers to pray that
enslaved children "may all be set free," and the remainder of the paper
included a wealth of abolitionist content that children might peruse
at a later age. The *Colored American* reprinted pieces from the *Slave's
Friend* and praised Southard's *Youth's Cabinet* as "an excellent little paper
for children," whose editor "always turns everything to anti-slavery account."[67] The same kind of didactic material emphasizing correct child
behavior, moral and spiritual awareness, and social and political respon-
sibilities would later appear in the Black-owned *Christian Recorder*'s
children's section, variously known as Our Children, the Child's Cabinet, and the Child's Portion.[68]

A handful of juvenile periodicals edited by antislavery men and
women kept abolition before young readers after the 1830s. The *Youth's
Emancipator* was edited by young people for young people at Oberlin
College, Ohio, one of the first US colleges to admit African Americans
and women. For most of its short run—only nine issues appeared between May 1842 and March 1843—the *Youth's Emancipator* was pub-

lished by members of the Oberlin Youth's Anti-Slavery Society, one of whom, John Giles Jennings, was seventeen at the paper's founding. Full of its editors' youthful fervor, the *Emancipator* was notable for printing first-person accounts of slavery by formerly enslaved people, for instance, H. H. Howard, a fugitive from Kentucky whose narrative was cut short when he left Oberlin unexpectedly.[69] Eliza Lee Follen's *Child's Friend*, created in 1843, occasionally brought up the subject of slavery. As Deborah De Rosa argues, Follen "maintained her popularity as a children's author by tactfully scattering her abolitionist juvenile literature throughout her works and embedding her attacks on slavery in . . . gender-appropriate spaces."[70] The *Child's Friend* provided one such space. Advertised as a monthly magazine for the use of families and Sunday schools, the *Child's Friend*, unlike the *Slave's Friend*, did not trumpet its abolitionism. A piece with a rather generic title, "How Shall Children Do Good?," first discusses how children can do good to the poor but then takes an antislavery turn as Follen laments that hundreds of children "are daily born to slavery, doomed to have all their rights trampled upon, to be bought and sold like four-footed animals." In a letter written from Liverpool, Follen briefly mentions a conversation with "an intelligent lad of fourteen years of age," who tells her "all he thought and felt about the wickedness of [US] slavery." "I could not but feel ashamed that one, almost a child, should throw this disgrace of my native land in my face," Follen comments. "Pic Nic at Dedham," with which this book opens, is an evocative description of a white child's entry into the antislavery world. Like Garrison and Tappan, Follen also used her magazine to amplify Black voices, reprinting George Moses Horton's 1829 poem "The Slave's Complaint."[71] Finally, the Wesleyan Methodist abolitionist Lucius C. Matlack made antislavery central to the *Juvenile Instructor*, a paper he edited in Syracuse, New York, between 1844 and 1858. The *Juvenile Instructor*, Matlack wrote in an 1853 advertisement for the paper, was meant to "give a proper direction to the youthful mind in these times of strife for the supremacy of slavery." He boasted, "It has moulded the minds of thousands of children who have grown up to manhood and womanhood, thoroughly imbued with the love of freedom for all men." Amid conventional children's fare— stories on honesty and poems on piety—Uncle Lucius, as Matlack called himself, mentioned the 1854 Kansas-Nebraska Act, praised Solomon

Northup's slave narrative *Twelve Years a Slave* (1853), and reported on the electoral results of antislavery politicians.[72]

Abolitionists did not condescend to children, nor did they dumb down their message when writing for them. One of the best illustrations of this is Jonathan Walker's *A Picture of Slavery, for Youth*, undated but probably published in 1846 or 1847. In July 1844, Walker, a sea captain, had attempted to take seven runaway slaves from Florida to the British West Indies. He was sentenced to the pillory and his hand branded with a double *S* for "slave stealer."[73] Walker published a brief account of the episode in the summer of 1845 and, later, another volume for children partially based on his experience. He felt that he had seen "but few anti-slavery publications adapted to the capacity of children."[74] Juvenile anti-slavery books such as Garrison's *Juvenile Poems* and Susan Paul's *Memoir of James Jackson* (1835), the latter discussed in chapter 4, were scarcer and less widely disseminated than periodicals. *A Picture of Slavery, for Youth* was meant to fill that void.

Walker's book is graphic in every sense of the term. Heavily illustrated, it discusses the treatment of the enslaved in explicit terms, showing how they are "compelled to work day after day . . . without having suitable victuals and clothes to satisfy their pressing wants—made to submit to all the demands of wicked and cruel masters, mistresses, overseers, or drivers—whipped, chained, bought and sold like cattle." Walker draws on a variety of sources commonly found in antislavery publications for a more mature audience, such as slave codes and southern newspapers, which he takes care to paraphrase and contextualize. How can the United States boast of being "the freest country on the earth," he asks, "while it has three millions of its own people in the markets for sale"? Attention is paid to the violence inflicted on the enslaved but also to acts of resistance and self-expression: at various points, Walker defers to the authority of Frederick Douglass, whose 1845 narrative he quotes from liberally. In an acknowledgment of the expressive power of Black letters, he also quotes from Phillis Wheatley's 1773 poem "To the Rev. Dr. Thomas Amory," which in this context becomes a call for juvenile abolitionism: "Oh! may each bosom catch the sacred fire, / And youthful minds to virtue's throne aspire!" Bridging the slave's cause and the Indian's cause, *A Picture of Slavery, for Youth* highlights the plight of Native Americans in its last pages, as Walker recalls the circumstances surrounding the Second Seminole War, deplores the misrepresentation of Indigenous people "by many prejudiced and bigoted writers . . . in this country," and reproduces a speech by the Seneca chief and orator Sagoye-watha, or Red Jacket. "The Indians," he declares, "have always been wick-edly and cruelly treated by the white Americans." The volume ends on a denunciation of the United States' imperialist war against Mexico, a war meant "to strengthen the hands of slave-holders." Targeted at a slightly older audience than Garrison's Juvenile Department and Tappan's *Slave's Friend*, Walker's *A Picture of Slavery, for Youth* exposes the stark reality of slavery and conveys a broad, radical vision of abolition and racial justice. Walker urges his "young friends," "Remember those who are in slavery, and make their case your own," though ultimately he leaves it to them to decide how to act.[75]

Slave Narratives and Their Juvenile Readers

Scholarly discussions of slave narratives and children's literature have rarely intersected. Yet children and youth formed an important—if unrecognized—part of the readership for narratives of formerly enslaved people in the nineteenth century. A number of these narratives, though not written especially for children, were circulated in juvenile contexts. As mentioned earlier, *A Narrative of Some Remarkable Incidents, in the Life of Solomon Bayley, Formerly a Slave, in the State of Delaware, North America* was marketed as a children's book by Harvey and Dar-ton. Cugoano's and Asa-Asa's narratives both made an appearance in the *Liberator's* Juvenile Department; Ball's did so in the *Slave's Friend* (it was lightly revised so as to eliminate words deemed too difficult).[76] Lengthy passages from Douglass's *Narrative* were embedded in Walker's *A Picture of Slavery, for Youth*. Northup's story was recounted in the pages of Matlack's *Juvenile Instructor*, whose readers were encouraged to procure a copy of the narrative: "This story is found in a large good book styled 'Twelve years a slave,' that your father would perhaps buy for you if he knew as well as I do, how thrilling it is. It is advertised in one corner of the Juvenile."[77] The antebellum "culture of reprinting" made it likely that children of abolitionists would encounter these texts, if only piecemeal.[78]

At least one slave narrative originally written for a general audience—though read, from the very first, by children, as seen in chapter 1—was repurposed as a children's book. In 1829, the Quaker abolitionist Abigail Mott published a twenty-five-page abridgment of *The Interesting Narrative of the Life of Olaudah Equiano, or Gustavus Vassa, the African* (1789) titled *The Life and Adventures of Olaudah Equiano*. The pamphlet was published specifically for African American children: students of the New York African Free School could obtain a copy as a "premium for good behavior."[79] *Life and Adventures* was issued under the imprint of Samuel Wood, one of the main publishers of children's books in the early US republic, along with Mahlon Day—both of them Quakers and both of them involved with the NYAFS's operations.[80] In 1826, Day had issued a previous volume by Mott for the use of (African American) schoolchildren. *Biographical Sketches and Interesting Anecdotes of Persons of Colour* told of the lives of Black people, some eminent, other obscure, whose "honesty, . . . attention to religious worship, temperance, and industry" made them models for young readers to imitate.[81]

In much the same vein, *Life and Adventures* portrayed Equiano as a role model for African American children: Mott's Equiano is "industrious, pious, eager for education, and successful in commerce." Comparing Equiano's narrative and Mott's abridgment of it, Valentina Tikoff finds that though Mott retains Equiano's criticism of slavery and cruel slaveholders, she mutes much of his social analysis and criticism, in particular of systemic injustice, racist thinking, and religious hypocrisy. On the other hand, Martha Cutter notes that Mott's text "figures black children as capable of both claiming power in their own lives and becoming active in abolition debates." Through such texts, NYAFS students came to see themselves as "potential abolitionist activists."[82] Indeed, many became leading abolitionists, perhaps spurred by their reading of Equiano's narrative. The only US edition of the *Interesting Narrative*, on which Mott's abridgment may have been based, had been published in New York as far back as 1791.[83] In publishing this new abridged edition of the volume, Mott both performed an act of recovery and pointed her young readers to the long history of antislavery activism, implicitly inviting them to occupy a place in that history. Besides Equiano, other narratives of enslavement and freedom were retold by children's authors. Two decades after Mott, another Quaker abolitionist, Ann Preston, narrated the dramatic escape of Henry Box Brown in *Cousin Ann's Stories for Children* (1849). Her brief story emphasized Brown's courage in mailing himself to freedom. "We call people heroes who do something that is brave and great," Preston explained, "and Henry is a hero."[84]

Even slave narratives that were neither reprinted in juvenile contexts nor abridged or retold for youth came to be read by children. As Beverly Lyon Clark has emphasized, strict divisions between juvenile and adult literature were not yet in place in the nineteenth century. Authors commonly assumed a broad readership of both adults and children.[85] Books that we would not spontaneously identify as children's literature were in fact often read by children. Such was the case, within the African American literary canon, of Harriet E. Wilson's *Our Nig* (1859), an autobiographical novel depicting the brutality of white racism in the North through the story of a mixed-race indentured servant. Eric Gardner has found in his quest for early readers of the novel that many copies of the book were owned by children, "some not even at reading age when *Our Nig* was printed." The phrase "children's book," he adds, "signified differently in the antebellum period than it does now and included a much wider range of texts."[86] Young abolitionists in the *Liberator*'s Juvenile Department and the *Slave's Friend* were often represented reading antislavery texts not specifically designed for them. In Chandler's "Edward and Mary," mentioned earlier, Edward reads Charles C. Andrews's *History of the New-York African Free-Schools* (1830) as well as poems by Phillis Wheatley and George Moses Horton, while Mary reads to him "the most interesting passages" of a "Memoir of the Blacks of America" written by the French abolitionist Jacques-Pierre Brissot de Warville.[87]

Reviewers in the antislavery press routinely recommended that slave narratives be placed in the hands of young readers. "Mr. Brown's book cannot fail to interest the young and the old," wrote a *Christian World* reviewer of *Narrative of William W. Brown, a Fugitive Slave* (1847). "Especially do we wish that the young may possess it, and to this end we should be glad to have it introduced into our parish libraries." A Lynn, Massachusetts, reviewer of *Narrative of the Life of Frederick Douglass* likewise predicted that the book's "stirring incidents will fasten themselves on the eager minds of the youth of this country with hooks of steel." Garrison confidently declared in the *Liberator* that *Narrative of the Life and Adventures of Henry Bibb, an American Slave* (1849) was "a book for the rising generation in particular."[88] Some authors of slave narratives themselves claimed to be writing for youth. In the preface to the third edition of *The Fugitive Blacksmith* (1849), penned in 1850, James W. C. Pennington noted, "My object was to write an unexceptional book of the kind for children in point of matter, and for the masses in point of price."[89] Literary scholars have characterized his book as a "popular autobiography" yet never as a "children's book"—a label only applied to an earlier publication of his, *A Text Book of the Origin and History . . . of the Colored People* (1841).[90] The Black intellectual James McCune Smith, in his introduction to Douglass's *My Bondage and My Freedom* (1855), assured that he would "place this book in the hands of the only child spared [him], bidding him to strive and emulate its noble example."[91] At over four hundred pages, *My Bondage and My Freedom*—a structurally and stylistically more complex text than the *Narrative*—might seem like an arduous read for ten-year-old James W. Smith. Yet it was James McCune Smith's belief that his son would benefit from such a reading experience. Douglass offered a model of "courage, resilience, perseverance, strength, and virtue," in Erica Ball's terms, and his autobiography illustrated the importance of both self-improvement and antislavery principles.[92] Similar reasons led the Congregational Church of Putnam, Connecticut, to purchase a copy of the book for its Sunday-school library: "We . . . wish to avail ourselves of a most powerful influence to arouse the youthful mind to vigorous exertions to obtain useful knowledge, and to form a noble, an energetic, and a stable character."[93] Slave narratives were seen as formative reading for young Black and white Americans.

Most of what precedes is prescriptive discourse, and one might wonder whether children actually read slave narratives. They did. Nathaniel Bowditch was nine years old when he received a copy of *Narrative of the Life of Frederick Douglass* from his father, the Boston abolitionist Henry Ingersoll Bowditch. The copy, held at the Massachusetts Historical Society, bears the following inscription: "Nath¹ Bowditch / from his father / March 1849 / Neither *be*, nor *own*, a slave!" (figure 2.6). Young Nathaniel's antislavery education had started when he was even younger. Three years earlier, his father had taken him to see the body of the abolitionist martyr Charles T. Torrey, who had died of tuberculosis in a Baltimore prison after being arrested for aiding fugitive slaves. "I carried Natty to let him see the revered face, and teach him to swear eternal enmity to slavery," Henry Ingersoll Bowditch wrote in his journal. He

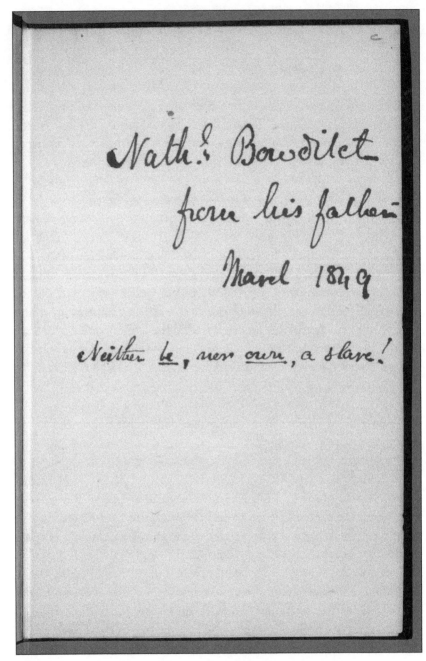

Figure 2.6. Copy of *Narrative of the Life of Frederick Douglass, an American Slave* owned by Nathaniel Bowditch. Courtesy of the Massachusetts Historical Society.

then made a reference, common among advocates of juvenile abolitionism, to the Carthaginian general Hannibal, whose father, Hamilcar, had
him swear an oath of eternal hatred against the Romans when he was
nine years old: "Like Hamilcar of old, I determined to make the young
Hannibal remember, as one of his earliest associations, his father taught
him to hate slavery. I think he will remember. I raised the little fellow
on my knee, and allowed him to look, and when I took him down he
asked to be allowed to look once more. I then told him the history of
the good man's life, at which he seemed deeply interested."[94] In 1851,
Henry brought his son to a demonstration against the rendition of the
fugitive slave Thomas Sims. The stories of fugitive slaves and their allies
that "Natty" heard and read as a child must have stayed with him. In
the fall of 1861, he enlisted in the Union army. A year and a half later,
the twenty-three-year-old officer died on a Virginia battlefield, "while
leading a charge in this war for free institutions, and for liberty," in his
grieving father's words.[95]

Douglass's *Narrative* was read by children on both sides of the Atlantic. The British member of Parliament Thomas Burt, in his 1924 autobiography, fondly remembered reading it as a boy. The book "impressed
and stimulated" him greatly, he wrote, and helped him "in [his] efforts
to live bravely and to use [his] life for noble ends."[96] This coal miner's
son later became a trade-union leader and one of the first working-class
members of Parliament. Of course, no direct link can be made between
Burt's reading of the *Narrative* and his upwardly mobile trajectory. Yet
it can be argued that young men in Britain and the United States saw
Douglass as an exemplar of self-affirmation and found in his autobiographies not only a critique of slavery but an encouragement to try
to overcome social and racial determinisms. As one reviewer of *My
Bondage and My Freedom* put it, the book "should be in the hands of
every young man . . . in an obscure and discouraging position."[97] Nor
were Douglass's autobiographies kept out of the hands of girls, despite
their graphic descriptions of sexual exploitation and the fact that young
women were generally expected to conform to the inferior position as-
signed to them in US and British society. When in 1848 the white abolitionist Samuel May Jr. was sent a copy of the first French translation
of Douglass's *Narrative*, he noted, "my daughter (who was away from
home when I received it, & who was 12 yrs. old yesterday, by the way,)

is . . . anticipating much pleasure from reading it this winter."[98] Adeline May was also an early reader of Jonathan Walker's *A Picture of Slavery, for Youth*, as the inscription on the copy held by the American Antiquarian Society indicates: "Adeline and Edward May / from their father / June 1, 1847" (figure 2.7). Adeline was going on eleven when she was gifted this book; her younger brother, Edward, had turned nine a few months before.

Not all youthful reading experiences of slave narratives were wholly positive. In 1855, the Illinois abolitionist Cynthia Potter Bliss decided to read one of Douglass's autobiographies—perhaps *My Bondage and My Freedom*, given the date—to her five-year-old son, Howard Clarkson Bliss. In a letter to Douglass, later published in *Frederick Douglass' Paper*, she confessed, "The story of your wrongs has deeply affected him, and his grief has sometimes been so passionate that I have been compelled to lay aside the book and use all the skill I had command of to soothe and quiet him without detracting from the interest of the narrative or the impression it was making."[99] Howard was understandably upset by Douglass's story. Juvenile antislavery literature and the archives of the abolition movement are full of children who were likewise moved to tears when their parents or teacher or an antislavery lecturer discussed slavery with them.[100] Yet Howard's mother was intent on communicating important information to him, and though she made sure to take breaks and gloss on the narrative so as to soften its effect, she persevered with her reading. Cynthia Potter Bliss was a key intermediary between Douglass's text and her son. She did so well that in the end, Howard not only overcame his grief but insisted on writing Douglass a letter (with his mother as amanuensis), also printed in Douglass's newspaper. "Father and mother have read your book to me," he wrote, "and I am very glad you have got away from the *Slaveholders*. I wish all the slaves could get away where they could run and play, and have books and papers, and houses and horses."[101] The boy commented on various episodes that had struck his attention: the fight with Edward Covey, Douglass's failure at driving an ox cart. A parallel he made with the narrative of Henry Bibb suggests that his parents had been reading other slave narratives to him. Narratives of fugitive slaves were an essential part of his antislavery education.

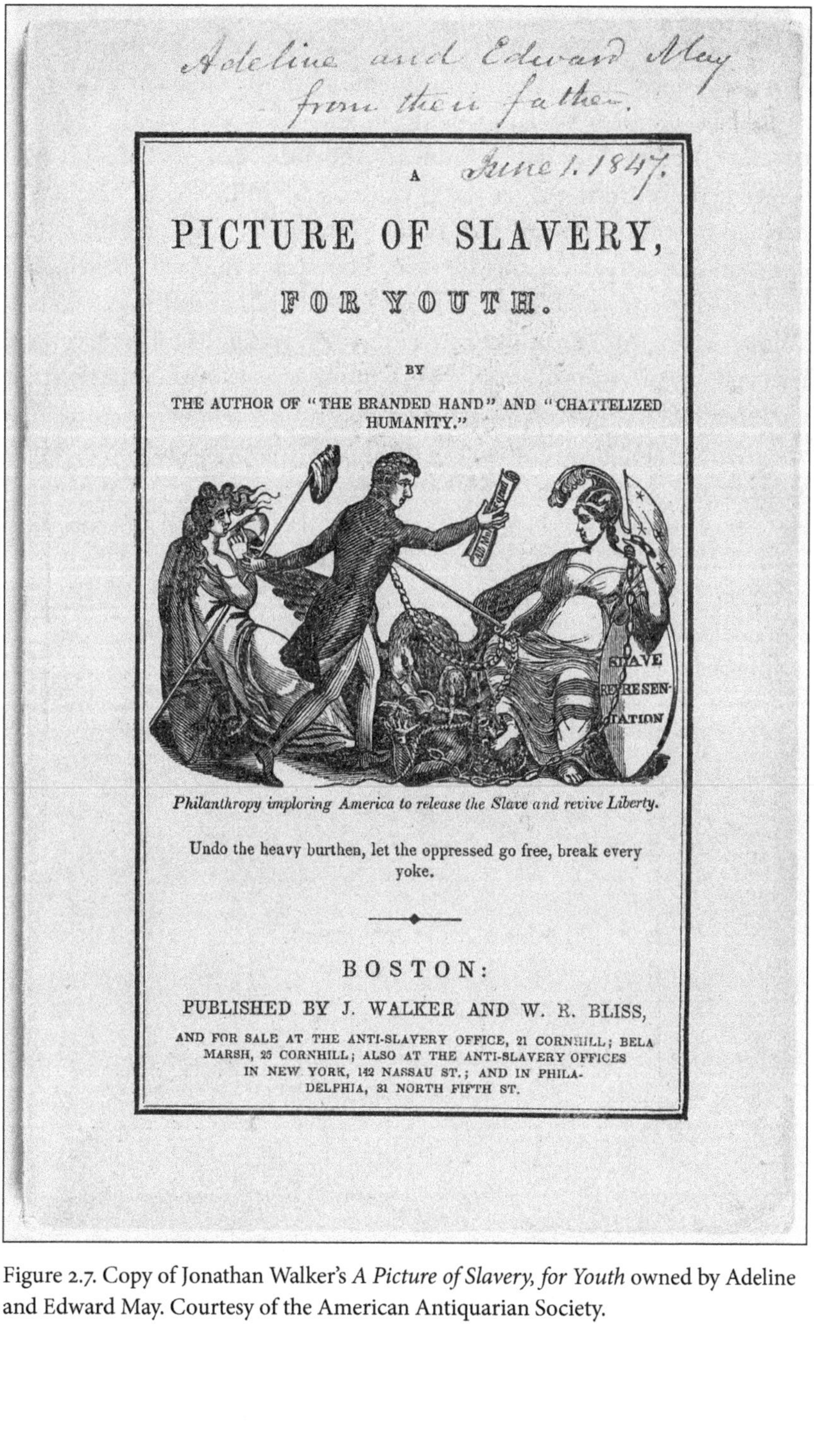

Adeline and Edward May
from their father.

A June 1. 1847.

PICTURE OF SLAVERY,

FOR YOUTH.

BY

THE AUTHOR OF "THE BRANDED HAND" AND "CHATTELIZED HUMANITY."

Philanthropy imploring America to release the Slave and revive Liberty.

Undo the heavy burthen, let the oppressed go free, break every yoke.

BOSTON:

PUBLISHED BY J. WALKER AND W. R. BLISS,

AND FOR SALE AT THE ANTI-SLAVERY OFFICE, 21 CORNHILL; BELA MARSH, 25 CORNHILL; ALSO AT THE ANTI-SLAVERY OFFICES IN NEW YORK, 142 NASSAU ST.; AND IN PHILADELPHIA, 31 NORTH FIFTH ST.

Figure 2.7. Copy of Jonathan Walker's *A Picture of Slavery, for Youth* owned by Adeline and Edward May. Courtesy of the American Antiquarian Society.

Given the racist history of infantilizing African Americans as a way to legitimize slavery, one might feel reluctant to read slave narratives as "children's literature." What is more, studies of the slave narrative have assumed an audience of adult, white, middle-class readers, a monolithic description that does not account for the variety of people who read slave narratives in the antebellum United States. Black and white children and youth composed part of their readership. To antebellum free children, narratives such as those of Equiano, Douglass, Brown, and Bibb made vivid the plight of the enslaved child and the injustice of slavery. Young African American and white working-class readers were also encouraged to read them for the moral lessons and examples they contained. Slave narratives were read with the assistance of educators and parents, alongside antislavery stories, poems, orations, and essays—some of which were designed for children but others not. Considered from this perspective, juvenile antislavery literature was a broad category from which children drew radical lessons.

3

"Anti-Slavery Success to the Juniors!"

Organizing Juvenile Abolitionists

Antebellum abolitionists did not just sensitize children to the question of slavery. They encouraged them to work for abolition—to actually *do* something for the slaves. Children, like their parents, formed their own antislavery associations. Associations had long been the primary mode for organizing antislavery activities. By the time William Lloyd Garrison formed the American Anti-Slavery Society in 1833, countless local groups had already been founded, from the Quaker-led pioneer societies of the early US republic (like the Society for the Relief of Free Negroes Unlawfully Held in Bondage, formed in Philadelphia in 1775) to the African American mutual aid societies and civil rights organizations that made antislavery an essential part of their platform (like the Massachusetts General Colored Association, formed in Boston in 1826).

Associations were popular beyond the abolition movement. They were a common feature of the early American cultural landscape, as the French political theorist Alexis de Tocqueville famously observed. Though it has passed unnoticed, Tocqueville, in his examination of associations in American civil life, mentioned age—rather than, say, gender or race—as a significant variable in the makeup of associations. "Americans of all *ages*, all conditions, all minds constantly unite," he wrote.[1] Indeed, middle-class children formed associations for all sorts of charitable goals in the antebellum United States. Juvenile newspapers reported on their activities. In 1829, several mothers in a Maine village formed their seven- to twelve-year-old daughters into a Juvenile Sewing Society. The group met twice a month, spending the afternoon and evening "in various kinds of sewing, the avails of which are given to some benevolent object." That same year, a Juvenile Missionary Society was organized by a group of twelve- to fourteen-year-old girls in an unspecified northern locale. They had become "particularly interested for the poor Burman children" after learning about their poverty and lack of access to education. Such societies existed in the South too. The Juvenile Industry Society of Charleston, South Carolina, prided itself on "distribut[ing] 200 garments to 22 poor women, for the use of their infants" in 1833.[2] This vigorous juvenile associational culture also included literary clubs, debating societies, religious societies, and political organizations.[3]

Juvenile antislavery societies multiplied in the 1830s. They were, in fact, one of the most salient features of juvenile abolitionism at the time. Yet historians of the abolition movement generally skim over them. One reason for this neglect may be that juvenile antislavery societies were not as durable as their adult counterparts were. Clearly, there was a "moment" for juvenile antislavery societies during the 1830s; most of them were formed between 1831 and 1838. Few of these societies lasted more than a few years, and most were defunct by the early 1840s. One other reason for the scant attention given to juvenile antislavery societies may be that historians have been reluctant to take them seriously. How could children possibly have the political and organizational skills, let alone the economic resources, necessary to form and maintain such societies? And what did it mean exactly for children to be part of an antislavery society? How old were these children, and what did they do? To what extent were adults involved in the management of such groups?

In this chapter, I explore the ephemeral world of juvenile antislavery societies and shed light on the activities of specific male and female groups. Drawing on newspapers, reports, minutes, and diaries, I show that the membership of these societies varied from the very young to the almost adult; the more or less sophisticated nature of their activities and the participation of more mature abolitionists varied accordingly. I discuss the promotion of these societies by the Black activist John W. Lewis and the white abolitionist Henry Clarke Wright, in the press and through antislavery lecturing. Most importantly, I highlight the activism of young African American children, whose societies did not always use the word "antislavery" in their names but whose devotion to abolition infused all of their activities. Though short-lived, these groups functioned in much the same way that adult antislavery societies did and therefore prepared the young for active participation in the abolition movement later in their lives.

African American Juvenile Abolitionists Organize

"Negroes of a tender age," Benjamin Quarles wrote in his foundational *Black Abolitionists* (1969), "shared in the abolitionist crusade from the beginning."[4] The first juvenile antislavery society, the Juvenile Garrison Independent Society (JGIS), was founded by young African Americans in Boston in October 1831.[5] Unlike white-led juvenile organizations, the JGIS did not explicitly focus on the issue of slavery, foregrounding education and racial uplift instead. A few months before it was created, delegates at the national Colored Convention in Philadelphia had touted "*Education, Temperance* and *Economy*" as virtues best calculated to further the elevation of the race.[6] Likewise, the JGIS sought to "encourage learning" and promote "honest, sober and virtuous" behavior among its members. The society's constitution, reprinted in the pages of Garrison's *Liberator*, reflected its strict code of conduct: anyone who did not keep "decent" company or who acted dishonorably could be expelled. The formation of "economical habits" was perhaps the most important aspect of the JGIS's mission. Members were expected to make weekly contributions of a few cents, which were then deposited in the bank. By early 1833, thirty dollars had been collected. JGIS membership was restricted to boys and young men "from the age of 10 to 20." Its most eminent member would turn out to be William Cooper Nell, who was fourteen years old at the society's founding and served as its secretary; an adult, William's father, William Guion Nell, held the purse strings as treasurer. JGIS members were youths rather than children, which explains why the word "juvenile" was occasionally dropped from the society's name in the press.[7]

In trying to foster an ethos of respectability and self-improvement among young Black Bostonians, the JGIS participated in the fight against slavery. As Erica Ball has argued, moral reform and antislavery activism were two faces of the same coin: one did not go without the other, as middle-class African Americans strove to transform themselves into "living refutations of proslavery doctrine."[8] That the JGIS named itself after Garrison, a leading abolitionist, signaled that antislavery was part and parcel of its agenda. In March 1833, the society, presumably drawing on its savings, presented its namesake with a heart-shaped silver medal on the occasion of his first trip to England (figure 3.1). The medal came

Figure 3.1. Silver medal presented to William Lloyd Garrison on his departure for England in 1833 by the Juvenile Garrison Independent Society. Courtesy of the Boston Public Library.

with a letter signed by the younger Nell, president Enoch L. Stallad, and vice president Nestor P. Freeman, expressing gratitude toward Garrison for his "valuable services in the cause of humanity" and wishing him success on his English tour.[9]

The JGIS not only supported Garrison in his antislavery labors but, through him, joined in the transatlantic fight for abolition. At the society's second anniversary in October 1833, the sixteen-year-old Nell delivered an eloquent address in which he further praised Garrison and paid tribute to the "ladies, who have exerted themselves earnestly in the defence of the oppressed—who have endured *persecution* and *imprisonment*, in endeavoring to instruct young ladies of color," an allusion to Prudence Crandall, the abolitionist schoolteacher who had been harassed by her community after admitting Black girls to her academy in Canterbury, Connecticut. Praising the past accomplishments of eminent

Black individuals such as the Jamaican scholar Francis Williams and the African American poet Phillis Wheatley and hailing the free and "happy republic" of Haiti as a model of Black autonomy, Nell encouraged fellow JGIS members to embrace all opportunities to elevate themselves, with a view to attacking white prejudice, precipitating "the downfall of the Colonization system," and working toward "the triumph of equal rights." "In all addresses on anti-Slavery—and by every philanthropist—a loud call is made to the young men of color *to assist themselves*, and by *their* influence, to renovate the minds of the public in the defence of their national rights and liberties."[10] Juvenile influence, a concept discussed in chapter 1, encompassed the ability of young African Americans to transform white minds. Observers found Nell's address all the more remarkable as its author was young. "We believe there is not one boy in a thousand, at *that age*, and having enjoyed no better advantages for education, who could have done as well," the editor of the *New England Telegraph* noted.[11] The JGIS proved essential to Nell's development as an antislavery orator.

Young Black New Yorkers were no less eager to organize than their Boston peers were. Early in 1834, they formed an association also named after the *Liberator's* editor, the Garrison Literary and Benevolent Association (GLBA). The GLBA's age range was even broader than that of the JGIS: any boy "of good moral character" between the ages of four and twenty could be admitted. The GLBA was mostly managed by young men—some over twenty—for the benefit of younger boys. Its list of officers included two eminent activists, twenty-four-year-old David Ruggles (already an important figure of the Underground Railroad in New York) and eighteen-year-old Henry Highland Garnet (fresh out of the New York African Free School). The association's young assistant librarian was William Howard Day, not yet nine years old at the time and later to become an Underground Railroad operator, participant in the Colored Conventions movement, and editor of the Cleveland-based *Aliened American*, whose masthead would bear the motto "Educate your Children—and Hope for Justice." Educating children was the GLBA's main mission. "The object of this Society," its constitution stated, "shall be, the diffusion of knowledge, mental assistance, moral and intellectual improvement." Dozens of children met on Saturdays to sing, pray, write compositions, and deliver addresses, under the supervision of men such as Prince Loveridge, a teacher and the association's librarian. In so doing, they absorbed some of their elders' abolitionism. When one of the trust-ees of the school where the GLBA held its meetings objected to the use of Garrison's name for the association, members were quick to react:

> This information [communicated by Loveridge to his students] seemed to shade every countenance with a cloud of gloom. After one or two min-utes silence, one of the members mustered courage to rise, and, said he, with an emphatic tone of voice, the name of "GARRISON" shall ever be cherished by me, and if you strike it off from that Constitution, you may strike me off; it shall be my motto as long as I *live*! Every countenance brightened, and the room rung with applause. . . . It was pleasant to hear the little ones cry—Garrison! Garrison! forever.[12]

The younger members of the GLBA may not have fully understood who Garrison was or what he stood for, but this did not matter. They under-stood that he was a friend to their community and a supporter of their educational endeavors. In time, and through contact with people such as Ruggles, Garnet, and Loveridge, these children would have a clearer grasp of what "abolitionists"—a bit of a mouthful for a five- or six-year-old—fought for. The name of Garrison was retained.

African American abolitionists made the case for the formation of juvenile antislavery societies. John W. Lewis, a minister and the GLBA's president, did so in 1837 in a series of four letters to children published in the white-owned *Herald of Freedom*, the organ of the New Hampshire Anti-Slavery Society. He was probably spurred by his own experience as president of an association maintained for youth and, more immedi-ately, by a series of four pseudonymous letters to children published in the same paper earlier that year, bemoaning the quasi-absence of juve-nile antislavery societies in New Hampshire. "The juvenile anti-slavery societies in Providence and Pawtucket [Rhode Island] have come up nobly to the work," the author noted. "I have received but little intel-ligence from other juvenile societies, except the one in Concord [New Hampshire]."[13] Lewis concurred that more such societies were needed, presenting his case in four points. First, he elaborated on the argument that children are naturally color-blind: white children, as opposed to adults, are "strangers to the deep-rooted prejudice and hatred toward the colored man." Yet their antiracist sentiments should be cultivated; otherwise, they are bound to dissipate as these children grow up in a society that condones slavery and perpetuates racial prejudice. "If [children] are formed into societies when young," Lewis argued, "they can keep their hearts in a right state towards all men." Second, antislavery societies provide an environment in which the child can develop a reform sensibility. By meeting and talking about slavery as it exists in the United States, children become attuned to other forms of exploitation elsewhere in the world, which causes them "to sympathize with all who are oppressed." Third, Lewis pointed out that the young have more time to devote to the antislavery cause than do adults, whose minds are "absorbed in mechanical, commercial or agricultural pursuits." That time should be employed wisely, for instance, "in thinking about, and acting for the slave." Fourth, juvenile antislavery societies foster a collaborative spirit among the young, who are led to realize how much more efficient concerted, rather than individual, action against a social ill can be. "There might be five hundred youth in New-Hampshire opposed to slavery and willing to see it abolished; yet unorganized, their efforts would be weak." In his final letter, Lewis asked the "noble youth of New-Hampshire" to "stand to [their] integrity" and keep in mind the promise of equality inscribed in the Declaration of Independence: "Let your opponents who say that . . . children are engaged in the anti-slavery cause know that although you are young yet you view with horror the abominations of the system."[14] Lewis did not say anything specific regarding the racial dynamics of juvenile antislavery societies, as he believed in the possibility of interracial cooperation. He would soon be disillusioned. In 1840, he left the position of lecturing agent for the New Hampshire Anti-Slavery Society that his series of letters had gained him, claiming that white abolitionist infighting, which in the early 1840s was at its peak, weakened the abolition movement as a whole. Like other African American activists, Lewis turned his attention to independent Black organizing. He became a traveling agent for the *Colored American* and entered the Colored Conventions movement.[15]

Still, Lewis's call seems to have been heard beyond New Hampshire. Several African American juvenile societies specifically devoted to abolition were formed in the late 1830s. The Pittsburgh, Pennsylvania, Juvenile Anti-Slavery Society was notable for being conducted by and for

African American children and youth. It was formed in July 1838 on the "cent-a-week" plan, devised by the AASS—and more specifically by Nathaniel Southard, mentioned in previous chapters—after a drop in income following the Panic of 1837 left the society's coffers depleted. As Teresa Goddu notes, "the low-cost plan enabled new segments of the population to be targeted as contributors," including children.[16] An article in the *Slave's Friend* taught them about the system: "Let each member of the Society be a collector. The collectors can ask their parents, their uncles and aunts, their grand parents, their brothers and sisters, and all their friends, to give a cent a week for the Anti-Slavery cause. Once a week ask them for the money. Get a collection-box, and drop it in. Once in three months open the box, take out the money, and hand it to the treasurer of the Society. He can send it to the treasurer of the American Anti-Slavery Society."[17] It is unknown who the treasurer of the Pittsburgh Juvenile Anti-Slavery Society was, but two of its leading figures were eleven- to twelve-year-old David J. Peck, who served as president, and fourteen-year-old George B. Vashon, who served as secretary; George's father, John B. Vashon, was a friend of Garrison's and an abolitionist himself. Young as they were, Peck and Vashon were readers of the Black press, and they raised money for the support of the *Colored American*: in November 1839, they forwarded five dollars to its editors, "as a small token of the esteem we have for your paper." By then, the Pittsburgh Juvenile Anti-Slavery Society consisted of forty members, "several of whom have addressed the Society, at different times."[18] Like the JGIS earlier in the decade, the group provided a safe space in which these young activists could hone oratorical skills that they would later demonstrate publicly.

Little is known about the Yates Juvenile Anti-Slavery Society—named after the white abolitionist William Yates, author of an 1838 treatise on racial discrimination—except for its participation in Emancipation Day celebrations in Troy, New York, on August 1, 1838. As pointed out in this book's introduction, Emancipation Day was a Black celebration before it was adopted by white abolitionists in the early 1840s. It replaced earlier Black festivities commemorating the end of the slave trade or emancipation at the state level. Music and prayers would alternate with orations and toasts in a sequence that lasted the entire day. Children came to play a prominent role in these rituals, as Julie Roy Jeffrey observes: "Youthful

participation ensured that children knew the wonderful facts of emancipation and encouraged them to believe in the possibility of freedom
for American slaves."[19] The Troy 1838 celebrations saw the children of
the Yates Juvenile Anti-Slavery Society walk in procession and deliver
recitations. Nine-year-old Peter F. Baltimore, later an important figure
in the local abolitionist community, addressed the assembly, and so did
another young boy named James Gardener. "The exercises of these dear
children were conducted with great decorum," the Colored American
noted, "and we enjoyed great delight in listening to the melodious sonnets which flowed from their lips in praise of Freedom's God."[20] The
son of a formerly enslaved man who had fled north years before, young
Baltimore had no personal knowledge of slavery. His antislavery education took place in the home, through stories told by his father, but also
at such public events, at which he was encouraged to express antislavery
sentiments. His very performance was part of the work of abolition in
that it demonstrated Black capacity for instruction and improvement.
The radical nature of such an education was not lost on racist whites.
Four years later, at a Philadelphia Emancipation Day parade, young
Black members of the local Youth Vigilance Committee unfurled an antislavery banner that opponents deemed provocative. The marchers were
attacked by a mob, leading to a three-day riot that must have left some
children traumatized.[21]

Juvenile antislavery societies were also formed within educational
contexts, as was the case in Carlisle, Pennsylvania. A school for African
American children was established there in 1835 as a response to white
exclusion. The institution soon thrived, with dozens of local children
from four years of age, as well as some adults, attending the classes taught
by the white instructor Sarah Bell in the basement of Bethel African
Methodist Episcopal Church. A juvenile antislavery society was formed
as part of the school, whose youthful members, like Peck and Vashon,
were consumers of the Black press. "The teacher informed us," an observer wrote in 1838, "that when the Colored American arrives every
child that can read is anxious to know what news the Colored American has brought." Some of the younger scholars, however, seem to have
struggled with the paper, which, after all, was primarily directed at an
adult audience. "Many of these children of whom we have just spoken,
often search the paper in vain for matter suited to their capacity." "Will

not our worthy Editor and excellent Proprietors give us a Children's or Juvenile Department?"[22] This suggestion was duly noted. In April 1840, a new column for children was included in the *Colored American*, as discussed in chapter 2. A year later, a different observer commented on the beneficial effect of the column on the Carlisle children. "It is delightful to see the amount of interest they have taken in that paper, especially since it contains the children's department." "We are convinced that this paper is exerting a very salutary influence, directly on the children, and indirectly on the parents," he added, in a nod to the theme of juvenile influence.[23]

Finally, the Juvenile Anti-Slavery Society of Salem, Massachusetts, provides a rare example of a society composed, perhaps entirely, of young African American women. Black women played a pioneering role in Salem, where in 1832 they formed the country's first female antislavery society; the Salem Female Anti-Slavery Society (SFASS) was reconstituted as an interracial society in 1834.[24] Two juvenile antislavery societies were formed in Salem later in the decade, and their members occasionally took part in SFASS meetings and were invited to participate in a fair organized in December 1838.[25] Part of the proceeds, it seems, was used by one of these two groups, referred to in the *Liberator* as a "Juvenile (colored) Sewing Soc.," to grant the white abolitionist schoolteacher William B. Dodge, a respected figure within the African American community, a life membership in the Massachusetts Anti-Slavery Society (MASS). As Erik Stumpf notes, a number of abolitionists received lifetime memberships to the MASS as a result of children's fund-raising efforts.[26] The two juvenile societies in Salem had provided memberships for three women, Eliza J. Kenney, Clarissa C. Lawrence, and Susan G. Roundey, a few months before, while the Plymouth Juvenile Anti-Slavery Society did the same for the Baptist minister Horatio N. Loring in 1839. Dodge sent "his very grateful acknowledgements to the colored females in the Juvenile Anti-Slavery Society of Salem," expressing the hope that these young women, "as a result of their labors in part," would live to see the end of slavery.[27]

The World of White-Led Juvenile Antislavery Societies

Juvenile societies served as a stepping-stone to the world of activism for Black children and youth. William Cooper Nell, William Howard Day, George B. Vashon, Peter F. Baltimore, and the young girls of the Salem Juvenile Anti-Slavery Society, depending on their age and sex, practiced their oratorical skills; they learned about organized abolition and its leaders; they participated in antislavery rituals; they managed fund-raising campaigns. Slavery and racial prejudice, however, were part of these children's daily lives. Many had formerly enslaved parents and knew all too well about the workings of racism. There was little they needed to be taught on the subject. Juvenile antislavery societies arguably played an even more crucial role for white children and youth, who may otherwise have remained ignorant of or indifferent to the realities of slavery. White abolitionist adults made sure that this would not be the case. Older and more enterprising children formed societies of their own initiative.

The earliest of the white-led antislavery societies seems to have been formed in Utica, New York. Two separate organizations were created in April 1833, one for boys, the other for girls.[28] Both were later integrated into the AASS's vertical institutional structure, entertaining relations with town, county, and state antislavery societies.[29] The Utica Female Juvenile Anti-Slavery Society mostly survives in the form of an 1838 petition penned by its eighteen-year-old secretary, Ellen W. Dorchester, on behalf of its members and sent to Congressman John Quincy Adams, a man of antislavery sympathies and an ardent defender of the right to petition. "We are young," the petitioners conceded, "but still we are old enough to know a little about the great question which is acting so powerfully upon the community at the present day." The petition alluded to the recent murder of Elijah P. Lovejoy, demonstrating these young abolitionists' familiarity with current events. Quoting from the Declaration of Independence, it drew attention to the plight of "3 millions of our fellow-beings, rational creatures, who have been endowed by their Creator with certain inalienable rights, among which are life, *liberty*, and *the pursuit of happiness*, inhumanely deprived of these rights, and held in the vilest servitude." "We are determined to do something to prevent our dearly beloved country from falling a prey to violence, daring cruelty and midnight assassination," the petitioners concluded.[30] Though the younger members of the Utica society may not have been involved in the wording of the petition, they probably discussed its contents with Dorchester and other more mature members of the group and in the process learned about the practice and rhetoric of antislavery petitioning. They also found out about the obstacles faced by abolitionists. The Utica petition, like all such petitions, was tabled as a result of the gag rule that was adopted in the House of Representatives in 1836 and renewed each year until 1844.

The AASS enthused over the appearance of these antislavery societies of a new kind in its second annual report. "The Committee have heard with great pleasure of the formation of Juvenile Anti-Slavery Societies, in Providence and Utica—others no doubt exist. And why should they not? . . . Every child understands the right and the wrong about Slavery, the moment the case is stated."[31] The Providence Female Juvenile Anti-Slavery Society, mentioned in the report, was founded in December 1834 by fourteen-year-old Sarah R. Miller, who had imbibed antislavery principles while visiting friends in Boston and returned to Providence "a staunch abolitionist." Secretary Almira F. Bolles reminisced about the formation of the group on the occasion of its first anniversary. "We knew very little about what had been done or was doing for the slaves," she explained, "but *this* we had learned, that 2,500,000 immortal beings were deprived of liberty, treated like brutes, and subjected to innumerable hardships." It was one thing to learn about the injustices of slavery; it was quite another to combat them. "At first, we hardly knew in what way we could bring our exertions to any valuable account." Eventually, members decided to meet weekly and "raise funds for the cause, by laboring as a Sewing Society." Small articles such as holders, pincushions, and work bags were made with pieces of silk and velvet donated by friends and family, while further information on the subject of slavery was acquired by having one member read antislavery publications to the others; reading and sewing often went hand in hand within female antislavery groups.[32] Once enough articles were manufactured, sales were organized in various places, for instance, at the home of the president of the Providence Anti-Slavery Society. The Providence girls' financial contribution to the cause was far from negligible: ninety dollars were raised during the society's first year of existence, most of which was transmitted to the AASS, and the remainder was given toward establishing an antislavery library in the city. By early 1836, the Providence Female Juvenile Anti-Slavery Society counted between thirty and forty members, including a few African American girls—making it, in effect, an interracial society. Most members were around twelve years of age. One was a two-year-old enrolled by her wealthy father, who promised that "his cash should make her an efficient member."[33]

Rhode Island was also home to one of the most long lasting of these societies. In late 1835, Pawtucket, a small village located not far from Providence, saw the formation of an energetic juvenile antislavery society "composed almost wholly of little girls," whose labors were directed by "half a dozen young ladies." It was common for such societies to have young adults, like Prince Loveridge in New York or Ellen W. Dorchester in Utica, acting as supervisors. The founders of the Bangor, Maine, Juvenile Anti-Slavery Society would later confess, "We did not feel ourselves capable of managing a society without assistance, and therefore solicited the help of some ladies."[34] In similar fashion to other female groups, the Pawtucket Juvenile Anti-Slavery Society met on Saturday afternoons, and occasionally in evenings, "to work in preparing various articles, by the sale of which they might raise money for the antislavery cause." These articles were sold at an annual fair that predated the large-scale women's antislavery fairs of the 1840s and 1850s. Over one hundred dollars were raised at the fair of August 1836, with several valuable articles left unsold. Historians of abolition have pointed to the lowly origins of the abolitionist rank and file, and the Pawtucket girls were no exception.[35] "None who have been engaged in this work, are the children of opulent parents," the antislavery *Pawtucket Record and Free Discussion Advocate* made clear, "but persevering industry has worked this wonder." Proceeds from the fair usually went to the *Liberator*. Twenty-five dollars were appropriated for the support of the newspaper in 1837, and double that sum in 1839, gifts duly acknowledged by a grateful Garrison. In 1840, the society pledged itself to raise twenty-five dollars toward defraying Nathaniel Peabody Rogers's expenses as a delegate to the World's Anti-Slavery Convention in London; Charles Lenox Remond, the sole African American delegate at the convention, also had some of his expenses paid with money raised by a Rhode Island juvenile society, the Young Ladies and Juvenile Anti-Slavery Society of

Newport. With nine increasingly professionalized fairs organized between 1836 and 1844, however, it is debatable whether the Pawtucket group remained a juvenile society or whether it grew into adulthood along with its members. It is unlikely, for instance, that children were involved in the production of the elegant antislavery gift book that was sold at the 1840 fair, *The Envoy*. Though its title page claimed that it was "published by the Juvenile Eman. Society," the book was edited by thirty-five-year-old Frances Whipple Green. Only one of its pieces, John Neal's "The Instinct of Childhood," discussed abolition in relation to children. By the early 1840s, it seemed that this "juvenile" society was firmly in control of young women, which might be why the white abolitionist Abby Kelley estimated that it "merits a more venerable name."[36]

Indeed, the age of members varied significantly within societies and from one society to another. The Mansfield and Foxborough, Massachusetts, Juvenile Society provides a rare example of an antislavery society for the very young. Naturally it was not formed by one of its members but on the initiative of an adult, the white abolitionist Experience Billings. The society, Billings explained to Garrison, included girls *and* boys, which was possible precisely because its members were so young: "None are fourteen—the largest number between ten and five." The little abolitionists met at Billings's house on a less frequent and formal basis than more mature groups did. Their activities, however, were similar: the children braided colored straw that was sold for the benefit of the antislavery cause. "Could the slaveholders take a peep into our little room and see these children all actively engaged," Billings went on, "they would have reason to fear that ere long these young Davids and Jaels will sever the heart of the monster Slavery." Though understandably modest, the group's donation to the MASS was duly recorded in the *Liberator* in the spring of 1839: the "product of labor of juvenile friends" in Mansfield amounted to sixty-eight cents. Other small contributions were listed in the paper.[37] By mid-1840, however, Billings felt less optimistic about the fate of the society than she had been a year earlier. "I have sent a line to our young Friends to meet," she wrote to Maria Weston Chapman. "I think that we shall do as much as we did last year tho their meeting together now, has lost its novelty & the parents do not encourage them as formerly." Interest in the society seems to have been fleeting, as the experience of another abolitionist, Fanny Skinner, also demonstrated: "I met with a friend in Mansfield Mrs. Horace Skinner that began with a few young friends last year but she says they have all left her." Downright opposition to juvenile antislavery fund-raising further threatened the existence of the Mansfield and Foxborough Juvenile Society: "There is a poor widow and her young daughter that have been friendly but are now at a stand, the daughter has been one of our number she also had a contribution box. Her uncle came on a visit from Westfield (a profest Methodist) saw the box told his sister it was the greatest imposition."[38] Like most juvenile antislavery "societies"—a term used even for such loosely organized groups as this one—the Mansfield and Foxborough Juvenile Society went defunct not long after it was created. Yet perhaps some of the antislavery seeds that Billings planted in the hearts of its young members developed into full-grown abolitionist sentiments.

At the other end of the age spectrum was the Junior Anti-Slavery Society of the City and County of Philadelphia (JASSP), formed in June 1836 as an auxiliary to the Pennsylvania State Anti-Slavery Society. Two manuscript versions of its constitution exist, one of which states that the society was open to "any person, over the age of fifteen." In the other version, the words "any person between the ages of 14 and 21 years" have been struck through and replaced by "any person under the age of 21 years," which may be an indication that persons under the age of fourteen applied for membership.[39] As far as we can ascertain from its list of members, the JASSP was mostly composed of young men on the cusp of adulthood. Thomas S. Cavender was fifteen at its creation; Samuel J. Levick and Edward Squibb, sixteen; Henry Peterson and Joshua L. Hallowell, seventeen.[40] In the Philadelphia *National Enquirer*, the veteran white abolitionist Benjamin Lundy printed a letter by a pseudonymous "Young Abolitionist," probably a member of the JASSP, who in November 1836 noted that "those who are now foremost in freedom's cause" would soon pass away. "We will tread in the footsteps of the Garrisons, the Thompsons, the Lundys, the Birneys, the Jays, and other pioneers in the cause," another "Young Abolitionist" declared later that month. Lundy himself concurred: "Time will soon remove *us* from the field of action; and *on you* will depend the consummation of the great reformation which by us has been but *commenced*."[41] These young abolitionists' activities resembled those of more mature activists. They engaged in debates about abolition, petitioned Congress against the annexation of Texas, circulated antislavery publications, held and addressed public meetings in Pennsylvania and nearby New Jersey, and helped with the establishment of Black schools.[42] Theirs was, in Deborah De Rosa's terms, "a highly structured and politically conscious organization."[43] More specifically, JASSP members debated such questions as "Is it consistent with the principles of Abolitionists to partake of the produce of Slavery?"; "Is it consistent for Anti-Slavery merchants to sell goods to Slaveholders?"; and "Is it *expedient* for colored persons to join Anti-Slavery Societies?"—the latter suggestive of some of the ambiguities of white abolitionism regarding interracial activism.[44] The JASSP was also notable for sponsoring the publication of two pamphlets based on addresses delivered by Henry Peterson before the society in 1836 and 1838. In his second address, the nineteen-year-old Peterson explained the rationale behind juvenile abolitionism:

> This is a subject which claims in an especial manner the attention of the young. Manhood, engrossed with business, and accustomed to the present condition of our country, will hardly think of evils which do not directly interrupt the even tenor of its money-getting way. Age, wearied with toil, or smiling and crying in the infirmities of second childhood, has neither vigor of mind nor strength of body for active exertion. It is for the young, then, to take up this cause in their morning, and cheerfully support it during the burden and heat of the day. . . . The young are also more particularly interested. Manhood and old age may pass away ere the tempest shall burst in its fury,—but the youth of the present, the men of the coming day, may be doomed to abide the storm.[45]

Abolition demanded youthful energies, Peterson argued, because young men such as himself might have to suffer the consequences of their elders' inaction.

The published diary of another JASSP member, Samuel J. Levick, gives us an idea of how antislavery activism fit into a young man's daily life. "Being ardent of temperament, . . . keenly sympathetic, and aglow with the aspirations of early manhood," a friend of his later commented, "it seemed not only natural, but highly probable, that he would be interested in the reformatory movements that were being started or advanced in his native city." Sam, as he was known among friends, was a committed abolitionist before he reached the age of twenty. In January and February 1839, he attended at least six JASSP meetings, including several meetings of the board of managers in his capacity as treasurer. Some of his evenings were spent "arranging [the] accounts" of the society, others "at the school for colored men" that Levick and his associates had opened in Clarkson Hall; Levick was frequently in contact with poor African Americans in Philadelphia. Whenever a debate was organized among JASSP members, he took the more radical side: he took the affirmative when the question "Is slave-holding under all circumstances, sinful?" was discussed and the negative when it was asked if intemperance was "a greater evil than Slavery." Levick was so devoted to abolition that he regularly attended the meetings of other local antislavery societies, including the city and county antislavery groups, the Northern Liberties Anti-Slavery Society, the Workingmen's Anti-Slavery Society, and the Association of Friends for Pleading the Cause of the Slave. He persisted in his activism even in the face of antagonism. He was met "with great opposition" from fellow Quakers when he asked if their meetinghouse could be used for the third Anti-Slavery Convention of American Women, to be held in Philadelphia in May 1839; his coreligionists' reaction must have been all the more painful as it was the first time that the young man had spoken at a Friends' meeting. A few weeks before, a JASSP meeting was disrupted by "a number of unruly boys and men" who unsuccessfully attempted to interrupt Levick. As a believer in nonresistance, the young man strongly disagreed when fellow JASSP managers resolved to ask the mayor for police protection. Though he confessed on December 31, 1839, that he still felt like "a babe" in moral and religious terms, the twenty-year-old already had strong convictions that would only increase with time.[46]

"Anti-Slavery success to the Juniors!" exclaimed the abolitionist poet John Greenleaf Whittier in the *Pennsylvania Freeman*. "We love to meet with these young men. Their feelings have not been chilled by the world's coldness, nor their principles warped by self-interest. They can always see clearly what is right, where justice and truth are concerned." In praising the work of the JASSP, Whittier deployed the same kind of rhetoric that was used to advocate for children's abolitionism. He believed that "the Juniors" were young enough that they remained untainted by the corrupting influence of society. For them, the "self-evident truths" that "all men are created equal" and that they are "endowed by their Creator with certain unalienable Rights," as the Declaration of Independence affirms, were truly self-evident. These truths "flash upon their minds, and the heart, uncorrupted and unsuspecting, yields its spontaneous assent." Children and youth thus had the almost uncanny ability to bring the nation back to its own infancy—to a time when it still acted in accordance with its professed principles of liberty and equality. Abolitionists should look to the young as the vehicle for the nation's political, spiritual, and moral regeneration. "Give us the *young men*," Whittier concluded, and the antislavery cause "will be carried forward triumphantly."[47]

Enter the Children's Agent

Hoping to turn abolition into a mass movement involving Americans of all ages, the AASS encouraged the formation of local juvenile antislavery societies throughout the 1830s. In late 1836, it appointed a juvenile antislavery agent to work with children and help them organize. The position was occupied by Henry Clarke Wright, a key figure in the history of juvenile abolitionism, who wrote several books on childhood, motherhood, and the family (figure 3.2).[48] "The American Anti-Slavery Society has been directed by the God of the oppressed, to turn their attention to the children and youth of our country," Wright told Joshua Leavitt, the editor of the *New York Evangelist*. "To aid in this holy work, they have appointed me to labor as a *Children's Anti-Slavery Agent*. They wish me to organize juvenile anti-slavery societies in every town and village in the land where parents are willing their children should be thus associated in this godlike enterprise."[49] Wright took to his new role with gusto. Starting from New York, which he noted already boasted four juvenile antislavery societies averaging a hundred members each, he embarked on a tour that took him from New Jersey to Massachusetts and then on to Rhode Island and Pennsylvania.

One of Wright's first meetings took place in a church in Newark, New Jersey, on January 8, 1837, gathering over 150 children and youth. Parents had been invited to attend: whether they stood at the back of the room or sat next to their offspring, adults were an essential presence in such events, and several ministers were also there. Wright's account of

Figure 3.2. Henry Clarke Wright (1797–1870) with an unidentified child. Frontispiece to Henry Clarke Wright, *Marriage and Parentage; or, The Reproductive Element in Man, as a Means to His Elevation and Happiness* (Boston: Bela Marsh, 1866). Courtesy of the American Antiquarian Society.

the meeting in the *Emancipator* suggests that it mostly followed a call-and-response pattern, with Wright asking questions and the children answering them:

> I wished to see whether the children understood what slavery was, and asked them "what is slavery?" . . . Some said "to hold and use men, women and children as property." "Children, to whom do the bodies and souls of men belong?" "To God and themselves." "What do slaveholders do when they seize the bodies and souls of men, and hold and use them as their property?" "They rob God and man." . . . "Children, what is emancipation or anti-slavery?" "To raise up the poor slaves from the condition in which wicked slaveholders hold and use them as property—and place them in that situation in which God placed them at first." "What situation was that?" "But little lower than the angels."[50]

The exchange must have been highly stylized, as it is unlikely that a large group of children, even sons and daughters of abolitionists well schooled in biblical and antislavery precepts, would have answered his questions in such language, let alone in unison. The dialogue, in fact, reads more like an antislavery catechism from the *Slave's Friend* than a faithful report of a children's meeting. Still, there is no doubt that it was based on actual interactions between Wright and his audience. The meeting ended with a vote to form the Newark Juvenile Anti-Slavery Society. Parents were appointed as officers; Alexander N. Dougherty, who would become the first president of the New Jersey Anti-Slavery Society upon its creation two years later, served as secretary of the juvenile association, and surely his fifteen-year-old son, Alexander, a surgeon in the US Volunteer Army during the Civil War, was in the audience that day.[51] Several resolutions were passed, including the following, apparently written by the adults in the voice of the children: "That when our parents are called *fanatics*, *incendiaries*, and enemies of their country for being abolitionists, we will only love them the more, and try to imitate their example." The children probably demonstrated more agency when they voted unanimously that each member of the newly created society would try to raise one cent a week for the antislavery cause. A "colored Juvenile" antislavery society was founded the same day, with the African American barber and activist Adam Ray as secretary.[52] "Who dare despise the efforts of those dear

children?" Wright asked the editor of the *Emancipator*. "By God's blessing, they will revolutionize Newark on the subject of slavery."[53]

Three months later, Wright could be found in Boston, lecturing to a
large audience composed of children of the Boston Juvenile Anti-Slavery
Society. The meeting lasted an hour and a half, yet the children showed
no sign of restlessness. "Children, every where, constitute my most attentive and sympathizing auditors," Wright assured Garrison.[54] A short
piece in the *Slave's Friend* about a juvenile antislavery meeting featured
an abolitionist mother congratulating her daughter, Elizabeth, for sitting
"very still at meeting to-day" and paying "a good deal of attention to
the minister [Wright] while he was speaking."[55] This did not mean that
Wright was never challenged by his audience. In Boston, a boy seemed
to question the soundness of immediatism. "Mr. Wright, would you
have all the slaves set free now?" the boy asked. "Yes—to-day," answered
the lecturer. "I would not." "Why?" "*They would cut all our throats.*"
"How do you know?" "*Father says so.*"[56] That the boy's father warned
his son about the dangers of immediate emancipation suggests that it
was the mother who enrolled the boy in the juvenile society and made
him attend this particular meeting, pointing to possible intrafamilial
conflict over the question of slavery. Another piece in the *Slave's Friend*
dramatized the situation of Daniel Tracy, whose father would not let
him attend a lecture by Wright on the grounds that "he is a fanatic, an
incendiary, a brawler, a cut-throat, a fool." The boy pleads with his father, arguing that Wright "is a temperance man, a peacemaker, a friend
to liberty," but his efforts are in vain. "You are too young to talk about
such things," the father retorts before sending his son to bed.[57] Not all
children were as determined as little Daniel: Wright himself recalled a
boy who had requested that his name be erased from the constitution
of a juvenile antislavery society after his friends had "laughed at him,
and called him a fanatic."[58] A little girl in the *Slave's Friend* was teased
by her classmates because her father was an abolitionist.[59] Abolition was
no more socially acceptable among children than it was among adults.

Dozens of children braved the taunts of friends and classmates and
persisted in what they perceived as a just cause. Such was the case in
Lynn, Massachusetts, where Wright supervised the formation of two
juvenile antislavery societies, the female one presided over by eighteen-
year-old Mercy T. Buffum, a member of the Lynn Female Anti-Slavery

Society; it counted over eighty members by 1838. The children of Lynn, Wright reported to Garrison, "are determined to put a good deal of money into the treasury of the Anti-Slavery Society." In a town known for its shoe-making industry, antislavery girls would bind shoes to get money, apparently with some success. In early 1839, the Lynn Female Anti-Slavery Society acknowledged a contribution of fifty dollars to its fair from the "Lynn Juvenile Society" (another smaller contribution from "Children in Weymouth," Massachusetts, was listed).[60] Overall, juvenile antislavery societies seem to have put significant sums of money into the "abolition treasury."[61] Under the heading "Money Received from Children," the *Slave's Friend* repeatedly listed financial contributions by various antislavery societies. The October 1837 issue mentioned contributions by societies in Rhode Island, Maine, New York, and New Jersey, totaling $71.99.[62]

The girls of Providence were just as dynamic as their Lynn sisters, as Wright discovered. The now sixteen-year-old Sarah R. Miller still served as the Providence Female Juvenile Anti-Slavery Society's "enterprising young President," and $150 had been raised the year before under her directorship. Miller made sure that a venue was available for Wright, who was able to hold several meetings, one of them attended by "more than 100 boys . . . and as many girls, and many adults."[63] Wright lectured not only on slavery and abolition but on peace, his other cherished cause; a few years later, he published a collection of children's stories advocating abstention from conflict, *A Kiss for a Blow* (1842), in which he claimed to have addressed "more than fifty thousand Children."[64] Wright explained to the children of Providence that antislavery and peace principles were interconnected: "I endeavored to show them how wicked it was for one man to attempt to *constrain others* by *violence*, as slaveholders and bloody warriors do; to show them that when they got angry, quarreled, struck each other and fought, they acted just like slaveholders." To the all-female, and more mature, audience of the Providence Female Juvenile Anti-Slavery Society, he explained the power of female influence: "I lectured to a full meeting of females here, and showed how much our mothers, daughters and sisters can do for our holy cause by instilling the principles of Anti-slavery into the minds of the little children." In the end, however, it was juvenile influence that would allow abolition to carry the day, according to Wright. Children, he affirmed, have "a mighty influence in Providence and will do more to make the whole city Anti-slavery, than any others can do." He made this point over and over again in the letters he wrote to antislavery editors during his lecturing tour. "I tell you children have an influence," he reiterated to William Goodell after lecturing to the boys and girls of Pawtucket.[65]

Wright then proceeded to Pennsylvania, writing to Benjamin Lundy about his labors there. The constitution of the Darby Juvenile Anti-Slavery Society, he found, "embodies the pure and heaven-born principles of peace as well as of abolition." The children he met in Darby had been well educated in both abolition and the "non-resisting spirit." In Kennet Square, Wright drew an impressive crowd of 250 children and youth, with adults in tow, a number of whom had come by carriage from the neighboring areas. His audience proved particularly receptive to his message. "It was a happy sight to me," he told Lundy, "to see these children and youth, with warm anti-slavery hearts and smiling anti-slavery countenances, meet to be instructed in the great principles of humanity and universal liberty."[66] Wright's travels for the rest of the year are harder to trace, and it appears his agency on behalf of the AASS was for 1837 only. From then on, however, he was known as "the Children's Preacher," and abolitionists remarked on his ability to talk to and interest young people.[67] As Garrison put it in 1842, "His great forte lies in addressing little children, over whom he exerts complete mastery. Place him in the midst of a crowded assembly of children, and he never fails to produce a deep impression upon their minds."[68] Jane Elizabeth Jones's *The Young Abolitionists; or, Conversations on Slavery* (1848) opens with young Charlie Selden begging his mother to take him to a meeting (not one for children) where Wright is going to lecture. Wright has just visited the Seldens and made quite an impression on the children. "I like *him*," says Charlie. "We chased each other all round the old pasture, he helped me sail my boat, he played with old Tig, and it was rare sport we had." While Mrs. Selden goes to the meeting alone, she promises her son, "At some convenient time I will tell you all about this visiter [*sic*]; how he loves little children, and is always teaching them to be good, and to follow peace principles."[69] On the eve of the Civil War, Wright was still extolling the virtues of juvenile abolitionism in the pages of the *Liberator*.[70]

Other abolitionists besides Wright addressed juvenile audiences. In September 1838, Philo C. Pettibone, an agent for the Essex County Anti-

Slavery Society, addressed the children of Haverhill, Massachusetts, who had already formed several antislavery societies. "About 300 children and youth were present at the meeting," Pettibone reported to Garrison. "Never before have I witnessed so interesting a group of children. Let all the children of our land become electrified with abolition and peace principles, and there will be no *materials for mobs or war in the next generation*."[71] Further north, the Congregational minister David Thurston lectured to the children and youth of the Winthrop, Maine, Anti-Slavery Society. It was Thurston's conviction that the young must be "well informed in regard to the true character of American slavery." He insisted that even "quite young persons" could be made to understand the immorality of the slave system, and in his lectures, he took care "to exhibit the [antislavery] principles in such a manner, that the youngest present might distinctly understand them."[72] Thurston adopted the same kind of didactic, catechismal lecturing style as Wright, asking questions to children and building on their answers. He gave them specific advice as to how to advance the antislavery cause.

Women were also involved in juvenile antislavery lecturing, though to a lesser extent. Sarah and Angelina Grimké, for instance, were present at a June 1837 meeting of the Boston Juvenile Anti-Slavery Society. Rather than interacting directly with the audience, the southern-born Grimké sisters drew on their firsthand knowledge of slavery. Sarah told the story of a little girl bought off a slave ship whom she had received as a present when she was a child. The daughter of an African princess, the girl had been abducted by white men and separated from her family. "She would not eat, and was very thin and poor," Sarah told her young listeners. "She said she was afraid if she ate and grew fat, the white people would kill and eat her," a common fear among kidnapped Africans. Though Sarah treated her kindly, the orphan died before reaching adulthood. Sarah further told the children that "she had seen twenty children chained together, and driven through the streets of Charleston to be sold in New Orleans, never more to see their parents—the driver whipping them with a whip." Wright, who was present, showed the audience a whip and fetters that he had brought with him. The children, as can be imagined, were "deeply affected" by what they saw and heard. On that day, the Grimkés and Wright adopted a more emotional mode of address based on visual elements and moving stories meant to capture the attention of their young audience. The tragic story of the African girl who was afraid to be eaten by white people, though authentic, had elements of the fairy tale in it that were sure to captivate at least some of the children. While the Grimkés and Wright presented the audience with a grim picture of slavery, J. Horace Kimball, an AASS agent who was just back from the British West Indies, ended the meeting on a more cheerful note by explaining to the children, based on what he had seen, "how safe it was to masters and slaves, to liberate the slaves immediately."[73] A collection was then taken and copies of the *Slave's Friend* distributed. In a letter to one of the secretaries of a British female antislavery society, Angelina Grimké commented on the usefulness of such meetings. "Even *Children* may be addressed with great effect now," she wrote, "for they are beginning in the Free States, to form themselves into associations, to lisp the wrongs of the Slave, and to throw their pennies into the coffer of the National Society."[74]

The abolitionists' promotion of juvenile antislavery societies, like their promotion of juvenile antislavery literature, provoked a furious backlash from antiabolitionists. In the pages of the *New York Commercial Advertiser*, a paper not known for its antislavery sympathies, one Equitas fumed against what he called "the climax of fanaticism, ignorance and downright prostitution of morals." Equitas had come across an account of a late-1836 meeting for the formation of a juvenile antislavery society in New York, at which Wright had addressed his audience with characteristically provocative rhetoric, declaring that "the Devil was the first slave holder, and that slavery originated in hell, that none but the Devil, and those influenced by the spirit of the Devil, could ever tear children from their mothers, and mothers for their children." A self-proclaimed "well-wisher to the rising generation," Equitas found it "perfectly disgusting and immoral—yes, IMMORAL"—that children should be exposed to such incendiary doctrines. "Can it be that there are parents in New York, who have no more regard for their children than to allow them thus to have their infant minds poisoned and prejudiced by ignorant and infatuated men?"[75] Any money raised by the children, he added, would end up not in the coffers of antislavery societies but in the pockets of abolitionists.

Not all critics of juvenile abolitionism were as aggressive as Equitas. Some seemed to understand the logic of such a project; indeed, they recognized that enlisting children in the antislavery cause was probably the best way for abolition to triumph in the long term. "I like [juvenile associations] less than any other feature of the times," one Tennessee congressman noted. "It is comparatively of little consequence what old men think; but boys, who have seventy years to live and do mischief in, are to be dreaded. I never hear of a juvenile anti-slavery society, without thinking of the infant Hannibal swearing eternal enmity to Rome."[76] In the event, some antiabolitionists created their own juvenile societies. Even before Wright went on his lecturing tour, white southern youth had considered the possibility of forming rival organizations. In mid-1835, a group of young men "between the ages of *seventeen and nineteen*"—the same age group as the JASSP—held a meeting in Charleston to discuss "the formation of an anti-abolition and constitutional society."[77] Colonizationists in the Old Northwest were not averse to juvenile organizing either. As early as 1830, a Juvenile Colonization Society was organized in Cincinnati, Ohio, for youth under sixteen.[78] Garrison wittily called it "a childish scheme," in the same issue of the *Liberator* in which he printed one of the first iterations of the Juvenile Department.[79] The juvenile associations of antiabolitionists and colonizationists, though, were never as numerous or as active as those of abolitionists.

Juvenile antislavery societies occupy a significant place in the annals of the abolition movement. Short-lived though they were, these associations helped create a generation of Black and white abolitionists who would be at their most vocal in the critical decades of the 1840s and 1850s. They familiarized children with aspects of the antislavery argument and introduced them to tried-and-tested antislavery tactics and strategies. With the help of more mature abolitionists, children learned about petitioning, speech-making, and fund-raising and about the day-to-day management of a reform organization and the kind of commitment needed to keep it alive. Young abolitionists would carry these lessons with them into adulthood.

4

"We Have Several School-Mates Who Have Been Slaves"

Abolition in the Classroom

Sarah Parker Remond longed to be educated. Yet educational opportunities were limited for a young African American girl growing up in
Salem, Massachusetts, in the 1830s. No private school would have her.
She understood why and felt the pain of repeated rejection. Finally,
Sarah and two of her sisters were admitted to one of Salem's public
schools. The white teachers treated them kindly; their classmates did
too, though Sarah could feel that these children had already imbibed
some of their parents' racist ideas. Not long after the Remond sisters
entered the school, a petition was put forward by white community
members asking that the girls be removed and a segregated school
for Black children be created. The Salem school committee complied.
One morning in 1834, Sarah's teacher told her that she could no longer
attend the school and walked her home. "I had no words for any one,"
Remond later recalled. "I only wept bitter tears; then, in a few minutes, I thought of the great injustice practiced upon me, and longed
for some power to help me to crush those who thus robbed me of
my personal rights."[1] Remond found this power in herself. The eight-
year-old later became a renowned abolitionist, who lectured on racial
prejudice and slavery internationally. She was quick to make the con-
nection between the two. "Prejudice against colour," she realized, was
"the legitimate offspring of American slavery."[2] Remond's humiliat-
ing childhood experience at the East School for Girls was arguably a
catalyst for her antislavery activism.

Racism did not stop at the door of the schoolhouse in the antebellum North; nor did abolitionism. Schoolrooms were highly political
spaces, where students were exposed to racially progressive or white
supremacist ideas, depending on where they were schooled and by
whom they were taught. Holly Keller writes, "Because of the conser-

vatism of all but the most progressive nineteenth-century schools, most antislavery, and surely all abolitionist, texts for children were read outside the classroom," seemingly ruling out any possibility that abolition would have been discussed in an educational context.[3] Indeed, there were probably many more conservative instructors who kept well away from such controversial topics than abolitionist teachers who acquainted their charges with the wrongs of slavery. Some white abolitionists homeschooled their children lest they be exposed to nefarious influences at school.[4] Yet there were educational institutions of many kinds in the antebellum United States, and some in the North came to serve as platforms for antislavery work. School segregation paradoxically meant that slavery could be discussed more or less freely in classrooms such as that of the African American teacher and abolitionist Susan Paul. Slavery was a tangible reality anyway at Boston Primary School No. 6. As some of Paul's young students noted, "We have several school-mates who have been slaves, and we try to make them as happy as we can."[5] Paul did bring up slavery with her students. She even had them sing antislavery songs. Education and abolition were tightly interwoven for antislavery activists. Education was not only the pathway from slavery to freedom, to paraphrase Frederick Douglass: it was the pathway from freedom to abolition.

Abolitionism was not always taboo in white schools either. With the aid of textbooks that addressed slavery and racial prejudice critically, some instructors, from the early years of the republic, infused their teaching with abolitionist values. Sunday schools were critical to the development of white juvenile abolitionism. In this chapter, I push the door of several abolitionist classrooms, going back to Quakers' early support for Black education. I show how the education of African American children was tied to the abolitionist project and more specifically how slavery and abolition were addressed in the early national and antebellum classroom. I pay close attention to the words of children who delivered poems and addresses or wrote compositions denouncing slavery. Abolitionists knew that any attempt at educating Black children—let alone nurturing Black and white children's antislavery sentiments—was fraught with danger. I end this chapter with a look at how slavery's defenders tried to thwart these attempts.

Education as Abolition

Quakers have long been recognized as pioneers of abolition in the United States. Inspired by acts of slave resistance, eighteenth-century Quakers such as Benjamin Lay, John Woolman, and Anthony Benezet played a leading role in the emergence of antislavery thought in the British North American colonies, urging fellow Friends to emancipate their slaves, recognize Black humanity, and work toward abolition. Objections to the suitability of the enslaved for freedom led antislavery Quakers to establish the first schools for free Black children. Education, they argued, was key to the abolitionist agenda: emancipation would no longer appear as a threat to the social order if the newly freed were properly educated.[6] The French American schoolmaster Anthony Benezet was the most influential of the early Quaker promoters of Black education (figure 4.1). As early as 1750, Benezet began providing evening classes for young Black people in his home. Two decades later, he was instrumental in convincing the Philadelphia Monthly Meeting to establish the African School, or School for Black People. He was intimately involved in its operations and ran it from 1782 until his death two years later.[7] At a time when slavery was only beginning to be abolished in the North—Pennsylvania's gradual emancipation law was adopted in 1780—his students did not need to be told about its injustice or what it did to their relatives who were still enslaved. Lessons in reading, writing, and arithmetic, as well as vocational education, were what they most urgently needed. Yet the African School's classroom was an abolitionist space insofar as its very existence was linked to the possibility of—and hope for—a future without slavery. Several of the school's young scholars, notably James Forten, became leading abolitionists.[8]

Quakers also made sure that white children knew about slavery and the slave trade. Born on Nantucket Island, Massachusetts, a decade after the judicial abolition of slavery in the state, young Lucretia Mott (née Coffin) had some contact with free African Americans but little with enslaved people. She ascribed her juvenile abolitionism to the texts and images shown to her at Quaker school in the late 1790s. "My sympathy was early enlisted for the poor slave by the class books read in our schools, and the pictures of the slave-ships as presented by Clarkson," she wrote in an autobiographical sketch.[9] Among these "class books" was Priscilla Wakefield's *Mental Improvement* (1794), discussed in chapter 2; a US edition

Figure 4.1. Anthony Benezet (1713–1784) teaching African American children. John W. Barber and Elizabeth G. Barber, *Historical, Poetical and Pictorial American Scenes* (New Haven, CT: J. W. Barber, 1850), 56. Courtesy of the New York Public Library, General Research Division.

had appeared in New Bedford, Massachusetts, in 1799. One passage in particular—Mrs. Harcourt's graphic description of the Middle Passage to her children—made such an impression on Mott that she could still recite it by heart in her old age, according to her granddaughter. Thomas Clarkson's visual representation of the slave ship *Brookes* made even more vivid Wakefield's textual account of the slave trade. One of Mott's biographers claims that the image adorned the classroom walls, along with a well-known picture of William Penn signing a peace treaty with the Lenape Indians. At the age of thirteen, Mott left Massachusetts for a Hudson, New York, boarding school, where she was introduced to the poetry of William Cowper by her English-born Quaker teacher, Susanna Marriott. An abolitionist, Marriott probably shared some of Cowper's antislavery verse with her students, including his 1788 "Negro's Complaint." Another white abolitionist and advocate of African American education, Emily Howland, credited Marriott for introducing her to the antislavery movement.[10]

Marriott may have introduced Wakefield's *Mental Improvement* in her classroom because the author, like her, was an English Quaker. But there was no shortage of locally produced antislavery schoolbooks in the newly independent United States. Revolutionary antislavery was still in the air in the 1790s, and students were likely to be exposed to abolitionist sentiment at a young age and with little controversy. As I have shown in chapter 1, most early juvenile antislavery publications were, in fact, school readers meant to be read in the classroom. Noah Webster wrote in the advertisement to *The Little Reader's Assistant* (1790) that he had been "repeatedly requested by the Instructors of Schools, to publish a small book, containing *familiar* stories in *plain* language, for the benefit of children." The title page of Caleb Bingham's *American Preceptor* (1794) made it clear that it was "designed for the use of schools." These readers strove to promote cultural values and inculcate moral principles— including, for Webster and Bingham, an abhorrence of slavery—as well as to enhance reading and language skills. Book historians have emphasized how popular they were: *The American Preceptor* sold 640,000 copies over its lifetime, *The Columbian Orator* (1797) another 200,000. Both of Bingham's volumes were in use for several decades. Untold numbers of young scholars may have been made to read and recite William Pitt and Samuel Miller's anti-slave-trade speeches in the *Preceptor* and the *Orator*, respectively. In time, both volumes succumbed to *The English Reader* (1799), by the wealthy New York Quaker Lindley Murray, the largest-selling author in the first half of the nineteenth century.[11] Amid didactic pieces on cruelty to animals and "the vanity of wealth," Murray reprinted a passage from Cowper's *The Task* (1785) about war, slavery, and other "national prejudices." Finding "his fellow guilty of a skin / Not colour'd like his own," man "chains him, and tasks him, and exacts his sweat / With stripes," Cowper's poetic voice deplored. It went on:

> I would not have a slave to till my ground
> To carry me, to fan me while I sleep,
> And tremble when I wake, for all the wealth
> That sinews bought and sold have ever earn'd.[12]

Teachers who adhered to Cowper's antislavery message could point their students to this particular section of the reader and use it as a starting point for a discussion on US slavery. Students could also stumble upon it by themselves. It did not take young Frederick Douglass long to locate the *Orator*'s "Dialogue between a Master and Slave," a piece reprinted in many other early US schoolbooks.

Throughout the first decades of the nineteenth century, Black schools remained a privileged space for juvenile abolitionism. The New York Manumission Society's African Free School, in particular, became an "incubator for black politics," molding Black children to serve as "ambassadors to the project of abolition" (figure 4.2). A vital institution in the long-term development of African American abolitionism, the NYAFS educated thousands of children and youth across six buildings between 1787 and 1834, with at least a third of New York's Black children affiliated with the school in the 1820s.[13] As slavery slowly receded in the state, leaving in its stead forms of indentured servitude that only gradually gave way to complete freedom, NYAFS leaders, like early Quaker educators, set out to prove that Black children were intellectually equal to white children and no less deserving of civic inclusion. Reading, writing, arithmetic, and geography were among the school's main areas of study. As was common at the time, each academic year ended with an exhibition meant to showcase the scholarly accomplishments of the students for parents, trustees, and the general public.[14] NYAFS leaders wasted no opportunity to publicize their students' hard work and dedication to their studies, in spite of endemic poverty among New York's African American families. In speech after speech, they emphasized the link between education and abolition. "We are convinced that the instruction and right education of the children of the African race, will do more to advance the cause of universal emancipation than all other means put together," they wrote.[15]

NYAFS students did not simply receive a classical education. They were also provided with the conceptual as well as rhetorical tools to participate in ongoing debates over slavery, colonization, abolition, race, and citizenship. From the school's earliest years, James Oliver Horton and Lois Horton write, "students . . . were encouraged to express antislavery ideas, and public oratory at special events was filled with abolitionism."[16] The practical and the political were often closely intertwined.

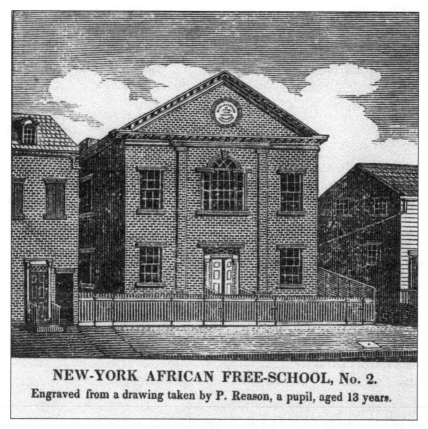

NEW-YORK AFRICAN FREE-SCHOOL, No. 2.
Engraved from a drawing taken by P. Reason, a pupil, aged 13 years.

Figure 4.2. New York African Free School No. 2. Frontispiece to Charles C. Andrews, *The History of the New-York African Free-Schools, from Their Establishment in 1787, to the Present Time* (New York: Mahlon Day, 1830). Courtesy of the Schomburg Center for Research in Black Culture, Photographs and Prints Division.

In 1820, sixteen-year-old Nicholas Bartom perfected his penmanship by copying an excerpt from Joseph Addison's *A Letter from Italy* (1701) reprinted in the 1819 edition of Murray's *English Reader* as "Liberty and Slavery Contrasted." Addison's praise of liberty—"thou pow'r supremely bright, / Profuse of bliss, and pregnant with delight!"—probably struck a chord with Bartom, a young Black New Yorker whose parents might still have been enslaved.[17] At a public examination in 1816, young James Anthony demonstrated his oratorical skills by reciting verses from Hannah More's poem "Slavery" (1788), originally written to coincide with the British parliamentary debate over the slave trade but frequently re-printed on both sides of the Atlantic.[18] Anthony creatively engaged with the poem by tweaking it slightly. If the NYAFS records are a faithful transcription of what he said that day, he started midpoem, perhaps as a way to capture the attention of his audience with More's apocalyptic vision of the ravages wrought on Africans by Europeans:

Whene'er to Afric's shores I turn my eyes,
Horrors of deepest, deadliest guilt arise;
I see, by more than Fancy's mirror shown,
The burning village, and the blazing town;
See the dire victim torn from social life,
The shrieking babe, the agonizing wife—

He then segued into an earlier part of the poem denouncing antiblack racism and affirming Black capacity for intellectual improvement: "Perish th' illib'ral thought which would debase, / The native genius of the sable race! / Perish the proud philosophy, which sought, / To rob them of the pow'rs of equal thought." Anthony's engagement with the poem appeared most clearly at the end of his recitation, when, instead of saying, "Shall Britain, where the soul of freedom reigns, / Forge chains for others she herself disdains?" he said, "Shall Columbia where the soul of freedom reigns, / Forge chains for others she herself distains? [sic]."[19] In a striking example of what the literary scholar Daniel Hack has termed the "African Americanization" of British texts, Anthony adapted More's poem to his and his audience's immediate context, turning a condemnation of the British slave trade into one of US slavery and the United States' betrayal of its republican principles.[20]

NYAFS students penned their own essays, poems, and addresses on slavery. In 1828, their white schoolmaster Charles C. Andrews forwarded a selection of such writings to the American Convention of Abolition Societies, then meeting in Baltimore, along with other "specimens of ingenuity and talent" such as a map of Turkey drawn by twelve-year-old Patrick H. Reason—later to become a renowned engraver—and a likeness of Benjamin Franklin. No history of juvenile abolitionism or anthology of juvenile antislavery literature would be complete without mentioning the NYAFS student essays and poems by twelve- to fifteen-year-old George R. Allen, George W. Moore, Thomas S. Sidney, Eliver Reason (Patrick's brother), and Isaiah G. De Grasse, first printed as an appendix to the convention minutes. Writing soon after the complete abolition of slavery in the state of New York on July 4, 1827, these young abolitionists thanked the convention for its work on behalf of the enslaved and expressed their pride at belonging to the NYAFS. Though they rejoiced at the end of slavery in their home state, they lamented its persistence elsewhere in the United States. Allen's essay was read out by Mahlon Day, a publisher of children's literature and NYMS delegate. "Liberty is an invaluable blessing to us," Allen wrote, "and we often feel compassion for the thousands of our brethren in the South who are groaning under the chains of bondage, while we are enjoying the benefits of freedom." De Grasse likewise spoke out against "the enormities which continue to be practised in many parts of our otherwise favoured country, on the ill-fated Africans, and their descendants, who are torn by the hands of violence from their native country, and sold like brutes to tyrannical slave-holders in different countries, where they are held in slavery and bondage."[21] Reason and Moore expressed similar sentiments. To the four essays were added two brief poems, Allen's "On Slavery" and Sidney's "On Freedom," demonstrating the schoolboys' mastery of prosody and familiarity with the poetical tropes of literary abolitionism. Finally, Andrews included as part of his sample of student work a copy of an earlier address delivered by eleven-year-old James McCune Smith to the Marquis de Lafayette. The hero of the American Revolution and antislavery advocate had visited the NYAFS during his 1824 tour of the United States. Smith thanked Lafayette for his visit and commended him as "a friend to African Emancipation."[22]

Scholars have pointed to the scripted dimension of such performances. Many of the pieces the students recited on public occasions were written for them or edited by white teachers. Students who composed their own pieces were generally asked to do so and had to conform to certain instructions if they hoped to achieve good grades. Allen did not spontaneously decide to write verses on slavery: he had been "required to produce something on Slavery . . . in half an hour," Andrews explained. Sidney was granted an hour to complete his own assignment. Still, the two young men were given a choice of writing "either in prose or verse" and thus exercised a degree of agency within the bounds set by their teacher.[23] Andrews later gave a different account of the episode, affirming that he had required Allen "to produce a piece of poetry on any subject he pleased," as if to downplay his own role in choosing this particular topic. At the same time, he noted that Allen had been "locked up in a room alone" while completing his task. The young man was all but coerced into composing an antislavery poem.[24] Nor are the essays free of such tensions. Again, they were produced as part of an assignment. Andrews had informed his students that the American Convention of Abolition Societies was to meet in Baltimore. He "intimated its objects and its labours" and "proposed to the senior boys the propriety of their attempting something in the form of an Address from them to that body." Though he insisted that Allen's essay was his "genuine, unaided production," he did admit to having erased "*a few superfluous words*" and did not comment on the other essays, which might be read as an indication that he edited them to some degree. There are obvious parallels between the essays—all four students refer to themselves as "a poor little descendant of Africa," "a poor boy of my description," or "a poor descendant of [the African race]"—suggesting that they drew from a repertoire of phrases and images taught to them by Andrews.[25] Carla Peterson finds them "so formulaic that it would be difficult to call them original."[26] Likewise, my reading of Anthony's recitation of More's "Slavery" is premised on the assumption that Anthony himself was responsible for reordering the poem. It is not impossible that Andrews reordered it for him.

It seems reductive, however, to describe the NYAFS students as "nothing more than ventriloquists, mouthing the words of their benefactors."[27] All education entails an element of imitation and constraint. The lessons in abolition that these students received empowered them, and they were keen to mobilize them in a variety of contexts. A few weeks after young Smith delivered his speech to Lafayette, he repeated it to the passengers of a steamer bound for Philadelphia, making some money out of it. Smith seized on his experiences at the school for his own purpose and in the process came to realize that he could use his intellect to make a living. James McCune Smith later became a leading abolitionist, physician, and author.[28] NYAFS students not only absorbed their teachers' antislavery message but took it further than was intended. In a eulogy to the Black abolitionist Henry Highland Garnet delivered on the occasion of his death in 1882, fellow NYAFS alumnus Alexander Crummell reminisced about their school days in the late 1820s and early 1830s in the following terms: "[Garnet] was one of a company of our school-mates in New York who at from thirteen to sixteen years resolved, that while slavery existed we would not celebrate the Fourth of July; and we did not. For years our society met on that day, and the time was devoted to planning schemes for the freeing and upbuilding of our race. The other resolve which was made was, that when we had educated ourselves we would go South, start an insurrection and free our brethren in bondage. Garnet was a leader in these rash but noble resolves."[29] At the very moment the school's white administrators were taking a conservative turn, aligning themselves with the American Colonization Society's program for sending free African Americans to Africa, its Black students were moving in the opposite direction and considering the radical possibility of fomenting a slave revolt. Garnet's famous 1843 "Address to the Slaves of the United States," in which he called for an open rebellion of the enslaved, should be understood as prolonging his youthful acts of resistance as an NYAFS student (and, before that, as an enslaved child). As Wilma King correctly notes, Garnet did not become an abolitionist "solely because of his enrollment in the school, but it is reasonable to posit that his ideas about enslavement and emancipation would have developed in an environment such as a school founded by an abolitionist society, the influence of which is demonstrated in the children's crafts and essays."[30]

The NYAFS students' essays took on a life of their own. Black abolitionists were quick to see their political potential: on March 14, 1829, they appeared on the front page of *Freedom's Journal*, whose editors, Samuel E. Cornish and John Russwurm, were firm believers in the importance of "training . . . children, while young, to habits of industry, and thus forming them for becoming useful members of society," to quote from their first editorial.[31] Originally written at the instigation of a white teacher and addressed to a white abolitionist organization, the essays could now reach a wider audience of Black readers across the North—and beyond, as *Freedom's Journal* was read by free and enslaved African Americans in the South.[32] Allen's, Moore's, Reason's, and De Grasse's productions were reprinted without editorial comment. The essays spoke for themselves: they testified to Black children's intellectual abilities as well as political savviness. If twelve-year-old Allen understood the antislavery implications of the Declaration of Independence, whose preamble he quoted in his essay, then surely the nation's leaders could understand them too? *Freedom's Journal* provided a gratis subscription to the NYAFS, which means the four young men would have seen their names in print.[33] This, in itself, was a valuable lesson regarding the role of print in the dissemination of ideas. Andrews published the essays and poems, along with Smith's address to Lafayette, as part of his *History of the New-York African Free-Schools* (1830), thus making sure that they would be recorded for posterity.[34] The following year, William Lloyd Garrison included De Grasse's essay in the *Liberator*'s Juvenile Department (Allen's was mentioned in a story by Elizabeth Margaret Chandler).[35] De Grasse, whom Garrison described as a "young colored lad," offered an example of a juvenile abolitionist for Black and white child readers to emulate. Indeed, his essay may have contributed to the rise of juvenile abolitionism in the early 1830s: a few months after it appeared in the *Liberator*, a group of young Black Bostonians formed the Juvenile Garrison Independent Society, discussed in chapter 3. De Grasse's essay bridged the gap between first- and second-wave abolitionism. A child of gradual emancipation who saw the end of slavery in New York, De Grasse inspired a new generation of young abolitionists who called for its termination throughout the land. De Grasse did not live to make his mark on the antebellum abolition movement; he passed away before his thirtieth birthday. His NYAFS essay, along with a later sermon on "the blessings of an early, sound, thorough education," remained as testimony to his youthful commitment to the intertwined goals of education and abolition.[36]

What Children Think

The *Liberator*'s Juvenile Department and the *Slave's Friend* gave significant attention to African American schools and their students' achievements. They also promoted the work of teachers who addressed slavery and racism in the classroom and amplified their students' calls for abolition. In the summer of 1831, Garrison reported on a visit to an "Academy for colored boys and girls" founded in Philadelphia by the Black educator Stephen H. Gloucester. Garrison was impressed by what he saw there: the young scholars performed well in a number of subjects, including history, grammar, and arithmetic. The highlight of his visit was an address delivered by twelve-year-old John E. Burr, which Garrison printed in full in the Juvenile Department. Burr's address demonstrated his familiarity with the antislavery world. The young orator started by paying homage to his illustrious auditor, "the man . . . who is endeavoring to relieve the deplorable condition of our colored brethren, . . . who is trying to show the white men, that we are not the race born for slavery, which they say we are." He continued by pointing to the labors of other white allies such as Benjamin Lundy, Arthur Tappan, and Simeon S. Jocelyn, who fought not only against slavery in the South but also for Black access to education in the North. Tappan and Jocelyn, as Burr noted, were then raising money for the establishment of a Black college in New Haven, Connecticut—what would have been the nation's first African American college had not white opposition thwarted the plan. Burr was just as familiar with Black activist networks. He referred to the National Convention of Free People of Color that had taken place in Philadelphia the week before. In a bold move that Garrison must have appreciated, he presented the contemporary Black freedom struggle as a more urgent endeavor than earlier efforts by American patriots to throw off the British yoke: "Fifty years ago, the white population, throughout the United States, met in the city of Philadelphia, to meliorate their condition. We can see they have gained their independence, by perseverance, by uniting themselves heart and hand. Our condition is as bad as was theirs, and in some cases worse: we are not only slaves to our country, but are slaves to every white man personally. We have the same intellect and the same prospect; then let us join heart and hand, and in a few years we may gain our independence."[37] Garrison himself would call the grievances of the revolutionary leaders "trifling in comparison with the wrongs and sufferings" of the enslaved, in the 1833 Declaration of Sentiments of the American Anti-Slavery Society.[38]

When Burr was finished, a proud Gloucester gave Garrison a manuscript copy of the address, insisting, like Charles C. Andrews of the NYAFS, that it "had received no emendation, neither had its topics been selected for the lad: it was all his own."[39] That Burr should have selected such topics comes as no surprise. His father, the barber John P. Burr, served as an agent for the *Liberator*, participated in the Colored Conventions movement, and worked with the Underground Railroad. His mother, Hetty Burr, was a founding member of the interracial Philadelphia Female Anti-Slavery Society. His teacher, born enslaved in Tennessee, was coproprietor of the *Colored American* for a time and formed an all-Black antislavery society in Philadelphia.[40] In school and at home, young Burr was surrounded by adults who were deeply immersed in antislavery activism, and in time, he developed an interest in abolition himself, of which his classroom address to Garrison was a shining example. Burr must have had a gift for oratory. A year later, the now thirteen-year-old boy was asked to deliver another address "on the subject of giving a preference to the production of free labor, over that of the unrewarded toil of slaves."[41] In 1839, he was elected as an officer of the Demosthenian Institute of Philadelphia, a literary society for African American youth formed at his father's home, whose aim was to prepare its members for the public platform.[42] Burr's later trajectory is harder to trace, but it seems he never reneged on his juvenile activism. In 1853, he signed the call for a national Colored Convention to be held in Rochester, following in his father's footsteps.

At Gloucester's academy, Garrison was also presented with a copy of an address by a slightly older student, the sixteen-year-old William H. Matthews, which he printed as well in the Juvenile Department. Matthews's address was of an altogether different cast than Burr's. Burr was deferential to white abolitionists, in particular to Garrison; he spoke in carefully chosen words, with what Garrison called "a propriety of gesture and intonation far beyond his years."[43] Matthews, on the other hand, sounded like a mini David Walker. He addressed not whites but his Black "brothers," both enslaved and free, whom he urged to shake off their apathy and fight for their rights. "Are you so lost in thought, that you stand like ideots [*sic*], and let the white man reign lord of the universe, when we were all born free and equal?" he asked. "Are you dumb, or do you intend to sleep forever in ignorance? Why do you not arouse, and shout for *liberty* or *death*? Or do you say within yourselves, that you will wait until the white man's poor, mean generosity extends so low, as to condescend to set you free, one by one?" Two years earlier, in 1829, Walker had published the first edition of his famous *Appeal to the Coloured Citizens of the World*, a militant call to action addressed to fellow African Americans. In terms that foreshadowed Matthews's, Walker stated his object: "to awaken in the breasts of my afflicted, degraded and slumbering brethren, a spirit of enquiry and investigation respecting our miseries and wretchedness in this *Republican Land of Liberty!!!!!*" Matthews's use of punctuation was more restrained, but he did refer to the United States as "this boasted land of liberty and independence." His use of the word "ignorance" in the preceding quotation is also reminiscent of Walker: in article 3 of the *Appeal*, Walker lambastes white Americans for keeping Blacks in a state of "abject ignorance." In the same article, he refers to Hannibal, predicting that "the Lord our God" will give the enslaved "a Hannibal" to deliver them from their "deplorable and wretched condition." Likewise, Matthews expected that Black freedom would not be attained "until God puts into each heart of the rising generation the spirit of a Hannibal." Given these parallels, it is not unlikely that Matthews read the *Appeal*, or read about it, for instance, in the *Liberator*. His essay was full of the same fiery rhetoric, and like the *Appeal*, it raised the specter of violent resistance to slavery. "When we see and feel the wrongs of our brethren in the south, and ask God to enable and strengthen us to draw the sword of liberty, and burst the bands of slavery asunder," Matthews wrote, "O, then will the white man begin to spare us and let us free." The sixteen-year-old saw himself as playing a leading role in the fight for racial justice. Though he admitted to being "but a young advocate" in the cause, he hoped that "before many years roll round" he "may be found conspicuous."[44] Matthews was not "found conspicuous"—his name is absent from histories of abolition and Black activism—but his essay, like De Grasse's, may have been read by children and youth who became more vocal later.

Garrison could have taken the two manuscripts home and never given them a thought again. Instead, he printed Burr's and Matthews's addresses in the *Liberator*, ensuring them a wide audience. That he did so testifies to his sincere interest in what children had to say on slavery. "What children think" mattered to abolitionists, and it was usually in the classroom that young people got the opportunity to express their views on the subject most fully. "What Children Think" was the title of an article published in the *Slave's Friend* of June 1838. A certain A.B. sent the text of an essay by "a little boy eleven years old," which had been read at the examination of a district school a few weeks before. In typical fashion, A.B. guaranteed, "The composition is entirely his own, with the exception that I have taken the liberty to make two or three very slight alterations in words, not at all changing the sense." It is easy to understand why this essay might have appealed to the magazine's editor, the evangelical abolitionist Lewis Tappan. This little boy not only claimed the name of abolitionist for himself—"Some call me a strong abolitionist," his essay began, "[and] I think I have good reason for it"—but his denunciation of slavery was firmly grounded in evangelical Christianity. Whereas George R. Allen, John E. Burr, and William H. Matthews had invoked the revolutionary ideals of liberty and equality, with Allen quoting the Declaration of Independence and Matthews alluding to Patrick Henry's "Give me liberty or give me death," this (probably white) juvenile abolitionist repeatedly quoted from the Bible, of which he provided an antislavery reading. Christ "never told any body to go and steal negroes from Africa and sell them to America," he insisted. "He never held slaves." Piling up verses from Exodus, Leviticus, Song of Solomon, Jeremiah, John, and Corinthians, he concluded that "the Bible proves that the slaveholders do wrong in every thing about slavery."[45] Juvenile abolitionism, as these essays demonstrate, was no less diverse in its rhetoric and arguments than the abolitionism of more mature people was. Children were exposed to a variety of antislavery traditions, which they appropriated and deployed in well-crafted essays.

A more spontaneous, less polished expression of juvenile abolitionism can be found in a series of "children's letters" first published in the proceedings of the Ohio Anti-Slavery Convention of April 1835 and later partially reprinted in the *Slave's Friend* and other juvenile and antislavery periodicals.[46] The convention had met in Putnam, Ohio, to form a state antislavery society and draft a declaration of sentiments. A committee "to report on the condition of the colored population in this state," chaired by the white abolitionist Huntington Lyman, was appointed as part of the convention. Its report laid bare the dire realities of Black life in Ohio, where the "combined oppression of public sentiment and law reduced the colored people to extreme misery." It paid particular attention to the restrictions placed on Black education, explaining how Black children were shut out from public schools in spite of their parents paying "their full proportion of taxes for all public objects." This made children's accomplishments at the few schools open to them all the more remarkable. A formerly enslaved girl named Rhoda had entered a school "not knowing her letters—in four weeks her reading book was the Testament"; ten-year-old Charles "at the second quarter had gone through Ray's arithmetic, and could do any sum which the book contained." A majority of these children, the report noted, had been enslaved themselves or were sons and daughters of enslaved parents. Slavery was never far from their minds, and "the remembrance of friends still in bondage, presses heavily on their hearts."[47]

At one school in Cincinnati—a stone's throw from the slave state of Kentucky—a group of students were asked to put in writing what they "*think most* about." Their compositions, which took the form of brief letters addressed to fellow schoolmates or to their teacher, were collected and included in the convention proceedings. The youngest of the group responded as follows:

> Dear school-mates, we are going next summer to buy a farm and to work part of the day and to study the other part if we live to see it and come home part of the day to see our mothers and sisters and cousins if we are got any and see our kind folks and to be good boys and when we get a man to get the poor slaves from bondage. And I am sorrow to hear that the boat of Tiskilwa went down with two hundred poor slaves from up the river. Oh how sorry I am to hear that. it grieves my soul so that I could faint in one minute.[48]

The letter started in fairly conventional manner for a seven-year-old, discussing such quotidian matters as studying and visiting family members, but then veered in a different direction as the child expressed his ambition to grow into a man who would "get the poor slaves from bondage." The tone shifted again as he recalled a distressing event—the sinking of a boat with a large number of enslaved people on board—of which he may have heard in school or at home. (No boat named the *Tiskilwa* seems to have sunk in the early 1830s, so perhaps he was thinking of another disturbing piece of news involving enslaved people.) His repeated use of the set phrase "poor slaves" suggests that he was familiar with abolitionist rhetoric and experimenting with it. His teacher may have been one of the white students at Cincinnati's Lane Theological Seminary, where most students had converted to abolition following a series of debates organized by the abolitionist Theodore D. Weld in 1834. Some of them started teaching in the local Black community soon after.[49]

The other four letters were written by students aged ten to sixteen. Their teacher assured that they were "a fair transcript of our pupils' hearts." One ten-year-old brought up their familial ties to slavery: "Dear Sir.—This is to inform you that I have two cousins in slavery who are entitled to their freedom. They have done every thing that the will required and now they wont let them go. They talk of selling them down the river. If this was your case what would you do? Please give me your advice."[50] The letter's opening and closing make it clear that its young author had received lessons in letter writing. There were plenty of letter-writing guidebooks, including some for schoolchildren, that the letter writer's instructor might have used to teach students about epistolary conventions.[51] The formal, businesslike tone of the letter contrasted with the tragic personal events recounted in it—a sadly common story of freedom promised in a will and then denied, with the additional threat of being sold further south. There was unintended irony in asking a white teacher, "If this was your case what would you do?" Two other students showed their awareness of the link between education and abolition. One twelve-year-old wrote, "Dear School-master, I now inform you in these few lines, that what we are studying for is to try to get the yoke of slavery broke and the chains parted asunder and slave-holding cease for ever." The oldest of the five students found in a ninth-century Anglo-Saxon king an unlikely model of industry and perseverance to be emulated by young African Americans: "Look at king Alfred and see what a great man he was. He at one time did not know his a, b, c, but before his death he commanded armies and nations. He was never discouraged but always looked forward and studied the harder. I think if the colored people study like king Alfred they will soon do away the evil of slavery." He signed off with a simple but powerful denunciation of American pretensions to liberty: "I cant see how the Americans can call this a land of freedom where so much slavery is." That these children had heard of the abolition movement and read abolitionist writings appears most clearly in a letter by a formerly enslaved eleven-year-old: "Bless the cause of abolition—bless the heralds of the truth that we trust God has sent out to declare the rights of man."[52] It is possible that one of these children was John Isom Gaines. Born in Cincinnati in 1821, Gaines attended a primary school operated by Lane students in the early 1830s and later became one of Black Cincinnati's foremost intellectuals and orators. "Undoubtedly," Nikki Taylor writes, "instruction by abolitionist teachers must have helped him develop his critique of slavery and honed his oratory skills."[53]

Perhaps the most well-documented instance of a teacher infusing their pedagogy with antislavery values is that of Susan Paul. The daughter of an African American minister and abolitionist in Boston, Paul was an activist herself. She participated in the activities of the New England Anti-Slavery Society and Boston Female Anti-Slavery Society in the early days of immediatism and would probably have made a more lasting mark on antebellum abolitionism were it not for her untimely death in 1841. It was arguably as a primary-school and Baptist Sunday-school teacher that Paul made her most significant—and original—contribution to the abolition movement. In 1833, she formed the Juvenile Choir of Boston, which in the following years performed at various antislavery meetings throughout Massachusetts with great success (figure 4.3). The choir was made up of three- to ten-year-old students from Paul's primary school and Black Beacon Hill community. Its repertoire was notable for including songs dealing frankly with slavery, racism, and colonization. It ranged, in Lois Brown's terms, "from gloomy and graphic depictions of enslavement to lively and mischievous critiques of the prejudice believed to be at the heart of the colonizationist platform."[54] "Ye Who in Bondage Pine," originally written by Garrison, painted a particularly bleak picture of the condition of the enslaved, "Whose limbs are worn with chains, / Whose tears bedew our plains, / Whose blood our glory stains." Yet the poem's authorial voice was confident that "the long, long night" of slavery was almost over and soon to be replaced by "The glorious dawn / Of FREEDOM's natal day"—a prophecy of rebirth and renewal that took on particular meaning when uttered by children.[55] "Mr. Prejudice," later reprinted in the Slave's Friend, was written by the white abolitionist Samuel E. Sewall specifically for the choir.[56] Its personification of racial prejudice "Scolding at little colored girls, / And whipping colored boys" must have resonated with the young performers, who on one occasion were refused access to the coaches that had been engaged to carry them to Salem when the drivers realized they were Black.[57] Other abolition songs interpreted by the choir included

JUVENILE CONCERT,

UNDER THE DIRECTION OF
MISS SUSAN PAUL.

☞ A JUVENILE CONCERT of the Colored Children, constituting the Primary School, No. 6, under the direction of Miss Susan Paul, will be given at BOYLSTON HALL, on MONDAY EVENING, January 20.

ORDER OF EXERCISES.

Overture.—Marseilles Hymn.

PART I.

1. *Duet & Chorus.*—If ever I see.
2. *Chorus.*—In school we learn.
3. *Duet & Chorus.*—The Lark.
4. *Duet & Chorus.*—Italian Hymn.
5. *Duet & Chorus.*—Pleasures of Innocence.
6. *Chorus.*—Sweet Home.
7. *Solo & Chorus.*—Strike the Cymbal.

—

Grand Symphony.

PART II.

1. *Chorus.*—O speed thee, speed thee.
2. *Recitative & Chorus.*—Suffer little children to come unto me.
3. *Chorus.*—Little Wanderer's Song.
4. *Chorus.*—The Little Weaver.
5. *Solo & Chorus.*—Prayer for the Commonwealth.
6. *Duet & Chorus.*—Good Night.

☞ Tickets 25 cents each; to be had at the Bookstore of Dea. James Loring, Washington-street; at the store of Mr. James G. Barbadoes, No. 26, Brattle-street; at the office of the Liberator; and at the door of the Hall.

Jan. 4.

Figure 4.3. Notice of Juvenile Choir concert conducted by Susan Paul. *Liberator*, January 4, 1834. Courtesy of the American Antiquarian Society.

"Hark to the Clank!," "Sons of Columbia," the anticolonization "This, This Is Our Home," and the pro-sugar-abstention "The Sugar Plums" and "The Petition of the Sugar-Making Slaves."[58] There was no facet of the antislavery campaign that the choir did not sing about, and many of its youngest members, who perhaps did not quite understand the words at first, gained an education in abolition by rehearsing and performing these songs with their teacher. Having attended one of the choir's last concerts in 1837, a correspondent for the *New York Evangelist* noted that "several of the pieces produced no small emotion, from their bearing upon a certain 'delicate subject,' coming as they did from those who must *feel* their meaning." Like most reviewers of the Juvenile Choir, the correspondent also emphasized the children's impressive musical ability. Indeed, Paul's choir not only sang about racial prejudice: it sought to undermine it through its virtuoso performances. The *Evangelist* correspondent confessed being "astonished and delighted" by a little girl of three or four years old who sang "all the pieces, with apparent ease, and pronounced the words with distinctness and propriety," even singing several solos. "I think such things well calculated to remove the unjust feeling that exists towards these people," he concluded.[59]

Paul opened a window onto her classroom in a pamphlet published in 1835, *Memoir of James Jackson, the Attentive and Obedient Scholar, Who Died in Boston, October 31, 1833, Aged Six Years and Eleven Months*. A blend of didactic narrative and juvenile biography, the *Memoir* chronicled the brief though exemplary life of one of Paul's students, James Jackson, who died of tuberculosis at an early age. Paul made her intentions clear in her preface to the book: by recounting the story of a pious and industrious African American child, she hoped to show that "the moral and intellectual powers of colored children" were equal to white children's and thereby to contribute "towards breaking down that unholy prejudice which exists against color."[60] Written for juveniles, the *Memoir* "imparted important lessons in abolition and antiracism," Manisha Sinha observes.[61] Paul addressed racism in the first chapter, lamenting that children were taught to fear people with a skin color different from their own. A mother who said to her unruly child that she would give him "to the *old black man*" was sure to instill into him a lifelong hatred of African Americans. Paul demonstrated the absurdity of racial prejudice to her young white readers. "Would you love your sister or brother less because they had black or brown hair?" she asked. "Or your father or mother because one had black eyes and the other blue eyes?" In her classroom, she exposed her students to the reality of southern slavery. Rather than speaking about it in general terms, she focused on how it affected children specifically:

> One day while at school, [Jackson's] teacher told the children that there were a great many thousands of their color who were not allowed to read, who had no schools, nor any books. These persons she said were slaves. The fathers and mothers of a *great great* many children could not do as they pleased with them, because other men said that they could sell them or do what they pleased with them; they are called slaves. These men did not want the slaves to know any thing about reading the Bible. So they kept the children from school, and while you are at school they make the slaves work very hard, and because they don't know any thing at all about the word of God they are sometimes very wicked. Then they are cruelly whipped. So they live and die without ever going to school, or being taught by kind Sabbath school teachers. "And now," said she, "will these children pray to God for the little slave children and their parents?"

Young James Jackson, for one, did not remain indifferent to this lesson. He told his mother about it and pondered how best he could pray for the enslaved. He came up with the following prayer: "O Lord, pity the poor slaves, and let them be free, that they may have their liberty, and be happy as I am,—and may they have good teachers to learn them to read, as I have, and make them all very good. Amen."[62] Jackson's prayer was perhaps less authentic than the children's letters discussed earlier: what we hear here is as much Paul's voice as it is Jackson's. Yet this passage from the *Memoir* could lead teachers to discuss slavery even with the youngest of children and children to express their disapproval of slavery, if only in the form of prayers. It was such passages about slavery and racism that Garrison selected for reprinting in the *Liberator*'s Juvenile Department.[63]

Evidence suggests that the *Memoir of James Jackson* was read in white educational contexts and led some children to embrace abolitionism. On July 4, 1836, the children of the Union Evangelical Sabbath School of Amesbury and Salisbury, Massachusetts, penned a letter to Paul's students with the help of their superintendent, A. Morrill. "We remember to-day . . . those who are 'in bonds,'" they wrote, "and we feel very sorry that there are so many children in our country, who have no kind teachers as you and as we have, but are obliged to live and die ignorant slaves."[64] The timing of their letter was not fortuitous. Morrill had probably prompted his pupils to think about the paradox of celebrating national independence in a country whose founding principles were so obviously flouted. He organized a countercelebration of sorts that involved writing to a group of Black schoolchildren whom they had read about and sending them some of the pocket money—three dollars in total—that they had received for the Fourth of July. In turn, Susan Paul had her own students respond to Morrill's to thank them for their "act of love." "It has made us very glad to know that you think of us, and of the dear little children who are slaves," Paul's students wrote back.[65] That the correspondence was published a few weeks later in the *Liberator* suggests that Morrill, Paul, or the two teachers acting in concert sent copies of their students' respective epistles to Garrison. Educator-activists from Andrews and Gloucester to Morrill and Paul used their classrooms to raise children's political awareness. In so doing, they helped fashion young abolitionists whose voices they made sure were heard beyond school walls.

Lewis Tappan celebrated these politically engaged teachers in the *Slave's Friend*. In a piece titled "A Good School," he first noted that "many teachers are afraid to have anti-slavery matters discussed in their schools" but then praised an unidentified New England teacher who had purchased books on the subject and encouraged his students to form an antislavery society. Tappan gave an antislavery spin to a fairly generic picture of white children in a schoolroom, one delivering an address or poem from the lectern, another in the audience standing up and raising his hand (figure 4.4): "Look at the picture. One little boy is reciting a piece on slavery which he has committed to memory. How the rest listen! By and by the good teacher will explain the subject to these dear boys. I am thankful that there is a school where . . . the principles of liberty are instilled into the youthful mind." Memorization was one of the main pedagogical techniques in nineteenth-century schools. As Tappan suggests, students were routinely asked to recite from memory pieces whose meaning they did not fully understand. Educational reformers lamented

THE
SLAVE'S FRIEND.

Vol. II. No. VI.   **Whole No. 18.**

A GOOD SCHOOL.

Many teachers are afraid to have anti-slavery matters discussed in their schools. They think that parents will take their children away if any thing is said or done on behalf of poor slaves. Thus this fear makes *them* slaves. *White* slaves !

Figure 4.4. An abolitionist classroom. "A Good School," *Slave's Friend* 2, no. 6 (1837): 1. Courtesy of the Schomburg Center for Research in Black Culture, Manuscripts, Archives and Rare Books Division.

that most teachers taught students to imitate or repeat rather than to think for themselves. Yet Tappan's teacher made sure that his students did get the antislavery import of the piece they had learned. He guided them while at the same time giving them some autonomy: "Sometimes he would propose questions to his class, and invite the boys to discuss it; and at other times he would let them select pieces to recite."[66] Tappan's model classroom was one where student participation was always welcome, as suggested by the boy raising his hand in the picture. Conversely, Jane Elizabeth Jones, in *The Young Abolitionists; or, Conversations on Slavery* (1848), has Charlie Selden complain about his teacher Mr. Gardner, "He don't like to answer our questions." When Charlie's younger sister, Jenie, reading her Bible, asks Mr. Gardner what it means to "hide the outcast"—a biblical phrase commonly used by abolitionists to justify assisting persons who escaped slavery—he retorts that she asks "quite too many questions." Later on, Mr. Gardner catches Charlie and his antiabolitionist schoolmate Ned Miller "talking about the slaves."[67] The displeased teacher cuts short his students' conversation. There is no place for debate or discussion in Mr. Gardner's classroom.

Tappan and Jones saw eye to eye with educational reformers such as the antislavery Whig Horace Mann, who called for "a new democratic pedagogy," in Johann Neem's terms—one that did away with rote learning and, most importantly for abolitionists, corporal punishment. The classroom should not be a site of violent contest between teacher and students, they believed, but a forum for exchange and debate.[68] Long before the antebellum period, Anthony Benezet had argued for reform in the realm of school discipline, "preferring kindness and moral suasion to any form of corporal punishment," as his biographer notes.[69] Later on, Henry Clarke Wright, an advocate of nonresistance, advised that the rod "should never be used when the teacher is in a passion," while Lucretia Mott opposed corporal punishment of children on the grounds that "a child, like all human beings, has inalienable rights."[70] Some abolitionists who joined utopian communities established their own schools, such as the Hopedale Home School (Massachusetts) and the Eagleswood School at Raritan Bay Union (New Jersey), where they rejected what they saw as harmful educational practices and attempted, as one of them put it, "to renovate education."[71] At Boston's Temple School, the Transcendentalist abolitionist Bronson Alcott developed his own alternative teaching

View of Mr. Alcott and the Children conversing.

Figure 4.5. Bronson Alcott's classroom at Boston's Temple School. Bronson Alcott, *Conversations with Children on the Gospels*, vol. 1 (Boston: James Munroe, 1836), 1. Courtesy of the American Antiquarian Society.

style based on conversations with children. With the help of Elizabeth Palmer Peabody, he recorded some of his exchanges on religion, which he published as *Conversations with Children on the Gospels* (1836–37); the book was savaged by commentators, who denounced Alcott's pedagogical heresies (figure 4.5).[72] Alcott, as he explained in the preface, avoided "dogmatizing" as much as possible. "It was no part of his intention to bring forward, except by necessary implication, his own favorite opinions as a means of biassing, in the smallest degree, the judgments and decisions of the children." Alcott "preferred to become the simple Analyst of the consciousness of the children," though he recognized he could not entirely withhold his own sentiments from them.[73] Perhaps no one in the antebellum United States was more interested in what children thought than Bronson Alcott.

The Perils of Classroom Abolitionism

Contesting slavery and racial prejudice in the classroom was not without its perils. Proponents of white supremacy—colonizationists and antiabolitionists—regarded Black education as a radical project that threatened the social and racial order. Nor were they entirely wrong. As the AASS itself acknowledged in its first annual report, "Every measure for the thorough and proper education of colored females is a blow aimed directly at slavery. As such it is felt both by slave-holders at the south, and their friends and abettors at the north."[74] The AASS was commenting on the recent controversy surrounding Prudence Crandall's female academy in Canterbury, Connecticut. In 1831, Crandall, a Quaker teacher, had established a school for the daughters of the town's elite, the Canterbury Female Seminary, which soon became one of the best in the state. When Crandall permitted Sarah Harris, a young African American woman, to attend, parents and community residents were swift to protest, urging Crandall to remove Harris. Rather than yielding to racist demands, Crandall dismissed her white students altogether and transformed her academy into a "school for young ladies and little misses of color." After the *Liberator* ran an advertisement for students in March 1833, young Black girls and women from Boston, Providence, New York, and elsewhere headed for Canterbury. Legislation banning the instruction of African Americans from out of state was hastily passed, while townspeople embarked on a relentless campaign of intimidation and persecution. Crandall was left with no choice but to close her academy.[75]

Sarah Harris was between twenty and twenty-one years old when she was admitted, but there were younger girls attending Crandall's seminary. Harriet Rosetta Lanson, for instance, was sixteen in late 1833; Mary Elizabeth Miles, later to marry the Black abolitionist Henry Bibb, was about thirteen.[76] Kabria Baumgartner estimates that the age range of students spanned some thirteen years. Their experience at Canterbury was both a painful and politically formative one. For perhaps the first time in their lives, these girls were the target of vicious racial prejudice; insults were heaped on them in the press, garbage pelted at them on the streets. What they may have seen only from afar they now came to confront face-to-face. At Crandall's academy, however, they also found the means to resist such attacks. The school was, in Baumgartner's terms, "a vibrant, intellectual, and politically engaging space" where a number of white abolitionists came to teach.[77] Teachers and students conversed on subjects such as slavery, as did students among themselves, with the older girls possibly teaching younger ones about the principles of the abolition movement. One student made what must have been her first appearance in print with an essay on slavery published in the *Liberator* in early 1833. She denounced "the awful, heaven-daring sin . . . of enslaving and destroying millions of our African brethren, tearing them from their native homes, sundering the most tender ties, parting parents and children, husbands and wives, friends and neighbors, binding them with chains, shutting them up in dungeons, branding them with red hot iron, depriving them forever of liberty, and placing them as low in the scale of human beings as the very beasts of the fields."[78] In the months that followed, these students honed their critique of racism in the light of what they endured. Crandall sent several of their writings—heartfelt addresses first delivered in the classroom—to the religious and antislavery press. One student called prejudice a "dark misty cloud, which is born [*sic*] by selfishness and ignorance." She rejoiced that a growing number of white allies had "stepped from within [its shadow], and are now pleading [Black people's] cause, in the midst of persecution, with great success." Another ascribed the students' struggles to "the prejudice the whites have against" African Americans that causes them "to labor under so many disadvantages." "Oh prejudice! prejudice!" she exclaimed, "Heaven grant thy reign may be short."[79] When Lanson died of tuberculosis two years later, her guardian and obituarist, Simeon S. Jocelyn, mentioned "her love for all the advocates of emancipation, and her sympathy for the poor slaves."[80] In the 1840s, Mary Elizabeth Miles became known, in her husband's words, for her "devotion to the antislavery cause" and her talents as an educator.[81] The time that Lanson and Miles had spent at Canterbury was one among many other experiences that made them abolitionists. Garrison, in turn, made the Crandall affair the subject of a family dialogue published in the Juvenile Department, using it as pedagogical material for converting more children to abolitionism.[82]

Antebellum Black classrooms were never insulated from the outside world. Racial prejudice tried to remove the Canterbury students from their classroom and eventually succeeded in doing so, strengthening rather than weakening at least some of the students' abolitionist resolve. Slavery itself could knock at the school's door—or, rather, barge in—in even more dramatic ways. The classroom abduction of seven-year-old Henry Scott, a student of the NYAFS, is a case in point. Scott was the victim of a network of professional slave catchers who operated in New York in the early 1830s with the complicity of law enforcement officials. David Ruggles nicknamed the group the "New York Kidnapping Club." In March 1834, Scott was forcibly taken from school by a sheriff and a Virginia businessman claiming property over him. The sheriff tore him from the arms of his teacher, the antislavery press reported, "and dragged him as a bullock is dragged to the slaughter—to bind him with the galling chains of slavery!" Fellow NYAFS students were not silent observers of the drama that unfolded. "The cries of the little victim for mercy, and the screaches [sic] of his little school mates filled the room with dismay. Some fainted and fell—some run [sic] for their parents, and some followed the kidnapper crying, 'Kidnapper! kidnapper!'—'Let him alone! let him alone!'"[83] Most of these children knew what slavery was and the dangers it posed to all African Americans. Some, like Scott, whose father had brought him from Virginia, were born enslaved themselves. The abduction of their classmate was a chilling reminder that none of them was completely safe, even in a northern schoolroom, as long as slavery was allowed to persist in the South.

Young Black New Yorkers played a key role in publicizing Scott's plight and working toward his release. Several meetings were held at the NYAFS in the days following the arrest. At African Free School No. 5, where Scott had been a student, Mary Ann Windt, Lydia Ann Scimmons, and other young women whose precise age is unknown raised money for the boy's legal defense.[84] Money was also collected at African Free School No. 6 but only after Thomas H. Tompkins, cofounder of the Garrison Literary and Benevolent Association, discussed in chapter 3, delivered a stirring antislavery address:

> My fellow school mates, Slavery is a thing which ought not to exist another day, but should be immediately abolished. I cannot see how a humane being [sic], can bear to hold his fellow men in bondage, and treat him more cruelly than brutes. . . . On Friday last, three of those "boy-stealers" came into school No. 5, and seized a little boy six years of age,

and in spite of all that his teacher and little school mates could do or say, dragged him from school to the police, and shut him up in prison, in order to carry him back to the land of tyrants. A sum of money is required to release him out of prison, and our teacher thinks that it would be serving the cause of bleeding humanity if we would contribute towards raising the sum required, so that the little sufferer may be let out of the cold dark prison! And my fellow school mates, I hope every one of you will give something. IF IT IS ONLY ONE CENT, IT WILL HELP.[85]

The juvenile campaign for Scott's release had literary as well as financial dimensions. Under the heading "Juvenile Composition," the *Emancipator* published a poem, "Little Henry Scott," written by a student of the NYAFS. Its young author returned to some of the same motifs found in children's antislavery writings discussed in this chapter: "Sons of freedom to you I *appeal*! / Who the blessings of 'liberty' so proudly claim, / And if your hearts are prone to feel, / Break! O break! the tyrant's chain." "Little Henry Scott" was read among members of the GLBA.[86] White children and youth did not remain strangers to this campaign. Antislavery newspapers teemed with letters by Sunday-school instructors who said they had read accounts of Scott's abduction to their pupils. John Dudley of New Haven, Connecticut, described such a scene in vivid detail: "I could see their little countenances gather indignation at the cruelty of the man who took the innocent little fellow from his school and shut him in prison." Though poor, these children voted to collect some of their money and make a donation to Scott's classmates.[87] So did children in Providence, Rhode Island; Pittsfield, Massachusetts; and Sherburne, New York. J. N. Sprague wrote of the latter that they "have become the friends of the colored people, and haters of slavery" from hearing about Scott.[88] Many a white child may have been sensitized to the question of slavery on that occasion.

As the preceding examples suggest, classroom discussions of slavery and abolition seem to have taken place more often at evangelical Sunday schools than at common weekday schools. Slavery was just as divisive a subject in the Sunday-school movement as it was in the rest of US society. In the 1830s, the American Sunday School Union (ASSU), one of the main purveyors of juvenile literature at the time, adopted an official position of neutrality on the slavery issue in its publications, which for abolitionists was tantamount to supporting the institution. Lewis Tappan, who had previously contributed to the union, withdrew his support when he joined the ranks of abolition.[89] Susan Paul had firsthand knowledge of the ASSU's conservative racial politics: the two ASSU affiliates she had first approached with the manuscript of the *Memoir of James Jackson* refused to publish it or to stock it at their depositories for distribution to Sunday schools nationwide. The *Memoir* came out under the imprint of a white abolitionist bookseller and printer in Boston, James Loring, which severely limited its dissemination.[90] That Paul's students eventually corresponded with those of the Union Evangelical Sabbath School of Amesbury and Salisbury, however, reveals that the union's national policy and teachers' practices on the ground were two different things; not all schools (and few Black-run schools) were even affiliated with the state or national Sunday-school organizations.[91] Evangelical abolitionists who taught Sunday schools saw it as their moral duty to discuss slavery with their pupils and point to its sinful nature.

Children latched on to such a message. When the children of the Christian Sabbath School of Union Springs, New York, were given a choice of which newspaper they would like to subscribe to, they unanimously voted for the antislavery *Juvenile Instructor*. "We like the Juvenile Instructor . . . because it talks about the evils of slavery," they wrote to its editor, Lucius C. Matlack. "What a cruel, wicked thing it is, to deprive men and women of their liberty when they have done nothing wrong. Buy and sell them like cattle. Whip them to make them work and pay them nothing for all their hard toil."[92] At least one paper for the use of Sunday schools, the Portland, Maine, *Sabbath School Instructor* (later the *Juvenile Reformer, and Sabbath School Instructor*), edited by Daniel C. Colesworthy, consistently included abolitionist materials. As Garrison noted in the *Liberator*, "A considerable portion of it is devoted to the cause of the colored population, both bond and free, and we hope they will patronize it in their Sabbath Schools. Mr. Colesworthy is a meritorious young man of considerable talent, who early espoused the anti-slavery cause."[93] Though Susan Paul had been refused ASSU sponsorship, she appended to the *Memoir of James Jackson* two poems on racial prejudice originally published in the *Sabbath School Instructor*, symbolically aligning herself with the Sunday-school movement.[94] As Garrison's comment suggests, African American Sunday schools made regular use of antislavery literature. Book-length slave narratives, for instance, were purchased for inclusion in African American Sunday-school libraries. Frederick Douglass's *My Bondage and My Freedom* (1855) was touted in the Black press as "A New Book for Sabbath Schools."[95] The *Weekly Anglo-African* hoped that "no Sabbath School library, and no colored youth" would be found without a copy of *The Rev. J. W. Loguen, as a Slave and as a Freeman* (1859).[96] Throughout the North—and sometimes even in the South, as the case of Douglass helping to teach a Sunday school in Baltimore attests—Sunday schools served as a vehicle for transmitting what some evangelicals saw as a core value of Protestantism, namely, opposition to the sin of slavery.

Slave narratives may have been all the more useful in the classroom as newly published schoolbooks could no longer be depended on for antislavery content. Americans of the 1820s and the early 1830s had inherited the textbooks of the revolutionary generation, produced at a time—the 1790s—when antislavery ideology was more consensual than it ever was in the antebellum period and even upper southern states boasted abolition societies. It is telling that the first edition of Murray's *English Reader* was published the year before Gabriel's Conspiracy, one of several slave conspiracies and rebellions between 1800 and 1831 (the year Nat Turner launched his own rebellion) that catalyzed white southerners' development of an aggressively proslavery stance. Some new readers published in the 1820s resembled those of the previous generation: *The American First Class Book* (1823), edited by the Unitarian minister John Pierpont, included antislavery verse by Cowper and James Montgomery, author of the 1809 epic "The West Indies," as well as a passage from an 1820 oration in which the Massachusetts lawyer Daniel Webster denounced the slave trade as "a traffick, at which every feeling of humanity must revolt."[97] Charles Dexter Cleveland's *National Orator* (1829) offered young readers an even broader selection of antislavery texts by Cowper, Montgomery, Webster, William Wilberforce, William Pitt, John Sergeant, and John W. Taylor (the latter two had opposed the admission of Missouri as a slave state into the Union in 1820); they appeared under explicit headings such as "The Atrocity of Slavery," "The Evils of Slavery," and "The Moral and Physical Powers of a Nation Weakened by Slavery."[98] But educators who compiled readers from the mid-1830s tended to tread more carefully. Such was the case of William Holmes McGuffey, creator of the

Eclectic Readers, the first of which appeared in 1836. McGuffey's *Readers* claimed to be more attuned to children's needs and perspectives. What that meant, in practice, was that they avoided any controversial topic. As Charles and Jennifer Monaghan note, "No arguments over moral issues such as slavery, . . . so prominent in Caleb Bingham's schoolbook, ever entered the McGuffey *Eclectic* series as its publishers strove to please audiences in all parts of the country."[99] The *Eclectic Readers* soon overtook other titles in popularity.

A similar pattern could be discerned in history and geography textbooks. In *The First Book of History, for Children and Youth*, first published in 1831, Samuel Griswold Goodrich, another popular schoolbook author, had made clear his disapproval of slavery. An account of a Georgia slave auction at which children were sold to a different bidder from their mother ended thus: "Such are some of the evils of slavery. It is a bad system altogether, and all good people believe that it is wrong."[100] Goodrich, who never identified as an abolitionist, removed the passage from editions published in the latter half of the decade, as sectional conflict over slavery mounted; the alteration was noted in the antislavery press.[101] The whole chapter on slavery and its introduction into North America, in fact, was rewritten in a way that would have made it less objectionable to white southerners.[102] An 1835 geography published in New York bluntly stated, "The slaves, in general, are humanely treated, well fed, and not overtasked."[103] Such statements did not escape the attention of the AASS, which in its 1837 annual report noted, "On looking into our present generation of revised and improved school-books, it will be seen, that those faithful finger-boards which used to point the young mind towards righteousness and liberty, and away from SLAVERY, as from a den of abominations, are mostly torn down, and in their stead, in some of the popular reading books and geographies, pleasant lanes are opened, through which 'Southern institutions' look beautiful in the distance. . . . Slaveholders dread the young abolitionists more than they do the old."[104] This became a common complaint among abolitionists. "What a burning shame it is," Charles Lenox Remond, brother of Sarah Parker Remond, observed in 1842, "that many of the pieces on the subject of slavery and the slave-trade, contained in different school books, have been lost sight of, or been subject to the pruning knife of the slaveholding expurgatorial system!"[105] Wendell Phillips likewise noted in 1853 that "old school books tainted with some anti-slavery selections had passed out of use, and new ones were compiled to suit the times."[106] Long after the adoption of the Thirteenth Amendment, the white abolitionist Thomas Wentworth Higginson remembered how, by the early 1850s, slaveholders "had torn the anti-slavery pages out of the school books."[107]

Northern textbooks were not entirely purged of antislavery sentiment, however, and whatever hostility to slavery remained in them incensed proslavery apologists. Calls for a homegrown pedagogical literature began to multiply in the South in the 1850s. "Our text books are abolition works," C. K. Marshall of Mississippi declared at the 1855 Southern Commercial Convention, taking the example of a British atlas republished in New York by Appleton, which he claimed contained "hidden lessons of the most fiendish and murderous character that enraged fanaticism could conceive or indite."[108] Edwin Heriott of South Carolina agreed, recommending that "school books be *written, prepared and published . . . by southern men.*" In the pages of *De Bow's Review*, the preeminent southern magazine at the time, Heriott ridiculed the "sickly sentimentality" of Cowper's poetry and railed against *The American First Class Book* and *The National Orator*—an indication that these readers, though published two decades earlier, were still being used throughout the country.[109] Not even Goodrich, whose criticism of slavery was considerably muted over time, found favor with Heriott: he "has eagerly seized upon every opportunity . . . to insult and misrepresent the institutions of the South," Heriott later wrote in an essay addressed to Marshall. The two men were engaged in an all-out "war against . . . Anti-Slavery Text Books."[110] So was J. W. Morgan of Virginia, who on the eve of the Civil War penned yet another essay in which he criticized the use of textbooks flying the "black piratical ensign of Abolitionism" in southern classrooms. His message was unambiguous: "Our school books should assume a positive . . . stand, on the momentous subject of slavery."[111]

The hundred or so schoolbooks produced by the Confederacy during the war filled what white southerners had long perceived as a void in textbook publishing. Confederate arithmetic books were proslavery by default in assuming a world where human beings could be enslaved and exploited. One problem in Samuel Lander's *Our Own School Arithmetic* (1863) went, "If 5 white men can do as much work as 7 negroes, how many days of 10hr. each will be required for 25 negroes to do a piece of work which 30 white men can do in 10 days of 9hr. each?"[112] Because enslaved people were inferior to whites, the author implied, it was only natural that they should work longer hours. After the war, history textbooks such as Rushmore G. Horton's *A Youth's History of the Great Civil War in the United States, from 1861 to 1865* (1866) denounced "the false teachings of the abolitionists" and their "mad crusade against the Union," while claiming that enslaved people, freed by a dictatorial president, had been unwilling to leave plantations.[113] White supremacy was embedded in these schoolbooks.

The contest between anti- and proslavery forces did not simply take place in the halls of power, in the pages of newspapers, and on Civil War battlefields. What children thought, heard, read, and said at school was no less important in determining the future of the country. Abolitionists envisioned the classroom as a place where slavery and racial prejudice should be openly discussed rather than avoided or normalized. This did not mean that children should be dictated what to think. Young people had their own ideas on these subjects: it was the job of educators to listen and help them voice their opinions. Children's expressions of antislavery sentiment in the classroom, once in print, served as a fuel for the abolition movement. Schools could be platforms for activism, as racist attacks on young African Americans hoping to educate themselves demonstrated in dramatic ways. Many Black children and youth had to go through experiences akin to Sarah Parker Remond's. Doing so was their baptism of fire into the abolition movement.

5

"She . . . Made All Her Children Abolitionists"

Antislavery Families

When Mary Whiting of Binghamton, New York, died at the ripe age of ninety-three, in 1873, her obituary in the *New York Evangelist* noted that "she was early and always a warm friend of the slave, and made all her children abolitionists."[1] Whiting had had eight children, born between 1801 and 1819, the so-called middle period of abolition. At a time of "relative quiescence" for antislavery activism, Whiting seems to have quietly raised her children so that they would come to see slavery as an unjust, cruel system that needed to be abolished.[2] By 1855, her oldest son, William E. Whiting, could be found mingling with some of the most radical abolitionists of the day—Frederick Douglass and James McCune Smith, Gerrit Smith and John Brown—at the inaugural convention of the Radical Abolition Party in Syracuse, New York.[3] Within a few years, Mason Whiting Tyler, grandson of Mary and nephew of William, would enlist in the Massachusetts Thirty-Seventh Volunteer Infantry Regiment.[4] Antislavery ran in the Whiting family.

Abolitionism often was a family tradition in the antebellum United States. What James Oliver Horton writes of Black activists is true of all abolitionists: "If one member of a family was involved in civil rights, antislavery or general social reform, other family members were likely to take part."[5] Commitment to antislavery activism ran over several generations, as it did for the Douglasses, the Garrisons, the Fortens, the Jays, the Pauls, the Remonds, the Nells, the Browns, and many other Black and white families.[6] Juvenile abolitionism started in the home, where children heard and saw relatives talk about and act against slavery. Dynamics varied from one family to another. Both parents could be equally involved in their children's antislavery education, or one parent—a mother, for instance—could come to play a more determining role. An abolitionist grandfather or older brother might also be an important influence on a child's burgeoning political consciousness. Notably, children were encouraged to act against slavery themselves. A domestic antislavery education was about much more than reading juvenile antislavery literature: it involved assisting parents in their antislavery labors, whether it be in the editing of a newspaper or in the organization of a petition drive. Abolitionist parents, like teachers, nurtured children's autonomy and agency. They associated their young sons and daughters to their own work. As children grew up, they developed their own approach to antislavery, which sometimes conflicted with their parents'.

In this chapter, I explore the intergenerational, intrafamilial transmission of antislavery values, focusing on four families whose lives have been well documented, though not as part of a study of juvenile abolitionism. I shed light on the experience of the children of William Lloyd Garrison and Helen Benson Garrison, Frederick Douglass and Anna Murray Douglass, Elizabeth Buffum Chace and Samuel Buffington Chace, and John Remond and Nancy Lenox Remond. I briefly discuss other lesser-known families whose children were brought into the abolitionist fold at an early age. As much as possible, I adopt the point of view of these sons and daughters of abolitionists, who at the end of their lives penned memoirs in which they reminisced about their childhood.[7] Many insisted on the influence of their mother, which some felt had been obscured by the more public and therefore more visible labors of their father. Finally, I explore the adult lives of these juvenile abolitionists before and after the Civil War, showing how their abolitionism both persisted and transformed as they got older and the political context around them shifted.

Inheriting Abolitionism

Some children were born abolitionists. William Lloyd Garrison, shortly after the birth of his first son, George Thompson Garrison, published a cycle of five sonnets "addressed to an infant born on Saturday last, February 13th, 1836," in the *Liberator*. The sonnets were as much about slavery as they were about young George. Garrison pledged the life of his week-old baby to the cause of abolition, declaring that the child would be raised to "abhor OPPRESSION." Should the father die an untimely death at the hands of his opponents, the son was to fill his "vacant post" and "charge valiantly OPPRESSION's mighty host"—that is, carry on his father's antislavery work. George's birth led Garrison to reaffirm his own commitment to the cause. He hated slavery even more, he said, now that he held his "dear babe" in his arms and could truly understand the grief of the enslaved parent torn from their own child: "To rescue thee from bondage, I would brave / All dangers, and count life of little worth."[8] That Garrison became a father, in turn, endeared him to the African American community. "Our colored friends . . . were particularly careful to let me know how happy they felt to hear that Mrs. G. had got a fine little son," he wrote to his wife, Helen Benson Garrison, after attending meeting at Boston's African Meeting House. "Indeed, that eve[nt] tickles them beyond measure. We are doubly dear to them on that account." "My Sonnets seem to be universally admired," he added, reporting that Bronson Alcott, father of three-year-old Louisa May Alcott, had "wept as he read them, with excess of feeling."[9]

George Thompson Garrison, like many children of abolitionists, was named after a leading antislavery activist and friend of the Garrisons. George Thompson was a British abolitionist whose tour of the United States in the mid-1830s had led to many an antiabolition mob; on several occasions, he was pelted with rotten eggs and garbage, while President Andrew Jackson, in his seventh annual message to Congress, portrayed him and other such British activists as "emissaries from foreign parts" sent to destabilize the Union.[10] Garrison and his wife named all of their children but one after prominent US and British abolitionists: William Lloyd Garrison Jr., Wendell Phillips Garrison, and Francis Jackson Garrison followed in their father's footsteps—the latter two authored a biography of their father, *William Lloyd Garrison, 1805–1879: The Story of His Life Told by His Children* (1885–89)—while Charles Follen Garrison and Elizabeth Pease Garrison died in childhood. Helen Frances Garrison (later Fanny Garrison Villard), who outlived all of her siblings, was named after her mother and grandmother. Such naming practices were common within the abolition movement—and beyond: British Chartists also named their children after leading figures in the Chartist movement.[11] Naming one's child after a family friend was meant as a mark of esteem toward their namesake; naming them after a well-known activist was a way to establish a form of continuity between the present generation of abolitionists and those who would have to vindicate African American rights in the future. Garrison put it best when he informed Francis Jackson, then the president of the Massachusetts Anti-Slavery Society, of his decision to name his last-born son after him: "To call him *Francis Jackson Garrison* is only to indicate, in a slight degree, my admiration of your character, and the strong desire that I feel that the new comer [*sic*] may, through life, be inspired by that rare example of moral courage and unbending regard for principle, in contending with popular injustice and oppression, which his namesake has so nobly given to the world."[12] Frederick Douglass named his youngest son Charles Remond after the Black abolitionist Charles Lenox Remond, who himself named one of his sons Wendell Phillips, showing that the name of a white abolitionist could be adopted by a Black family (the reverse was less likely to happen, if it ever did). Some even combined several names in one: Peter F. Baltimore, mentioned in chapter 3, named his son Garnet Douglass, after two of the most eminent representatives of antebellum Black activism.

As Harriet Hyman Alonso has shown in an illuminating book on the Garrison family, William Lloyd Garrison and Helen Benson Garrison supplied their five children "with the necessary education to ensure . . . their dedication to social justice causes," including abolitionism and racial equality. Garrison and his wife, Alonso writes, were "absolutely determined to teach their children about the evils of slavery and the need for the abolitionist movement."[13] The Garrison children's acculturation to the abolition movement took place primarily in the home. There, they were exposed to a range of people, ideas, and texts that they were unlikely to come across elsewhere. Many Black and white abolitionists visited the Garrisons for more or less extended periods of time. On the visits of Jonathan Walker, mentioned in chapter 2, he shared the tale of his trials with the children and allowed them to touch the double *S* branded on his hand; perhaps it was as a result of these encounters with the young Garrisons that Walker was led to publish the undated *A Picture of Slavery, for Youth*. Wendell Phillips, Frederick Douglass, Harriet Tubman, and the Grimké sisters also frequented the Garrisons' home. The Garrison children listened in as adults discussed a coming antislavery convention or some piece of proslavery legislation that had been recently passed, and in time they came to participate in these conversations. "What we learned was an undying devotion to the principles of justice and humanity, never-to-be abandoned, come what may," Fanny Garrison Villard wrote in her late-life recollections of her father.[14] Her older brother William Lloyd Garrison Jr., for his part, reminisced about the fugitives who regularly showed up on the family's doorstep: "How many of these I have seen and how my childish heart throbbed with pity and sympathy at these evidences of barbarism! It was a common thing in my father's house for the maid to announce, 'There's a colored man in the kitchen who has run away from slavery.' Sometimes it was a colored woman, sometimes a mother with her baby in her arms. It was so interesting to listen to the story of the escape, to hear of the long journey in the night, before the free states were reached."[15] It is unknown whether William Jr. read any of the published slave narratives as a child—he probably did—but he and his siblings certainly got to hear many a tragic life story from the mouths of the formerly enslaved themselves.

Even when there were no guests visiting, abolitionism was virtually inescapable at the Garrisons'. William Lloyd Garrison's own devotion to the cause shaped his personal relations with his children and how he spent his time with them. For instance, Fanny recalled how, as a game, her father would place her on his shoulders and have her recite the names of the people—family and friends, including many abolitionists—whose pictures hung on the walls of the library.[16] On Saturday evenings, after supper, the children helped Garrison proofread the latest issue of the *Liberator*. One of them would "follow copy" while Garrison "read aloud from the proof-slip and corrected the typographical errors, which were apt to be pretty numerous." No doubt he answered quite a few slavery-related questions during these proofreading sessions. It was also common for the children to spend time at their father's workplace: Fanny would bring him lunch on Wednesdays, which was when the *Liberator* went to press. Garrison was a doting father who loved to play with his children, "either romping games when small, or games of skill when older," in Wendell and Francis's terms, but he was also a committed activist who was determined that his children feel compelled to act against slavery.[17] The playful and the political often mingled in his day-to-day interactions with them. In an 1857 letter to eight-year-old Francis sent from New Hampshire, where he was lecturing, Garrison responded to his son's account of his summer holiday and reminisced about his own fondness of "bat and ball, or flying the kite, or playing at marbles" as a boy. He then wrote about his latest lecture, regretting that there were not more people supporting the antislavery cause. "You, my dear boy, I trust, will grow up a good abolitionist," he added, "and should your father's voice be hushed in death before the wretched slaves are set free, you must lift up, in the loudest tone, your own voice."[18] Over two decades had elapsed since Garrison had composed his sonnets to Francis's older brother George. Now aged fifty-one, and with slavery still on the books, he felt the need to pass on his antislavery principles to his youngest child with even more intensity.

The Douglass children were no less exposed to their parents' abolitionism than the Garrison children were. Frederick Douglass and Anna Murray Douglass had their five children roughly at the same time as the Garrisons did, between the latter half of the 1830s and the 1840s; the youngest, Annie, died at the age of ten, on the eve of the Civil War. Douglass's status as an iconic, towering figure of African American activism, however, has meant that historians have only recently started paying attention to the people around him, including his wife and children, and his dealings with them.[19] "The told story of the father, Frederick Douglass," Celeste-Marie Bernier and Andrew Taylor argue, "is the untold story of the daughters, Annie and Rosetta, and sons, Lewis Henry, Frederick Jr., and Charles Remond Douglass."[20] Fragments of their childhoods emerge in various documents penned by them. What they show is a family deeply invested in what we usually perceive as Douglass's individual antislavery labors.

The Douglass children participated in the making of Douglass's *North Star* (and later *Frederick Douglass' Paper*) in crucial ways. As Douglass's youngest son, Charles, noted in a speech delivered toward the end of his life, "To maintain this paper every effort was put forth by every member of the family."[21] Rosetta, Lewis, Frederick Jr., and Charles himself all helped with the folding and mailing of the paper at some point. As they grew up, Lewis and Frederick Jr. took a more active role. According to Rosetta, it was Anna Murray Douglass who first suggested that they be employed at the newspaper's office. Prejudice ran rampant in 1840s Rochester, and their mother did not want the two boys roaming the streets when not at school. Frederick Douglass "acted upon the suggestion and at the ages of eleven and nine they were perched upon blocks and given their first lesson in printer's ink."[22] Such childhood experiences proved formative, especially for Lewis: he was apprenticed as a printer at the age of sixteen and was entrusted with the newspaper's management and business operations in late 1859 and early 1860, when his father was away to avoid prosecution following John Brown's raid on Harpers Ferry. "Though only nineteen years old," Benjamin Fagan writes, "Lewis had been helping make *Frederick Douglass' Paper* for most of its existence." Douglass's children, he adds, were probably "the most consistent presences in the newspaper office" during the second half of the 1850s.[23] Their introduction to printing and the newspaper business was also an introduction to the world of abolition. Working alongside their father, they understood the role of the press in the fight against slavery and racial proscription, as well as the challenges of publishing a Black abolitionist newspaper in the face of opposition from proslavery opponents and white Garrisonian allies who failed to see the point of another such publication. They heard and read about Colored Conventions, fugitive slave rescues, and the rise of political antislavery. They absorbed Douglass's views as expressed in countless editorials.

Like the Garrison home in Boston, the Douglass home in Rochester was an abolitionist hub. The residence served as a stop on the Underground Railroad. It was, as Charles recalled, "the last Station on that road before reaching Canada the goal of the fleeing slaves ambition [*sic*]."[24] When it came to aiding fugitives, everyone was involved. Douglass had a secret room built to conceal runaways. Anna Murray Douglass, whom her daughter called "one of the first agents of the Underground Railroad," was "called up at all hours . . . to prepare supper for a hungry lot of fleeing humanity."[25] Should a fugitive arrive in the middle of a cold winter night, the children would get up and start a fire. During the day, the boys went about collecting funds for the fugitives' fare on the steamer across Lake Ontario. "Every member of the family had to lend a hand to this work and it was always cheerfully performed," Charles noted. "We felt that we were doing a christian and humane duty."[26] No doubt there was some degree of mythologizing to the children's late-life reminiscences of their home as sanctuary. Yet it cannot be denied that they were involved in the operations of the Underground Railroad through their parents. As Lewis put it, "For years the family worked on ~~and~~ only encouraged by the thought that they were working for the cause in which their father and mother were interested—namely the emancipation of the slave."[27]

Countless antislavery activists stayed at the Douglasses' home, adding to Anna's already heavy workload. One of its most illustrious visitors was John Brown, who in early 1858 spent several weeks with Douglass and his family (he insisted on paying board). The Douglass children enjoyed the presence of this strange old man under their roof. Charles, aged thirteen at the time, became his "errand boy." Twice a day he went to the post office to receive Brown's mail, sent to Douglass's box under a pseudonym.[28] Brown confided in the children about his plan to arm enslaved people and spirit them to the mountains of Virginia. One day, he asked Douglass to put out two planed boards on which he could illustrate the system of forts and secret passages he meant to adopt. "I was less interested in these drawings than my children were," Douglass wrote in *Life and Times of Frederick Douglass* (1881), a remark which was meant to convey the impracticability of Brown's plan but which incidentally shines a light on the children's natural penchant for his brand of radical abolitionism.[29] Brown had many significant interactions with children, including his own, throughout his life. A year before, he had visited the Boston home of the wealthy businessman and abolitionist George Luther Stearns, one of his most steadfast benefactors. Stearns's twelve-year-old son, Harry, was present when Brown recounted his recent experiences in Kansas. "I listened attentively to the conversation," Harry later wrote, "and young as I was I had some idea of the meaning of it."[30] The boy offered Brown what pocket money he had, becoming in effect a funder of his antislavery endeavors. A few months later, Brown wrote Harry a letter in which he recalled how, as a child, he had witnessed the neglect and abuse of a boy by his enslaver. This incident, he explained, made him "a most *determined Abolitionist*."[31]

Like Harry Stearns, little Annie Douglass was drawn to Brown (figure 5.1). A letter written to her father five days after Brown's execution testifies to the centrality of abolition to her young existence. Ten-year-old Annie told Frederick about a piece she was to recite at school: "It is an Anti Slavery [sic]," she wrote. She took care to copy its words, taken from a poem published in Wilson Armistead's *The Garland of Freedom* (1853):

Figure 5.1. Annie Douglass (1849–1860) with her father, ca. 1854. Courtesy of the John B. Cade Library, Southern University and A&M College.

O he is not the man for me
    Who buys or Sells a slave
Nor he who will not set him free
    But send him to his grave
But he whose noble heart beats warm
    For all men's llife [sic] and liberty
Who loves alike each human form
    O that's the man for me.

Annie then mentioned the execution of John Brown in a way that showed her precise knowledge of the event: "Poor Mr. Brown is dead. That hard hearted man [the governor of Virginia, Henry A. Wise] said he must die, and they took him in and open field and about a half mile from the Jail and hung him."[32] Annie's budding abolitionism might have bloomed into full-fledged activism but for her premature death of what was perhaps meningitis three months later. Though Annie was not able to publicly express her antislavery sentiments, her family did it for her by connecting her death to Brown's and thus giving it political significance. Frederick Douglass suggested that "deep sorrow for the death of dear old JOHN BROWN upon whose knee she had often sat only a few months before" contributed to his daughter's decline and ultimate death. The *Douglass' Monthly* noted that two of Brown's followers, Aaron D. Stephens and Albert Hazelett, had been executed on the day of Annie's funeral, and at the same hour too. The funeral itself saw the officiating clergyman launch into an antislavery diatribe. "We hope the multitude who listened to him, resolved to enter upon the work of Abolition in right earnest," the *Douglass' Monthly* reporter commented.[33] The Douglass family honored Annie's juvenile abolitionism by ensuring that her death would serve the cause of abolition.

Antislavery Mothering

Abolitionist homes, as these examples demonstrate, were far from private enclaves cut off from the public world of antislavery agitation. Quite the contrary, they were vibrant, welcoming spaces where fugitives found a refuge and traveling activists found a place to stay when other houses were closed to them. Fanny Garrison Villard referred to her childhood home as a "hotel," noting the essential role played by her mother in its daily management: taking care of their home, she wrote, was one of Helen Benson Garrison's "great contributions to the cause of the slave."[34] As Hélène Quanquin and Daina Ramey Berry have argued, women such as Helen Benson Garrison and Anna Murray Douglass were abolitionists in their own right, who used the domestic space as a site of political activism.[35] Though they rarely assumed a public role, their behind-the-scenes efforts were integral to the antislavery enterprise.

As mothers, these women took an active part in raising antislavery children. Indeed, many an antebellum child who turned to antislavery activism did so through the agency of their mother. Throughout the period, as discussed in chapter 1, abolitionists enjoined women to use their "female influence" in the family circle and sensitize children to the problem of slavery. White mothers should "guard . . . the minds of their children from the ruining influences of the spirit of pro-slavery and prejudice," as one delegate at the first Anti-Slavery Convention of American Women, Abby Cox, put it in 1837.[36] All mothers were expected to involve their children in the business of abolition. One of the most eloquent proponents of this view was the white abolitionist and women's rights advocate Lucy Stone, who, at the 1857 annual meeting of the American Anti-Slavery Society, assured women that they could do much for the cause. Women might not be willing to speak on the antislavery platform, nor might they be able to vote for antislavery political parties; but as mothers, they could exert "a better and more powerful influence" than men within their homes. "It is not possible for the child that comes tottling to your side, that sits listening upon your knee and hears your words of instruction, not to be influenced in its future action by your teaching," Stone argued. The kind of teaching Stone had in mind was not simply moral or religious: it was unabashedly political. She insisted that children should be made aware of recently adopted legislation concerning slavery. "When there is a Personal Liberty Bill before the country, tell it in your household, and explain to your little child the reason of it," she said, referring to the personal liberty laws that had been passed by northern state governments to counteract the effects of federal fugitive law. A lesson on the personal liberty laws, she suggested, could double as a lesson on the political disfranchisement of women: "Forget not, at the same time, to tell them that, to the shame of the community, woman can have nothing to do with making that Personal Liberty Bill, but is utterly shut out from all political action by the theory of the government." State racism and proslavery violence were not subjects to be avoided either: "When the Dred Scott decision springs upon us, . . . tell your household what will be the result, and the smallest child can comprehend you. And when men are shot down in Kansas, tell your children why it is." The 1857 *Dred Scott* decision of the Supreme Court established that African Americans were not US citizens, while Kansas saw repeated outbreaks of bloody guerrilla warfare between pro- and antislavery forces during the mid-1850s. Stone did not consider the possibility that such topics might be age-inappropriate or beyond the grasp of children. She was confident that children would come to detest slavery as long as mothers seized every opportunity they had of showing their "little ones" the iniquities of the system.[37]

Juvenile antislavery literature also stressed the role of mothers. In Jane Elizabeth Jones's *The Young Abolitionists; or, Conversations on Slavery* (1848), it is Mrs. Selden rather than her husband who discusses slavery with her children. In fact, the two parents initially diverge on whether the topic should even be brought up at home. Mr. Selden does not want "the joyousness of [his children's] young spirits . . . checked by the contemplation of such terrible cruelties." Returning home one day, he finds his daughter, Jenie, examining a picture of an enslaved person being whipped, perhaps put into her hands by her mother; Jenie, he realizes on closer inspection, is weeping, making him fear that "at too early an age she was becoming acquainted with the history of crime." Mrs. Selden, on the other hand, reminds her husband that "their children would be learning these sad stories from one and another, and it was best for parents to instruct them in regard to slavery and other evils, that . . . they might have a just abhorance [sic] of wrong."[38] Two conceptions of childhood vie against each other in these pages. To borrow from Steven Mintz's terminology, Mr. Selden cherishes the ideal of a "protected childhood": children, he believes, need to be "insulated from adult realities." Mrs. Selden emphasizes a "prepared" childhood, one in which children are "prepared from a very early age for the kinds of threats they will face."[39] The spirit of slavery posed a direct threat to both children and the country they lived in. Like Mrs. Selden, abolitionist mothers had a responsibility to raise their children's antislavery consciousness and prepare them for future action against the slave system. Mr. Selden eventually aligns with his wife, at least as far as his eldest son, Charlie, is concerned. She "might as well make thorough work of it," he concludes, "and tell him as much about the system of slavery as he was able to understand."[40]

Antislavery women heeded these calls to action. Many were part of what Julie Roy Jeffrey has termed "the great silent army of abolitionism" and have left few direct traces of their investment in their children's antislavery education.[41] Such work was possible precisely because it was done privately, within the confines of the home. Yet their children's public antislavery labors testify to their otherwise invisible work. The Quaker abolitionist Aaron M. Powell, born in 1832, reminisced in his 1899 memoirs about his introduction to abolitionism through his mother, Catherine Macy Powell:

> My attention was first called to the subject of slavery, in my boyhood, by an illustrated pamphlet, upon the first page of which was shown the picture of a negro slave woman, with her baby in her arms, who was being severely whipped by a cruel slave-driver . . . until her bared back was lacerated, and blood was flowing from the wounds. . . . Though myself but a child at the time, this picture, with the interpretation of it which my mother gave to me, as she read from the anti-slavery pamphlet which had found its way into our rural home . . . made a deep and lasting impression upon my memory.[42]

Although he mentions his mother only in passing, and without naming her, Powell highlights her key role as the person who selected, read, and decoded an antislavery pamphlet for him. In his own telling, Powell did not fully engage with the abolition movement until hearing the abolitionists Abby Kelley Foster and Stephen S. Foster lecture in his community of Ghent, New York, when he was eighteen. "Theirs were the first anti-slavery addresses to which I had ever listened," he notes. Powell became an avid reader of the *Liberator* and the *National Anti-Slavery Standard*, which "became the basis of [his] anti-slavery education, commenced with the visit of the Fosters."[43] Yet the young man may never have taken an interest in abolition without the early seeds planted by his mother when he was a boy. It was with Catherine Macy Powell's reading of an abolitionist publication to him that his antislavery education truly "commenced." Powell became a committed abolitionist—he edited the *National Anti-Slavery Standard* for a time—while his sister, Elizabeth Powell Bond, also "developed the spirit of a reformer" at an early age, working on behalf of antislavery and temperance, probably under the joint influence of her mother and older brother (figure 5.2).[44] Likewise, the white abolitionist, freethinker, and women's rights advocate Lucy N. Colman remembered being taught an

Figure 5.2. Aaron M. Powell (1832–1899) and Elizabeth Powell (1841–1926), ca. 1849. Aaron M. Powell, *Personal Reminiscences of the Anti-Slavery and Other Reforms and Reformers* (New York: Caulon Press, 1899), 219. Courtesy of the American Antiquarian Society.

antislavery song by her mother—Hannah Newhall, unnamed in her 1891 reminiscences—in her childhood. Newhall did her best to answer her daughter's pressing questions regarding slavery, such as "Why did God let children be slaves?"[45]

While Catherine Macy Powell's and Hannah Newhall's antislavery mothering of their children has remained more or less hidden in the archives, there is ample evidence of the tremendous efforts deployed by Elizabeth Buffum Chace to "make" her children abolitionists. As Elizabeth Stevens argues, Chace saw motherhood as an important aspect of her life, one that was intimately connected to her activism. Like other nineteenth-century abolitionist mothers, Chace "saw both domestic childrearing and public work as an integral whole" rather than as two distinct areas of life. Motherhood, for Chace, was a truly "subversive" activity.[46] The story of the Buffum Chace family spans several generations of antislavery activism. Chace was the granddaughter of William Buffum, a member of the Providence Abolition Society, founded in Rhode Island in 1789. Of her father, Arnold Buffum, she wrote in her memoirs that he "became an abolitionist in his childhood," hearing stories about the Middle Passage told by a New York fugitive whom the Buffums had helped settle with his family not far from their farm in Smithfield, Rhode Island.[47] As an adult, Arnold Buffum participated in what Richard Newman identifies as the transformation of US abolitionism from a gradualist elite movement focused on strictly legal tactics into a radical interracial movement calling for the immediate end of slavery. Around the 1820s, Buffum grew increasingly dissatisfied with the conservative strategy of his organization, the venerable Pennsylvania Abolition Society, which he accused of tolerating colonizationism and failing to confront racial prejudice; an admirer of African American activism, Buffum became the first president of the integrated New England Anti-Slavery Society, founded in 1832.[48] "Thus was I born and baptized into the Anti-Slavery spirit," Chace wrote. "Our family were all Abolitionists."[49]

Elizabeth pushed her father's uncompromising antislavery even further, renouncing Quakerism when it became clear that the Society of Friends was no longer as willing to denounce slavery as it had been in the past.[50] Abolitionism, rather than Quakerism, became "the guiding principle that informed her mothering in the 1850s."[51] Indeed, though her husband, the industrialist Samuel Buffington Chace, came to espouse her views, it is clear that Elizabeth was the most dedicated of the two parents to her offspring's antislavery education; a "silent man" who was busy with his textile manufactories, Samuel seems to have had fewer interactions with his children anyway.[52] Elizabeth Buffum Chace made her home of Valley Falls, Rhode Island, into an antislavery home, where her children would naturally be led to think and talk about slavery and the need to abolish it. Far from being an enclosed, secluded space, the Chace residence, even more so than other such residences, was opened to both antislavery family and friends. Chace's parents often visited their daughter. In her memoirs, Chace noted with satisfaction that her father was as much an abolitionist in old age as he had been when younger. He could be heard reciting antislavery lines from William Cowper as he strolled about the house—those same lines from *The Task* (1785) that had appeared in Lindley Murray's *English Reader* in 1799 and that Arnold Buffum may have taught his grandchildren. The Chace house also provided a "resting place for the advocates of freedom" happening to lecture in Rhode Island: Garrison, Stone, Douglass, Remond, and Phillips counted among its most eminent visitors. The Chace children were "born and bred in the atmosphere which these lovers of freedom helped to create in [their] household."[53] The visitors brought something of the larger antislavery world into the children's necessarily more limited domestic world. The house itself bore many traces of its occupants' political convictions. Portraits of Garrison, Phillips, and the Transcendentalist abolitionist Theodore Parker hung on the walls. A silk-covered box with a verse of Cowper's on it and the picture of a kneeling slave, sent from Scotland and purchased at an antislavery fair, sat on a shelf in the parlor.[54]

Elizabeth Buffum Chace worked hard to instill strong abolitionist principles into her children. She made sure that their ordinary reading comprised not only such juvenile classics as *Robinson Crusoe* and *The Swiss Family Robinson* but also antislavery novels such as Harriet Beecher Stowe's *Uncle Tom's Cabin* (1852) and Richard Hildreth's *The White Slave; or, Memoirs of a Fugitive* (1852).[55] The Chace parents subscribed to the *Liberator* and the *National Anti-Slavery Standard*. Their daughter Lillie (later Lillie Chace Wyman), born in 1847, in her own reminiscences recalled turning the pages of these newspapers "for hours at a time" and reading "with a fascinated attention the reports of stirring debates and eloquent speeches." Elizabeth also took her children to public antislavery events. "I first saw William Lloyd Garrison in an antislavery meeting in Providence," Lillie further recalled, "and the eagerness with which I waited his entrance into the hall testified to the constancy" of her mother's abolitionist teaching.[56] Though we tend to imagine antislavery meetings (other than the juvenile meetings organized by Henry Clarke Wright) as being attended mostly by adults, parents often went with their children in tow. On these occasions, children of abolitionists

would have been introduced to antislavery oratory—perhaps not an entirely enjoyable experience, given that lectures commonly ran for several
hours—as well as to antiabolitionist violence. When Wright visited Falls
River for a meeting in April 1861, he was prevented from speaking by a
mob of "rough[-]looking men" who then pursued the attendees as they
were forced to regain their homes. As Chace later wrote, "We Abolitionists formed a solid phalanx around our speaker, the children among us,
while we walked quietly, . . . the mob following close upon us, with yells
and shouts and threats of violence."[57] Threats soon gave way to acts, and
thirteen-year-old Lillie got hit by a stone.

Abolition had long been an intimate part of the Chace family's identity, and as such, it came to be embraced by Elizabeth Buffum Chace's
children, who otherwise might have resisted an education centered on
such a heavy—and seemingly distant—subject as slavery. Abolition was
the family's religion: it provided the Chaces with a common language, a
set of shared values, and a sense of purpose. It was woven into the fab-
ric of their daily lives, to the extent that even moments of leisure were
"infused with antislavery content."[58] Elizabeth Buffum Chace's placing
a copy of *Uncle Tom's Cabin* in the hands of her children was both a
political act on her part and a way to keep them entertained. Likewise,
the Chace children must have enjoyed the near-constant presence of
antislavery guests at their house. Henry Clarke Wright was a favorite,
"because he held sportive sessions with them, called 'rollicking conventions.'"[59] Even the business of aiding fugitive slaves could be thrilling
from a child's perspective. The Chace home, like so many abolitionist
homes, served as a stop on the Underground Railroad. Doors would
sometimes be locked when a fugitive was sheltered, making it clear to
the Chace children that, under the Fugitive Slave Law, the enterprise was
a secret and potentially dangerous one. "We told our children, all, at that
time, under fourteen years of age, of the fine of one thousand dollars,
and the imprisonment of six months, that awaited us, in case the officer
should come, and we should refuse to give these poor people up," Chace
wrote.[60] The children promised to be good if such a thing should happen. "Possibly in their relish for martyrdom," Lillie added, "they almost
hoped it would."[61]

Antislavery politics was another popular topic among the boys.
Thirteen-year-old Samuel, eleven-year-old Arnold, and seven-year-old

Edward Chace entered heartily into the presidential campaign of 1856, which pitted the Democrat James Buchanan against John C. Frémont of the Republican Party, then a newly formed political movement opposing the extension of slavery into western territories. Young Samuel and Edward came out in favor of Frémont and made a "Frémont and Freedom" banner that they flew from the top of the well house. Arnold, on the other hand, strictly adhered to the Garrisonian principle of nonparticipation in the political process and refused to align himself with the Republican—let alone the Democratic—candidate; his own flag, placed on the housetop, bore Garrison's motto of "No Union with slave-holders."[62] The Chace boys inherited the same dedication to abolition from their mother but interpreted her antislavery teaching differently, thus demonstrating their capacity to think for themselves and come to their own conclusions regarding the best way to abolish slavery. Elizabeth Buffum Chace may have welcomed such (relatively minor) disagreements within her household. Lillie later wrote of the two flags, "These two emblems of the divided nature of the family anti-slavery faith floated serenely on the breeze during the campaign," which—to everyone's dismay—ended with the election of the proslavery Buchanan to the presidency.[63]

Chace's education of her children, though focused on abolition and other related doctrines such as nonresistance, was at heart a civic education. What Chace taught her children was that as citizens-to-be, they should feel a duty to engage with the world around them and help to correct social wrongs. That they were still young did not mean that they could not publicly express their opinions either. Elizabeth Buffum Chace encouraged her sons and daughter to take part in public debate through petitions and the press. At roughly the same time that her brothers were flying pro-Frémont and disunionist flags around the Chace property, Lillie wrote to the editor of one of her favorite children's newspapers, *Merry's Museum*, after he had published a rebus preceded by the question, "Why is our Hieroglyphical Rebus like the bright side of slavery?"[64] "I never knew slavery had any bright side" was Lillie's forthright answer to the rebus, in a letter otherwise complimenting Robert Merry for his entertaining paper. When Merry published Lillie's response in his "Monthly Chat with His Friends" the following month, he omitted the comment on slavery, leading the eight-year-old to send another letter: "I ask why you did not publish the *whole* of my letter? In my opinion, you left out the best part of it. . . . Mother says a magazine which is helping to educate the children of this country should speak out plainly against so great an evil as slavery." This second letter never appeared in the *Museum*, and like Lillie's earlier comment, it has survived only because Henry Clarke Wright decided to publicize the affair in the *Liberator*. In his write-up, Wright included a third letter to *Merry's Museum* by one of Lillie's older brothers, probably Arnold: "I think it is quite time that the American youth should be made acquainted with the horrible deeds perpetrated every day upon four millions of innocent men and women by slaveholders." Wright himself berated the magazine for pandering to the proslavery sentiment of its southern readership.[65] If the Chace siblings had not already been aware of the severe limitations on democratic debate in a slaveholding society, now they were. This did not deter Lillie from making herself heard. A few years later, the now eleven-year-old girl could be found signing petitions against school segregation. Lillie informed her brother Samuel, "[Those] who are old enough to understand it can sign these petitions under the heading of nonvoters. I have signed it."[66] It seems that the petition controversy of the 1830s had abated and minors could now exercise their right to petition without causing as much of a stir. The important thing was that minors "understand" what they signed, Lillie argued, implicitly making a point on the arbitrariness of age as a criterion for civic participation. After years of abolitionist training, Lillie—admittedly a politically precocious child—had a perfect understanding of what she was doing.

Lillie Chace paid tribute to her mother in her writings. So did Sarah Parker Remond. Remond, born in Salem, Massachusetts, in 1826, was the daughter of Nancy Lenox and John Remond, who, as leading members of Salem's Black community, had long been involved in self-help organizations and fighting for equal rights.[67] John was an agent of *Freedom's Journal*, and he subscribed to Garrison's *Liberator* as soon as it was created; in 1833, he became a life member of the New England Anti-Slavery Society. John Remond, Sibyl Ventress Brownlee argues, was a "role model for all his children," including Sarah Parker Remond, "in regards to political activism."[68] Another role model was Sarah's brother Charles Lenox Remond, born in 1810. Charles played an increasingly visible role in the abolition movement from the early 1830s. His younger sister, who was close to him, followed his career with great interest. All of Sarah's numerous siblings, in fact, were involved to some degree in antislavery work.[69] Susan Remond, born 1814, was a fancy-cake maker by trade, whose "kitchen was a Mecca where gathered radicals, free thinkers, abolitionists, female suffragists, fugitives"—as well as children, who were allowed to play and treated with goodies, as a family friend, Maritcha Lyons, recalled.[70] Young Sarah probably visited her sister's abolitionist kitchen on numerous occasions. Yet it was to her mother that Sarah Parker Remond gave pride of place in the autobiographical essay that she penned in 1861.[71] Nancy Remond was a member of the initially all-Black Salem Female Anti-Slavery Society. A committed abolitionist, she "hailed the advent" of Garrison "with enthusiasm."[72] It must have been in her and her sisters' company that Sarah attended her first antislavery meetings as a child.

At the same time that Nancy Remond introduced her daughters to the abolition movement, she provided them with a rigorous domestic education. "We were all trained to habits of industry, with a thorough knowledge of those domestic duties which particularly mark the genuine New England woman," Sarah wrote. Nancy's "home discipline"—her insistence that her daughters be able to knit, sew, and cook and that "the most trifling affair" be "well done"—had political dimensions, as Sarah later realized: "Her aim seemed to be to guard, and at the same time strengthen her children, not only for the trials and duties of life, but also to enable them to meet the terrible pressure which prejudice against colour would force upon them."[73] The fight against racial prejudice began at home, as Black conduct writers made clear. Parents were urged to raise exemplary children whose very lives would challenge white supremacist notions.[74] Nancy Remond took this message to heart, teaching her daughters to be just like her—models of energetic, politically engaged womanhood. Such an education would also serve as a shield against the demoralizing effect of racism, of which Sarah, even as a child, had firsthand knowledge. "Her discipline taught us to gather strength from our own souls, and we felt the full force of the fact, that to be black was no crime, but an accident of birth."[75] For Black abolitionist mothers, discussing personal liberty laws with their children or taking them to antislavery meetings was only part of the job of raising juvenile abolitionists, as Anna Murray Douglass also very well knew. Murray Douglass was not only an agent of the Underground Railroad and a member of several antislavery societies in Massachusetts and upstate New York. She was also, in her daughter's words, "a woman who strove to inculcate in the minds of her children the highest principles of morality and virtue both by precept and example."[76] Industry, morality, and virtue were instruments in the Black abolitionist toolbox of which mothers made systematic use in the domestic fight against slavery and racism. They raised children who both fought for and embodied abolition.

Juvenile Abolitionists Grown Up

Though Sarah Parker Remond's parents had been active on the local antislavery scene, their activism was always distinct from their professional life. John and Nancy Remond ran a catering business in Salem. Sarah, on the other hand, followed the example of her older brother Charles, who in 1838 had become the first African American AASS agent, and decided to step out in the public role of antislavery lecturer. That she waited until the age of thirty to do so suggests that this was not an easy decision to make. Even if antislavery reform was a family tradition, Sarah was a middle-class woman, and as such, she had to comport with prevailing gender norms. Activism was fine, and even encouraged, as long as it did not transgress these norms too blatantly. Remond's biographer hypothesizes that her father may not, in fact, have supported her public speaking.[77] It was one thing to participate in the activities of female antislavery societies in and around Salem; it was another to lecture before faraway mixed-gender audiences, as Charles had been doing. Sarah, however, felt a calling to play a more prominent role in the abolition movement. The family encouragement she did receive primarily came from her brother, who also happened to be an early ally of the women's rights movement. A self-described "woman's rights man," Charles Lenox Remond was eager to help Sarah pursue her vocation of public participation in the antislavery cause.[78] Through him, Sarah was hired as an agent of the AASS, and in 1856, the two siblings embarked on a joint lecture tour that took them as far away as Canada. Sarah was a success. Soon she would strike out on her own and cross the Atlantic without a protector for an even more ambitious antislavery tour of Britain.[79] The case of Sarah Parker Remond is illustrative of the sometimes uneasy transition from juvenile to "adult" abolitionism. Remond had received an abolitionist education, yet class and gender expectations interfered with her desire to do more for the cause. All of Remond's siblings but Charles had established themselves as independent business owners, either as caterers, bakers, or hairdressers; all of her sisters fought against slavery and racial prejudice in ways deemed suitable by their community. In turning to public lecturing, Remond both continued the family tradition of antislavery activism and departed from it.[80]

As juvenile abolitionists grew up, they gained in autonomy and decided for themselves if and how they would fight against slavery and, after the Civil War, for Black civil and political rights. Some, especially among whites, did not embrace an activist career. Their trajectories are, by definition, hard to reconstruct: little of their lives remains besides their youthful expressions of antislavery sentiment. Others strayed off the path traced by their parents. George Thompson Garrison, for instance, did not quite follow in his father's footsteps. From the day of his birth, George had been expected to devote his existence to racial justice. His own name was a constant reminder of what he was meant to accomplish. Like his siblings, George imbibed the ideas of his father, working alongside him at the *Liberator* for several years; his commitment to abolition was total. Yet the young man strove to express his individuality and independence, and on one point, he came to differ with his father. William Lloyd Garrison had long been an advocate of nonresistance, a form of radical pacifism that translated into a rejection of all human governments. "Moral suasion" was his privileged strategy: Garrison hoped to awaken public opinion on slavery and prejudice and thus convert white Americans, including slaveholders, to abolition; the name of Garrison became virtually synonymous with this approach.[81] George, however, came of age during the 1850s, a critical period when moral suasion lost ground in favor of a more aggressive response to slavery. Black abolitionists, as Kellie Carter Jackson has shown, played a leading role in this ideological shift, to which young George was not immune.[82] His father had converted from gradualism to immediatism under the influence of Black Baltimoreans thirty years earlier. Now George felt that the abolition movement needed to be pushed in a more militant direction. He "began to move away from his family's nonresistant philosophy," Harriet Hyman Alonso writes, "toward embracing the idea that if violence was needed to free the slaves, he could not only sanction it but also participate in it."[83]

Violent confrontations around the slavery issue multiplied throughout the decade, some of which, like the 1854 rescue of Anthony Burns, happened close to the Garrison home. Burns was a fugitive from Virginia who had settled in Boston. When he was arrested under the Fugitive Slave Law, local Black and white activists such as Lewis Hayden and Thomas Wentworth Higginson organized to remove Burns from the prison where he was held; their meetings took place in the *Liberator* office, perhaps in George's presence.[84] The Burns rescue left one of the prison guards dead, which did not deter abolitionists from trying to rescue other fugitives. George reconsidered his family's nonresistant views in the light of these developments. When civil war came, he was the only one of the Garrison sons to enlist. William Jr. affirmed, "[I could] no more take a gun into my hand to kill a fellow creature than I could do any other horrible deed which my soul abhors." Wendell, when he was drafted in 1863, paid a commutation fee releasing him from his military duty: "The doctrine of the inviolability of human life, which I accept, will probably forever debar me . . . from using a musket," he wrote in the *Liberator*. Both brothers, like their father, supported the Union war effort and followed the war's progress, but neither would participate in the fighting. Even Fanny tried to convince abolitionist friends not to take part in the war. If George had any qualms about enlisting, they lifted after Lincoln made it clear, by signing the Emancipation Proclamation, that the war was no longer just about restoring the Union but about ending slavery. He accepted an invitation to become a second lieutenant in the Massachusetts Fifty-Fifth Volunteer Infantry Regiment, one of the first two regiments of African American soldiers.[85] Garrison respected his son's decision: "Though I could have wished that you had been able understandingly and truly to adopt those principles of peace which are so sacred and divine to my soul," he wrote in a letter to George, "yet you will bear me witness that I have not laid a straw in your way to prevent your acting up to your own highest convictions of duty."[86] Abolitionists raised children to stand up for their beliefs, even when those beliefs conflicted with their own. Their children never blindly followed their parents' teachings but critiqued them, refined them, and adapted them to new contexts.

On several occasions throughout the postwar years did the Garrison children differ from their father politically. In 1865, twenty-five-year-old Wendell, who had contributed articles to the *Liberator* during the war, joined the editorial staff of the *Nation*, a newly created New York weekly that many people imagined to be the *Liberator*'s successor (it was founded with the financial backing of abolitionists). Yet the *Nation*'s first editor, Edwin L. Godkin, soon proved to be a conservative elitist with little concern for racial justice. By the early 1870s, Godkin was calling the Black voter in South Carolina "as ignorant as a horse" and excusing Ku Klux Klan violence. While Wendell did not espouse such extremist views himself, he defended Godkin when his father rebuked him for the paper's "evident contempt for the colored race."[87] Alonso calls Wendell Phillips Garrison "the most politically conservative of the Garrison children."[88] Overall, however, the Garrison children upheld the family's abolitionist legacy, especially after the death of their father in 1879 and the rollback of Black rights following the end of Reconstruction. During the late nineteenth and early twentieth centuries—the "nadir" of African American history, in Rayford Logan's formulation—they were promoters of Black education and critics of lynching, segregation, and disfranchisement.[89] William Jr. and Francis raised funds for Tuskegee Institute, the first institution of higher learning for African Americans, founded by Booker T. Washington in 1881, while Fanny and her son Oswald Garrison Villard were patrons of Manassas Industrial School, founded by the Black Virginian Jennie Dean in 1894. William Jr. was one of the main speakers at the inaugural meeting of the Massachusetts Anti-Lynching League in 1894. Francis was president of the Boston branch of the National Association for the Advancement of Colored People (NAACP), created in 1909. Many of the names present on the roster of the Boston branch, as James McPherson notes, had appeared on the membership list of the New England Anti-Slavery Society: Garrison, May, Bowditch, and Foster, among others. Albert E. Pillsbury, nephew of the white abolitionist Parker Pillsbury, compared the NAACP national convention in Boston in 1911 to "an old-fashioned anti-slavery meeting."[90] If Pillsbury ever attended an antislavery meeting, it was as a child, as he was born in 1849. Antebellum juvenile abolitionists were at the forefront of the postwar struggle for Black equality.

Douglass's children, like Garrison's, did not always agree with their father politically. The Civil War saw the same kind of tensions between Douglass and his oldest son, Lewis, as it did between Garrison and his son George, though on a different matter than nonresistance, a principle to which few Black abolitionists fully adhered. In the fall of 1862, Lewis was one of five hundred free African Americans who signed up to go to Central America as part of a colonization scheme supported by Lincoln. Douglass, though he had briefly considered emigrating to Haiti in 1861, had always been a virulent opponent of state-sponsored colonization. He was particularly incensed at some of the blatantly racist arguments used by Lincoln to justify the removal of African Americans. In *Douglass' Monthly*, he denounced the president's "inconsistencies, his pride of race and blood, his contempt for negroes and his canting hypocrisy."[91] It must have come as a shock when his twenty-one-year-old son announced that he wanted to try his luck in Panama (or Lincolnia, as the settlement was to be named). Lewis felt that his prospects in the United States were too limited. He may also have aspired for a degree of independence from his parents, especially from his father, with whom he had been working on *Frederick Douglass' Paper* for several years; George Thompson Garrison had likewise spent time in Minnesota and Kansas in his early twenties so as to escape the office of the *Liberator* for a while.[92] Whatever Lewis's reasons, Douglass was no less respectful of his choice than Garrison had been of his own son's. He went as far as recommending Lewis to Senator Samuel Clarke Pomeroy, the administration's chief promoter of colonization. Douglass made no mystery of his conflicted sentiments in his letter to Pomeroy. "I assent to neither the justice nor the wisdom of colonizing the free colored people in Central America," he wrote. "To see my children usefully and happily settled in this, the land of their birth and ancestors, has been the hope and ambition of my manhood," he went on, "but events stronger than any power I can oppose to them, have convinced my son that the chances here are all against him, and he desires to join your colony." "I shall follow him with my blessing, if I do not follow him personally," he concluded, signing off, "Sadly and truly yours, Fred'k Douglass."[93] Lewis's plan to move to Panama was not an endorsement of colonization per se: it is better interpreted as a pragmatic decision motivated in part by his young age. Still, it was probably the cause of many a heated discussion in the Douglass household—discussions that paralleled those taking place in more public fora such as the Black press and the Colored Conventions. In that sense, the episode marked an important moment in Lewis's intellectual and political maturing.

In the end, the scheme ran into diplomatic problems and had to be abandoned. Lewis never left the country. Instead, he and his younger brother Charles did something that their father was already too old to do: they enlisted in the Union army as soon as it opened to Black soldiers. The two brothers were recruited personally by their father into the Massachusetts Fifty-Fourth Volunteer Infantry Regiment, while Frederick Jr. went to Mississippi as a recruiter of Black troops, also at his father's behest.[94] Born and raised as abolitionists, the Douglass brothers helped make the war an abolition war and through their actions paved the way for Black citizenship. Research into the postwar lives of the Douglass children is still ongoing, and much new information is likely to surface in the multigenerational biography of the Douglass family currently being written by Ezra Greenspan.[95] As biographers of Douglass have shown, however, the Douglass children, who had been early associates of their parents' antislavery labors, never stopped fighting for civil rights. Black abolitionists could ill afford to abandon activism after the war: their material well-being and that of their own children depended on the continuation of the struggle for equality. Black juvenile abolitionists grew into committed activists who brought about the gains of Reconstruction and then did their best to preserve them in an increasingly hostile racial climate. The Douglass children were determined "to combat the survival of what Frederick Douglass interpreted as the 'spirit of slavery,'" Celeste-Marie Bernier and Andrew Taylor write. In the postemancipation era, "they delivered speeches and wrote essays on a variety of subjects," including discriminatory legislation, scientific racism, lynch law, capital punishment, unfair housing, and segregated schools.[96] Their antislavery education served them well. Lewis and Frederick Jr. shared editorial duties with their father when he launched the *New National Era* in Washington, DC, in 1870. They were participants in the Colored Conventions movement, stepping into the leadership roles that their father had previously occupied. In 1896, over a year after Douglass's death and barely a few weeks after the Supreme Court had rendered its notorious *Plessy v. Ferguson* ruling, Rosetta delivered a stirring speech at the founding meeting of the National Association of Colored Women. She had become, as one contemporary noted, "a restless agitator for the cause of humanity."[97]

Lillie Chace turned eighteen in the days preceding the adoption of the Thirteenth Amendment. The immediate postwar period was a time of rejoicing for the Chaces, as the war was over and the long-pursued goal of abolition finally attained, but it was also one of doubt and depression for Lillie. As far as the young woman could remember, the abolition movement had given structure to her life, providing "not only ideals and visions, but friendships, an extended family, meaningful work, in short, a protected and certain world in which she had grown to maturity," in the words of her biographer Elizabeth Stevens. Its demise was, paradoxically, "a great personal disaster for her." That it coincided with the end of her childhood—and with several deaths in the family— made the transition particularly difficult. Lillie herself put it eloquently when she wrote that children like herself "were trained for a conflict in which they were not permitted to fight." Except that the abolition movement was not dead. Its egalitarian ethos survived the Civil War, as has already been made clear, and led abolitionists not only to press for Black equality but also to engage in a host of other causes, as they had done before the war. William Lloyd Garrison Jr. was an ardent defender of women's suffrage, while Wendell Phillips Garrison reverted to his former radical outlook and became an anti-imperialist in the last years of his life. Lillie Chace was also involved in women's rights activism to some degree, contributing pieces to the *Woman's Journal* in the decade following the war, but most importantly she used her pen to draw attention to the plight of women and children operatives in the textile mills of Rhode Island, where she still lived. The daughter of a cotton manufacturer, Lillie Chace had firsthand knowledge of life in and outside the mills; she knew about the brutal working conditions, the long hours, the squalid housing. She portrayed these harsh realities in a series of short stories first published in the *Atlantic Monthly* and later collected in a volume entitled *Poverty Grass* (1886). She also published several essays on the same topic, including the four-part "Studies of Factory Life" (1888–89), in which she tentatively endorsed labor unions and strikes. In 1893, Lillie Chace Wyman, as she was then known, traveled to Providence to testify on behalf of the Factory Inspection Act, a bill that would regulate child labor, sanitary conditions, and hours of employment and mandate a woman factory inspector to oversee implementation. It was passed the following year.[98]

Wyman's antislavery education had prepared her for her later career as an activist writer concerned with the effects of unfettered capitalism on northern women textile workers. At the same time, Wyman's postwar interest in labor issues was also a reaction against the insufficiencies of her antebellum education. She suggested as much in "Luke Gardiner's Love," the only story in *Poverty Grass* not previously published in the *Atlantic Monthly*. Though primarily focused on the relationship between a poor Irish woman operative, Eden Ronian, and the eponymous character, an American man of English descent, the story is notable for a scene taking place at the home of Mr. Comstock, the Quaker mill owner. The Comstock home is clearly modeled on Wyman's own childhood home: there are "portraits, in oval gilt frames, of Wm. Lloyd Garrison, Wendell Phillips, and Theodore Parker" hanging on the walls.[99] As Mr. Comstock is reading the *Liberator* and his wife is sewing, a ghastly-looking girl—Flit, Eden's disabled sister—slips into the house, begging for money and frightening Mrs. Comstock. She is soon ushered out with one cent in her pocket. The scene can be read as a variation on what Charles Dickens, in his 1852–53 novel *Bleak House*, famously called "telescopic philanthropy."[100] As attuned as Mr. Comstock is to the antislavery cause, he seems indifferent to the economic hardships of his own workers. Of course, Wyman did not question the sincerity of her parents' devotion to abolition; rather, she pointed out what she identified as its blind spots. She herself, however, might not have been able to see these blind spots but for her early lessons in abolition, which had sensitized her to injustice. In a striking reversal of roles, Wyman sensitized her mother to the labor question. Elizabeth Buffum Chace did not address the grim conditions of textile workers before late in her life. She did so under various influences, including that of her daughter, who began writing about the plight of the mill workers a few years before her mother spoke out on the subject. One of Elizabeth Buffum Chace's most important contributions was a paper titled "Factory Women and Girls of New England," which was read at the 1881 congress of the Association for the Advancement of Women in Buffalo, New York.[101] Perhaps the best proof of the success of Lillie Chace Wyman's political education was that she was, in turn, able to educate her aging mother on the reform issue that most mattered to her after the Civil War.

Wyman also understood the importance of raising political matters such as slavery and racial prejudice with children, as her mother had done with her. She did so in the *Brownies' Book*, the first US magazine explicitly targeting African American children, edited by W. E. B. Du Bois between January 1920 and December 1921. In "Girls Together" (1921), she recalled the rise of immediatism in the antebellum period, noting children's interest for and involvement in abolitionist work. She mentioned the "half-grown children" of the Plymouth Juvenile Anti-Slavery Society, such as Abby Morton Diaz, later an author of children's literature, who "went without butter to save money to give to the anti-slavery cause." She discussed her and her siblings' encounters with abolition.[102] Du Bois himself, who had worked alongside Francis Jackson Garrison and Oswald Garrison Villard at the NAACP's founding, was convinced that children were key actors in the Black freedom struggle. Between 1912 and 1934, the *Crisis*, which he edited for the NAACP, included a yearly "Children's Number," which provided young readers with stories, poetry, and games but also accounts of political occurrences and lynchings.[103] The *Brownies' Book*, an offshoot of the "Children's Number," likewise imagined a "politically savvy and involved child reader."[104] Its regular news column, "As the Crow Flies," written by Du Bois in the voice of an anthropomorphized bird, harked back to the caged birds of pre–Civil War juvenile antislavery literature.[105] As Wyman's contribution made clear, there were continuities between antebellum juvenile abolitionism and Du Bois's attempt at centering African American children in the fight against racism, social and legal injustices, and antiblack violence. The *Slave's Friend* and the *Brownies' Book*, despite their differences, belonged to the same generic "family." They were distant cousins, perhaps, rather than direct descendants. Du Bois's philosophy of childhood, as expressed in his essay "The Immortal Child" (1920), was consonant with the abolitionists'. Like them, Du Bois realized that the "great battle . . . against color prejudice" would be won not in his day but in the day of his generation's children's children. Like them, he believed that racial issues should be frankly discussed with African American children; their survival depended on it. Du Bois was certain that children were intellectually equipped to understand such matters. "Your child is wiser than you think," he wrote to parents. Children would be all the stronger—and all the more inclined to act—for their knowledge of the workings of racism. "Is democracy a failure?" Du Bois asked. "Train up citizens that will make it succeed."[106] It was that very same lesson that abolitionists had put into practice close to a century before.

Epilogue

"IN YOUR HANDS. CLIMATE CHANGE DEMANDS ACTION. NOW."
So ran the front-page headline of "The New York Times for Kids," a
monthly section of the *New York Times* for readers aged eight to thirteen, in August 2022. The whole issue was devoted to the environmental
crisis, with articles on a deadly drought in Somalia and yet another
heat wave in Europe. The idea that children might have a role to play
in the climate movement would have seemed odd to some people until
recently. Yet one of the most visible faces of environmental activism in
the past few years has been that of Greta Thunberg, a young woman
born in 2003. The activist was fifteen when she staged her first protest outside the Swedish Parliament. Her early "school strikes" have
developed into global strikes organized by the international youth-led
movement Fridays for Future. Young people have good reasons for calling for urgent climate action. They, rather than their parents, will suffer
the worst consequences of the environmental crisis. "What can children do for climate?" is the question that the *New York Times* set out to
answer.

Juvenile involvement in social movements, as this book has shown,
is not a novel phenomenon. It has a long history that begins with the
participation of children and youth in the Anglo-American abolition
movement. Antebellum abolitionists, in keeping with the new, positive
conception of childhood that emerged in the eighteenth century, saw
children as allies of the antislavery effort. They devoted considerable
energy to making sure northern children knew about the horror and
injustice of slavery and the legal and political system protecting it. Abolitionist parents read slave narratives to their children and took them
to antislavery meetings; teachers had their pupils recite antislavery orations and write essays about racial prejudice. Children themselves, as
they grew up, engaged in the struggle for freedom on their own terms.
A number of them became committed abolitionists and, after the Civil

War, campaigned for other social justice causes. Their youthful activism might serve as an inspiration for today's young climate activists.

Scholars and activists have long drawn parallels between the nineteenth-century abolition movement and twentieth- and twenty-first-century environmental activism. As early as the 1960s, Rachel Carson's *Silent Spring* (1962), an exposé of the hazards of synthetic pesticides, was touted as "an *Uncle Tom's Cabin* of a book,—the sort that will help turn the tide."[1] Carson's book helped ignite the environmental movement in much the same way that Stowe's novel led a number of hitherto-unconcerned Americans to denounce slavery. More recently, environmentalists such as Naomi Klein have proposed abolition as a model for the climate movement. "As an international movement that created a paradigm shift similar to the one needed globally today on climate," Teresa Goddu writes, "antislavery serves as an inspirational success story for many." Among other things, the climate movement needs to radically transform people's perspectives on climate change. One way to achieve this, Goddu argues with the precedent of slave narratives in mind, would be to "foreground eyewitness testimonies of places and people."[2]

Abolitionists have another lesson for us. They took children seriously. They provided children with the intellectual tools to understand slavery and racial prejudice and paid attention to what children had to say in return. They saw childhood as a force for social change. Likewise, the climate movement needs the fervor and determination of young people. Children should be encouraged to act, and their perspectives should be taken into account. Juvenile abolitionists of the past sometimes speak to us in strangely prophetic ways. The words pronounced by Henry Peterson in relation to slavery in 1838, quoted in chapter 3, take on new meaning in the age of global warming: "Manhood and old age may pass away ere the tempest shall burst in its fury,—but the youth of the present . . . may be doomed to abide the storm." The youth of our present will certainly have to abide a more literal storm. Their calls for *immediate* action have largely been ignored.

The abolitionist past resonates with our environmentally concerned present. Before Greta Thunberg, there was Anna Elizabeth Dickinson (figure E.1). Dickinson was born in Philadelphia in 1842. Both her parents were abolitionist Quakers who regularly opened their home to

Figure E.1. Anna Elizabeth Dickinson (1842–1932), ca. 1863. Courtesy of the National Portrait Gallery, Smithsonian Institution; gift of Laurie A. Baty.

fugitive slaves and reform-minded visitors such as Frederick Douglass and Robert Purvis. Dickinson's father died when she was five years old, leaving his wife in reduced financial circumstances, though no less committed to antislavery. Dickinson herself was thirteen when she first took a public stance against slavery. She did so in the pages of William Lloyd Garrison's *Liberator*. A newspaper reader, Dickinson had come across a story describing how a schoolteacher in Lexington, Kentucky, had been tarred and feathered after he had denounced slavery in the Ohio press. "I could not help expressing my feelings upon reading of this barbarous atrocity," Dickinson wrote to Garrison. The young girl emphasized freedom of the press rather than the horrors of slavery, yet she made her detestation of the institution explicit. "If this is done in the State 'nearest to emancipation,' what must be the condition of that the *farthest* from it?" she asked. "And yet we are told to sit down quietly and fold our hands, and have *patience*, for in God's good time, the bright hour of freedom and the slave, for which we have prayed so long, will surely come!"[3]

Youthful impatience with slavery and the means used to silence its critics was what drove Anna Elizabeth Dickinson, as well as her friend Lillie Chace, with whom she had a regular correspondence, to act. The latter confessed to her friend that she felt it hard to be heard as a child. In 1860, Chace, soon to turn thirteen herself, wrote to Dickinson, "I come to command with thee, dear Anna, with a heart throbbing with indignation, and cheeks burning with suppressed excitement. Father and a friend are discussing the all absorbing slavery question in the parlor, and, as a last resort, I have fled from the scene of contention, to vent my justly excited anger (!) on paper. Not lately have I had to struggle so hard, to keep back the indignant words that sought expression, as tonight: and yet I felt that it would ill become me, a *child*, and a comparative stranger, to oppose the views of a man."[4] Dickinson had fewer qualms about speaking out as a young woman. Earlier that year, she had given her first antislavery lecture at the annual meeting of the Pennsylvania Anti-Slavery Society, sharing a platform with more mature activists. She soon became known for her fiery speeches on slavery and women's rights. In 1864, she was invited to lecture in the Capitol. For over an hour, the young orator railed against what she perceived as the administration's overly cautious approach to emancipation and civil rights. She did so in front of a crowd of two thousand people that included President Abraham Lincoln and his wife.[5]

Young climate activists demanding action on the part of world leaders have deployed the same kind of rhetoric that Dickinson did over a century and a half ago. Like juvenile abolitionists of old, they have formed organizations and signed petitions. Some, including in the United States, have taken their governments to court over climate inaction: in *Held v. State of Montana*, sixteen plaintiffs aged five to twenty-two sued their home state, arguing that the government was violating their constitutional right to a clean and healthful environment. The trial was held in June 2023.[6] As children and youth are making themselves heard on climate change as well as other issues such as gun violence and racial justice, scholars in various fields have considered the possibility that all age restrictions on voting be removed and children be enfranchised.[7] Such a bold proposition is unlikely to materialize in the near future; it is also unclear what effects it would have. In the meantime, we would do well to take a leaf out of the abolitionists' book and listen to what young people have been trying to tell us.

ACKNOWLEDGMENTS

This book would not exist without the help and support of many people and institutions. It is my pleasure to acknowledge them here.

I have had the opportunity to present my work on juvenile abolitionism at various seminars and conferences, where I received useful critical feedback. Many thanks to Hélène Quanquin and Jesse Olsavsky for inviting me to discuss this book as it was still being written at Université de Lille and Duke Kunshan University, respectively; to Anna Mae Duane for including me on her panel at the eleventh biennial conference of the Society for the History of Children and Youth; to Esther Cyna and Nora Nafaa for organizing the "Education in the United States" symposium at Université de Versailles Saint-Quentin-en-Yvelines in June 2023, where I was able to present parts of chapter 4.

An early draft of this book was submitted as part of my *habilitation à diriger des recherches*, supervised by Marie-Jeanne Rossignol at Université Paris Cité. Fabrice Bensimon, Laurence Cossu-Beaumont, François Furstenberg, Claire Parfait, and Will Slauter kindly agreed to sit on the evaluation committee. They were the manuscript's first readers, and I am grateful for their comments and criticisms, which have helped me rethink some of my arguments. Completing this book would have been a much more painful process without the time and funding provided by the Institut Universitaire de France. Robert Levine and Manisha Sinha recommended me for a fellowship there, for which I cannot thank them enough. I owe them an intellectual debt too: their scholarship has been a constant source of inspiration.

For assistance and encouragement at various stages of researching this book and for conversations that have shaped it in a number of ways, I am thankful to Susanna Ashton, Alke Boss, Claire Bourhis-Mariotti, Nathalie Caron, Marissa Carrere, Mark Cheathem, Myriam Cottias, Marlene Daut, Elsa Devienne, Brigitte Fielder, Daniel Foliard, David Gellman, Molly Hardy, Mischa Honeck, Nicolas Martin-Breteau,

Sandrine Parageau, Allan Potofsky, Frédéric Régent, Cécile Roudeau, Nele Sawallisch, Jonathan Senchyne, Bryan Sinche, Maria Beliaeva Solomon, Elizabeth Stevens, Julie Vatain-Corfdir, Michael Winship, and Natalie Zacek. I gratefully acknowledge my colleagues in American studies at Université Paris Nanterre, including Auréliane Narvaez, Caroline Rolland-Diamond, Bradley Smith, and Agnès Trouillet. Special thanks to two wonderful colleagues who have become close friends, Hugo Chatellier and Cécile Viollain.

Working with Clara Platter at New York University Press has been a fantastic experience. She has believed in this project from the moment I reached out to her, for which I am deeply thankful. I thank Andrew Katz, Veronica Knutson, and Alexia Traganas for their work on the manuscript. The illustrations were obtained thanks to the help of Brianne Barrett at the American Antiquarian Society; Sean Casey, Jay Moschella, and Kathleen Monahan at the Boston Public Library; Eddie Hughes and Angela Proctor at Southern University and A&M College's John B. Cade Library; and Helen Gunn at Indiana University's Lilly Library.

My final thanks go to my friends Laura Ménard, Mathias Degoute, Juliette Dorotte, Anne-Florence Quaireau, and Agathe Bernier-Monod, and to my family, Lucile Roy, Jean Roy, Claudine Ruimi, Jennifer Ruimi, and Pierre Troullier. Everything I write, I write for my mother, Jacqueline Nacache, whom I love and admire. My partner, Thomas Merly-Alpa, has provided love, support, and stability. He is the kindest, most patient person I know. Thank you for being here.

* * *

A version of chapter 3 was first published in *American Nineteenth Century History* in 2023. I acknowledge Taylor & Francis for granting me permission to reprint this material.

NOTES

INTRODUCTION

1 "Pic Nic at Dedham," *Child's Friend* 1, no. 1 (October 1843): 21–27. For Charles Christopher Follen's age, see Eliza Lee Follen, *The Life of Charles Follen* (Boston: Thomas H. Webb, 1844), 177–78.

2 "Pic Nic at Dedham" was reprinted in Eliza Lee Follen, *The Liberty Cap* (Boston: Leonard C. Bowles, 1846), 10–21.

3 See J. R. Kerr-Ritchie, *Rites of August First: Emancipation Day in the Black Atlantic World* (Baton Rouge: Louisiana State University Press, 2007).

4 "The First of August at Dedham," *Liberator*, August 11, 1843; "Dedham Picnic in Continuation," *Liberator*, August 18, 1843.

5 John A. Collins, preface to *The Anti-Slavery Picknick: A Collection of Speeches, Poems, Dialogues and Songs* (Boston: H. W. Williams, 1842), 4. Collins first called for the organization of antislavery picnics in "The First of August," *Liberator*, June 24, 1842.

6 "Juvenile Anti-Slavery Societies," *Liberator*, January 14, 1837.

7 "Juvenile Anti-Slavery Societies," *New York Evangelist*, December 24, 1836.

8 "Juvenile Anti-Slavery Societies" (*Liberator*).

9 William Lloyd Garrison, preface to *Juvenile Poems, for the Use of Free American Children, of Every Complexion* (Boston: Garrison and Knapp, 1835), n.p.

10 Steven Mintz, *Huck's Raft: A History of American Childhood* (Cambridge, MA: Harvard University Press, 2004), 76.

11 Colin Heywood, *A History of Childhood: Children and Childhood in the West from Medieval to Modern Times* (Cambridge, UK: Polity, 2001), 23–27; Mintz, *Huck's Raft*, 3, 75–77. On the establishment of a public school system, see Johann N. Neem, *Democracy's Schools: The Rise of Public Education in America* (Baltimore: Johns Hopkins University Press, 2017).

12 Collins, preface to *Anti-Slavery Picknick*, 3.

13 On the *Slave's Friend*, see chapter 2; on the *Anti-Slavery Alphabet*, see, for instance, Martha L. Sledge, "'A Is an Abolitionist': The *Anti-Slavery Alphabet* and the Politics of Literacy," in *Enterprising Youth: Social Values and Acculturation in Nineteenth-Century American Children's Literature*, ed. Monika Elbert (New York: Routledge, 2008), 69–82; James G. Basker, introduction to *American Antislavery Writings: Colonial Beginnings to Emancipation*, ed. James G. Basker (New York: Library of America, 2012), xxxvi. The most sustained examination of juvenile

abolitionism from a literary perspective is Deborah C. De Rosa, *Domestic Abolitionism and Juvenile Literature, 1830–1865* (Albany: State University of New York
Press, 2003).

14 "Uncle Tom's Cabin: or, Life among the Lowly," *National Era*, April 1, 1852.

15 De Rosa, *Domestic Abolitionism and Juvenile Literature*, 121.

16 Barbara Hochman, *"Uncle Tom's Cabin" and the Reading Revolution: Race, Literacy, Childhood, and Fiction, 1851–1911* (Amherst: University of Massachusetts
Press, 2011).

17 "Pic Nic at Dedham," 21.

18 Corinne T. Field, "Why Little Thinkers Are a Big Deal: The Relevance of Childhood Studies to Intellectual History," *Modern Intellectual History* 14, no. 1
(2017): 280. Scholars of slavery, abolition, and African American culture have
considerably broadened the scope of intellectual history in recent years. The
African American intellectual historians Brandon R. Byrd, Leslie M. Alexander,
and Russell Rickford have suggested that we "reconsider existing definitions
of and assumptions about intellectual history by foregrounding Black actors,"
while Peter Wirzbicki, in his book on abolitionism and Transcendentalism,
has sought to "take seriously the traditional history of ideas—texts, arguments,
writers—while simultaneously examining how those ideas left the page, so to
speak, went out in the open air, and rambled around in the world of people and
things." In a study of Black-led vigilance committees and the fugitives they
assisted, Jesse Olsavsky has called runaway slaves "the leading . . . intellectuals
of abolitionism." I see Black and white children as part of this newly conceived,
more inclusive intellectual history. Brandon R. Byrd, Leslie M. Alexander, and
Russell Rickford, introduction to *Ideas in Unexpected Places: Reimagining Black
Intellectual History*, ed. Brandon R. Byrd, Leslie M. Alexander and Russell
Rickford (Evanston, IL: Northwestern University Press, 2022), 3; Peter Wirz-
bicki, *Fighting for the Higher Law: Black and White Transcendentalists against
Slavery* (Philadelphia: University of Pennsylvania Press, 2021), 6; Jesse Olsavsky,
*The Most Absolute Abolition: Runaways, Vigilance Committees, and the Rise of
Revolutionary Abolitionism, 1835–1861* (Baton Rouge: Louisiana State University
Press, 2022), 49.

19 Susan Paul, *Memoir of James Jackson, the Attentive and Obedient Scholar, Who
Died in Boston, October 31, 1833, Aged Six Years and Eleven Months*, ed. Lois Brown
(Cambridge, MA: Harvard University Press, 2000), 70.

20 My own work is largely indebted to two foundational studies of abolition centering African Americans, namely, Benjamin Quarles, *Black Abolitionists* (New York:
Oxford University Press, 1969); and Manisha Sinha, *The Slave's Cause: A History
of Abolition* (New Haven, CT: Yale University Press, 2016). Both authors offer brief
but useful discussions of juvenile abolitionism.

21 James Oliver Horton and Lois E. Horton, *In Hope of Liberty: Culture, Community
and Protest among Northern Free Blacks, 1700–1860* (New York: Oxford University
Press, 1997), 217.

22 Jim Casey, "'We Need a Press—a Press of Our Own': The Black Press beyond Abolition," *Civil War History* 68, no. 2 (2022): 117.

23 Patrick Rael, *Black Identity and Black Protest in the Antebellum North* (Chapel Hill: University of North Carolina Press, 2002), 118–208; Erica L. Ball, *To Live an Antislavery Life: Personal Politics and the Antebellum Middle Class* (Athens: University of Georgia Press, 2012).

24 "Education. No. II," *Freedom's Journal*, April 6, 1827.

25 Corinne T. Field and Nicholas L. Syrett, introduction to "Chronological Age: A Useful Category of Historical Analysis," *American Historical Review* 125, no. 2 (2020): 371–84; James Marten, ed., *Children and Youth during the Civil War Era* (New York: New York University Press, 2012); James Marten, *The Children's Civil War* (Chapel Hill: University of North Carolina Press, 1998); Jon Grinspan, *The Virgin Vote: How Young Americans Made Democracy Social, Politics Personal, and Voting Popular in the Nineteenth Century* (Chapel Hill: University of North Carolina Press, 2016); Corinne T. Field and Nicholas L. Syrett, introduction to *Age in America: The Colonial Era to the Present*, ed. Corinne T. Field and Nicholas L. Syrett (New York: New York University Press, 2015), 4.

26 Wilma King, *Stolen Childhood: Slave Youth in Nineteenth-Century America*, 2nd ed. (Bloomington: Indiana University Press, 2011); Crystal Lynn Webster, *Beyond the Boundaries of Childhood: African American Children in the Antebellum North* (Chapel Hill: University of North Carolina Press, 2021); Vanessa M. Holden, "Generation, Resistance, and Survival: African-American Children and the Southampton Rebellion of 1831," *Slavery and Abolition* 38, no. 4 (2017): 673–96; Kabria Baumgartner, *In Pursuit of Knowledge: Black Women and Educational Activism in Antebellum America* (New York: New York University Press, 2019).

27 Sinha, *Slave's Cause*, 254.

28 Michael E. Jirik, "Abolition and Academe: Struggles for Freedom and Equality at British and American Colleges, 1742–1855" (PhD diss., University of Massachusetts Amherst, 2019).

29 William Henry Webb to Henry Clarke Wright, n.d., Henry Clarke Wright Letter Book, Cape Ann Museum.

30 V. P. Franklin, *The Young Crusaders: The Untold Story of the Children and Teenagers Who Galvanized the Civil Rights Movement* (Boston: Beacon, 2021), 2. See also Rebecca de Schweinitz, *If We Could Change the World: Young People and America's Long Struggle for Racial Equality* (Chapel Hill: University of North Carolina Press, 2009); Mintz, *Huck's Raft*, 302–8, 310–11, 317–19.

31 Quoted in Jon N. Hale, *A New Kind of Youth: Historically Black High Schools and Southern Student Activism, 1920–1975* (Chapel Hill: University of North Carolina Press, 2022), 1.

32 On the "wave" terminology, see Patrick Rael, *Eighty-Eight Years: The Long Death of Slavery in the United States, 1777–1865* (Athens: University of Georgia Press, 2015), 2.

33 "For Children. Anti-Slavery Children of Providence," *Friend of Man*, June 28, 1837.

CHAPTER 1. "WHAT CAN CHILDREN DO FOR THE SLAVES?"

1 "A Talk by the Fireside.—No. III. What Can Children Do for the Slaves?," *Liberator*, April 7, 1837. See De Rosa, *Domestic Abolitionism and Juvenile Literature*, 11, 108, 114.

2 Sinha, *Slave's Cause*, 256–65, 285–87.

3 Brigitte Fielder, "Frederick Douglass's Narrative of Childhood," *Black Perspectives* (AAIHS), April 23, 2019, www.aaihs.org.

4 Frederick Douglass, *Life and Times of Frederick Douglass*, ed. Celeste-Marie Bernier and Andrew Taylor (Oxford: Oxford University Press, 2022), 68.

5 King, *Stolen Childhood*, 262–313.

6 Holden, "Generation, Resistance, and Survival," 676. King writes that "children and youth played no role in the insurrectionary plans of Gabriel Prosser, Nat Turner, or Joseph Cinqué" (*Stolen Childhood*, 296).

7 Sarah Levine-Gronningsater, "Delivering Freedom: Gradual Emancipation, Black Legal Culture, and the Origins of Sectional Crisis in New York, 1759–1870" (PhD diss., University of Chicago, 2014), 9, 137.

8 Paul J. Polgar, *Standard-Bearers of Equality: America's First Abolition Movement* (Chapel Hill: University of North Carolina Press, 2019), 122–65.

9 Absalom Jones and Richard Allen, *A Narrative of the Proceedings of the Black People, during the Late Awful Calamity in Philadelphia, in the Year 1793* (Philadelphia: William W. Woodward, 1794), 24. See Polgar, *Standard-Bearers of Equality*, 181.

10 Leslie M. Harris, *In the Shadow of Slavery: African Americans in New York City, 1626–1863* (Chicago: University of Chicago Press, 2003), 132.

11 See Anna Mae Duane, *Educated for Freedom: The Incredible Story of Two Fugitive Schoolboys Who Grew Up to Change a Nation* (New York: New York University Press, 2020).

12 William Hamilton, *An Oration Delivered in the African Zion Church, on the Fourth of July, 1827, in Commemoration of the Abolition of Domestic Slavery in this State* (New York: Gray and Bunce, 1827), 8.

13 François Furstenberg, *In the Name of the Father: Washington's Legacy, Slavery, and the Making of a Nation* (New York: Penguin, 2006), 41–42.

14 See Debra Jackson, "A Black Journalist in Civil War Virginia: Robert Hamilton and the *Anglo-African*," *Virginia Magazine of History and Biography* 116, no. 1 (2008): 42–72.

15 Sinha, *Slave's Cause*, 107–8.

16 Paula T. Connolly, *Slavery in American Children's Literature, 1790–2010* (Iowa City: University of Iowa Press, 2013), 21.

17 Noah Webster Jr., *The Little Reader's Assistant* (Hartford, CT: Elisha Babcock, 1790), 40–43, 45–46 (quote at 46).

18 Caleb Bingham, *The American Preceptor* (Boston: Manning and Loring, 1794), 84–88, 113–14.

19 Frederick Douglass, *Narrative of the Life of Frederick Douglass, an American Slave*, ed. Celeste-Marie Bernier (Peterborough, ON: Broadview Press, 2018), 117.

20 Caleb Bingham, *The Columbian Orator*, ed. David W. Blight (New York: New York University Press, 1998), 256.

21 Jedidiah Morse, *The American Geography* (Elizabethtown, NJ: Shepard Kollock, 1789), 530; Susanna Rowson, *An Abridgment of Universal Geography* (Boston: John West, 1806), 272. Morse's anti-slave-trade diatribe is actually lifted from the second volume of a book by the British author Thomas Percival, *A Father's Instructions to His Children* (1777). Rowson had used almost identical terms in an earlier collection of tales, *The Inquisitor* (1788). On Morse, see Anne Baker, *Heartless Immensity: Literature, Culture, and Geography in Antebellum America* (Ann Arbor: University of Michigan Press, 2006), 125; on Rowson, see Basker, *American Antislavery Writings*, 116. For a more detailed treatment of the representation of slavery in early US schoolbooks, see Ruth Miller Elson, *Guardians of Tradition: American Schoolbooks in the Nineteenth Century* (Lincoln: University of Nebraska Press, 1964), 88–93.

22 Robert Robinson, *Slavery Inconsistent with the Spirit of Christianity: A Sermon Preached at Cambridge, on Sunday, Feb. 10, 1788* (Cambridge, UK: J. Archdeacon, 1788), 24–25. See David Turley, *The Culture of English Antislavery, 1780–1860* (London: Routledge, 1991), 24.

23 Thomas Clarkson, *The History of the Rise, Progress, and Accomplishment of the Abolition of the African Slave-Trade by the British Parliament*, vol. 2 (London: Longman, Hurst, Rees and Orme, 1808), 349–50. See Seymour Drescher, *Abolition: A History of Slavery and Antislavery* (Cambridge: Cambridge University Press, 2009), 221.

24 Esther Copley, *A History of the Slave Trade and Its Abolition* (London: Sunday-School Union, 1836), 295.

25 Kathryn Gleadle and Ryan Hanley, "Children against Slavery: Juvenile Agency and the Sugar Boycotts in Britain," *Transactions of the Royal Historical Society* 30 (2020): 97–117 (quote at 111).

26 Vincent Carretta, *Equiano, the African: Biography of a Self-Made Man* (Athens: University of Georgia Press, 2005), 355.

27 Margaret Escott, "Corbett, Panton," in *The House of Commons, 1820–1832*, vol. 4, ed. D. R. Fisher (Cambridge: Cambridge University Press, 2009), 749.

28 J. R. Oldfield, *Popular Politics and British Anti-Slavery: The Mobilisation of Public Opinion against the Slave Trade, 1787–1807* (London: Routledge, 1998), 147–48.

29 Gleadle and Hanley, "Children against Slavery," 103–4.

30 Clare Midgley, *Women against Slavery: The British Campaigns, 1780–1870* (London: Routledge, 1992), 61.

31 John W. Frick, *Theatre, Culture and Temperance Reform in Nineteenth-Century America* (Cambridge: Cambridge University Press, 2003), 64.

32 On the redemptive child in temperance fiction, see Karen Sánchez-Eppler, *Dependent States: The Child's Part in Nineteenth-Century American Culture* (Chicago: University of Chicago Press, 2005), 69–100.

33 Donald Yacovone, "The Transformation of the Black Temperance Movement, 1827–1854: An Interpretation," *Journal of the Early Republic* 8, no. 3 (1988): 282–83.

34 American Anti-Slavery Society, *Second Annual Report of the American Anti-Slavery Society* (New York: William S. Dorr, 1835), 52.

35 "Juvenile Anti-Slavery Society," *Slave's Friend* 2, no. 5 (1837): 4.

36 "Progress of Temperance," *Boston Recorder*, December 2, 1829; *Boston Commercial Gazette*, June 16, 1831; "Napoli, Cattaragus Co.," *Boston Recorder*, September 28, 1831.

37 "Hartford Colored People's Temperance Societies," *Liberator*, February 22, 1834; National Convention of Colored Citizens, *Minutes of the National Convention of Colored Citizens* (New York: Piercy and Reed, 1843), 38. Susan Paul's Juvenile Choir, discussed in chapter 4, sang temperance as well as antislavery songs. Paul, *Memoir of James Jackson*, 126.

38 Collins, preface to *Anti-Slavery Picknick*, 4.

39 Charles J. Warren, *The Cold Water Army* (New Haven, CT: Hitchcock and Stafford, 1842), ii.

40 Thomas P. Hunt, *Life and Thoughts of Rev. Thomas P. Hunt: An Autobiography* (Wilkes-Barre, PA: Robert Baur and Son, 1901), 10, 262; John Marsh, *Temperance Recollections: Labors, Defeats, Triumphs. An Autobiography* (New York: Charles Scribner, 1866), 143. On Hunt, see William P. White, "A Historic Nineteenth Century Character," *Journal of the Presbyterian Historical Society* 10, no. 5 (1920): 161–74.

41 Warren, *Cold Water Army*, 28.

42 Connecticut Temperance Society Pledge, ca. 1842, MS 73428, Connecticut Historical Society.

43 "Temperance Celebrations on the Fourth of July," *Emancipator*, July 22, 1841; "The Glorious Anniversary of Independence," *Journal of the American Temperance Union*, August 1841, 116, 114.

44 On the abolitionist critique of noise on the Fourth of July, see W. Caleb McDaniel, "The Fourth and the First: Abolitionist Holidays, Respectability, and Radical Interracial Reform," *American Quarterly* 57, no. 1 (2005): 134–38.

45 "Letters from the Editor. No. II," *Liberator*, August 18, 1843.

46 "Juvenile Temperance Meeting," *Herald of Freedom*, March 18, 1837.

47 "Juvenile Temperance Meeting," *Emancipator*, March 11, 1841.

48 Teresa A. Goddu, "Reform," in *The Oxford History of Popular Print Culture*, vol. 5, *US Popular Print Culture to 1860*, ed. Ronald J. Zboray and Mary Saracino Zboray (Oxford: Oxford University Press, 2019), 602.

49 Anne Scott MacLeod, *A Moral Tale: Children's Fiction and American Culture, 1820–1860* (Hamden, CT: Archon Books, 1975), 108.

50 Charles Jewett, preface to *The Temperance Toy* (Boston: Whipple and Damrell, 1840), ii.

51 Charles Jewett, *The Youth's Temperance Lecturer* (Boston: Whipple and Damrell, 1841), 23.

52 John C. Crandall, "Patriotism and Humanitarian Reform in Children's Literature, 1825–1860," *American Quarterly* 21, no. 1 (1969): 9, 10.

53 Hannah Townsend and Mary Townsend, *The Anti-Slavery Alphabet* (Philadelphia: Printed for the Anti-Slavery Fair, 1846), 16.

54 "Twenty-Five," *Genius of Universal Emancipation*, January 1, 1830.

55 William Lloyd Garrison to Helen E. Benson, March 12, 1834, in *The Letters of William Lloyd Garrison*, vol. 1, *I Will Be Heard! 1822–1835*, ed. Walter M. Merrill (Cambridge, MA: Harvard University Press, 1971), 291.

56 Henry Mayer, *All on Fire: William Lloyd Garrison and the Abolition of Slavery* (New York: St. Martin's Press, 1998).

57 "Sonnets," *Liberator*, February 20, 1836; William Lloyd Garrison, "On Completing My Thirtieth Year," in *Sonnets and Other Poems* (Boston: Oliver Johnson, 1843), 78; William Lloyd Garrison, "On Completing My Thirty-Fifth Year," in *Sonnets*, 79. On the sonnets commemorating the birth of his son, see chapter 5.

58 "Juvenile Anti-Slavery Societies," *Liberator*, January 14, 1837.

59 Fanny Garrison Villard, *William Lloyd Garrison on Non-Resistance* (New York: Nation, 1924), 2.

60 "Juvenile Anti-Slavery Societies."

61 "Children All Abolitionists," *Slave's Friend* 1, no. 5 (1836): 15.

62 Quoted in Charles Strickland, "A Transcendentalist Father: The Child-Rearing Practices of Bronson Alcott," *History of Childhood Quarterly* 1, no. 1 (1973): 11.

63 Mintz, *Huck's Raft*, 76.

64 "Wants of the Church—Education of Children," *Christian Recorder*, March 19, 1855. See Chanta M. Haywood, "Constructing Childhood: The *Christian Recorder* and Literature for Black Children, 1854–1865," *African American Review* 36, no. 3 (2002): 419.

65 Quoted in Heywood, *History of Childhood*, 24.

66 Henry Clarke Wright, "Reminiscences: My First Acquaintance with Garrison and Anti-Slavery," in *The Liberty Bell*, ed. Maria Weston Chapman (Boston: National Anti-Slavery Bazaar, 1848), 155–56.

67 Frederick Douglass, *My Bondage and My Freedom*, ed. Nick Bromell and R. Blakeslee Gilpin (New York: W. W. Norton, 2021), 104.

68 Nicholas Buccola, *The Political Thought of Frederick Douglass: In Pursuit of American Liberty* (New York: New York University Press, 2012), 80–81.

69 Frederick Douglass, "The Color Line," *North American Review* 132 (June 1881): 575. For a deeper exploration of how Douglass "locates in child subjects emancipatory and anti-segregationist claims and treats those claims as politically legitimate," see Marissa Carrere, "'Little Conversations': Child Communities and Political Agency in the Writing of Frederick Douglass," in *Literary Cultures and Nineteenth-Century Childhoods*, ed. Kristine Moruzi and Michelle J. Smith (Cham, Switzerland: Palgrave Macmillan, 2023), 139–56 (quote at 155).

70 "To Parents and Friends of Youth," *Liberator*, July 19, 1839. On white supremacy in antebellum children's books, see Donnarae MacCann, *White Supremacy in Children's Literature: Characterizations of African Americans, 1830–1900* (New York: Routledge, 1998).

71 "Juvenile Anti-Slavery Societies," *Emancipator*, December 29, 1836.

72 "To Parents and Friends of Youth."

73 Quoted in Paul Goodman, *Of One Blood: Abolitionism and the Origins of Racial Equality* (Berkeley: University of California Press, 1998), 251.

74 Hosea Easton, *A Treatise on the Intellectual Character, and Civil and Political Condition of the Colored People of the U. States* (Boston: Isaac Knapp, 1837), 40–41. See Bruce Dain, *A Hideous Monster of the Mind: American Race Theory in the Early Republic* (Cambridge, MA: Harvard University Press, 2002), 191–95; Elizabeth Stordeur Pryor, *Colored Travelers: Mobility and the Fight for Citizenship before the Civil War* (Chapel Hill: University of North Carolina Press, 2016), 10.

75 *Anti-Slavery Bugle*, November 17, 1848.

76 Reprinted in Eric Gardner, "Two Texts on Children and Christian Education," *PMLA* 123, no. 1 (2008): 161.

77 Michael Hines, "Learning Freedom: Education, Elevation, and New York's African-American Community, 1827–1829," *History of Education Quarterly* 56, no. 4 (2016): 634.

78 Robin Bernstein, *Racial Innocence: Performing American Childhood from Slavery to Civil Rights* (New York: New York University Press, 2011), 68.

79 F. Douglass, *My Bondage and My Freedom*, 39.

80 "Look at This!," *Liberator*, May 12, 1832.

81 Bernstein, *Racial Innocence*, 36.

82 Rebecca de Schweinitz, "'Waked Up to Feel': Defining Childhood, Debating Slavery in Antebellum America," in Marten, *Children and Youth during the Civil War Era*, 17.

83 Ivy Linton Stabell, "Innocence in Ann Plato's and Susan Paul's Black Children Biographies," in *Who Writes for Black Children? African American Children's Literature before 1900*, ed. Katharine Capshaw and Anna Mae Duane (Minneapolis: University of Minnesota Press, 2017), 78–79.

84 *A Tribute to the Memory of Fitzhugh Smith, the Son of Gerrit Smith* (New York: Wiley and Putnam, 1840), 32, 32–33, 33.

85 Juvenile Anti-Slavery Society Records, Massachusetts Historical Society. See De Rosa, *Domestic Abolitionism and Juvenile Literature*, 110. Bartlett died "aged 27" in 1843. *Liberator*, October 6, 1843.

86 "Youthful Philanthropy," *National Enquirer, and Constitutional Advocate of Universal Liberty*, March 25, 1837.

87 Maria Weston Chapman, "Sonnet," in *The Liberty Bell*, ed. Maria Weston Chapman (Boston: Massachusetts Anti-Slavery Fair, 1841), 99, 100.

88 Wendell Phillips Garrison and Francis Jackson Garrison, *William Lloyd Garrison, 1805–1879: The Story of His Life Told by His Children*, vol. 1, *1805–1835* (New York: Century, 1885), 85.

89 "What Females Can Do?," *Advocate of Freedom*, January 31, 1839.

90 "Address to the Ladies," *Liberator*, January 14, 1832.

91 "What Have Ladies to Do with the Subject of Anti-Slavery?," *Liberator*, March 29, 1834.

92 Martha S. Jones, *All Bound Up Together: The Woman Question in African American Public Culture, 1830–1900* (Chapel Hill: University of North Carolina Press, 2007), 23–57. See also Rael, *Black Identity and Black Protest*, 150–55.

93 "To Juvenile Anti-Slavery Societies," *Slave's Friend* 3, no. 2 (1838): 8–9.

94 Townsend and Townsend, preface to *Anti-Slavery Alphabet*, iii.

95 "A Father Converted through the Influence of His Own Child," *Sunday-School Journal*, August 17, 1836.

96 Nazera Sadiq Wright, *Black Girlhood in the Nineteenth Century* (Urbana: University of Illinois Press, 2016), 53.

97 "Two Good Boys," *Slave's Friend* 2, no. 12 (1837): 6.

98 "Newark Juvenile Anti-Slavery Society," *Emancipator*, January 19, 1837.

99 "For Children. Anti-Slavery Children of Providence," *Friend of Man*, June 28, 1837.

100 Jane Elizabeth Jones, *The Young Abolitionists; or, Conversations on Slavery* (Boston: Anti-Slavery Office, 1848), 21.

101 "'The Young Abolitionist,'" *North Star*, December 8, 1848.

102 "How Children Can Do Good," *Juvenile Instructor*, September 28, 1854.

103 "To a Young Lady, Who Refused to Give Her Name as a Member of a Benevolent Society, Because She Thought Her Influence Too Small to Be of Any Service," *Slave's Friend* 3, no. 3 (1838): 13–14.

104 Kate Masur, *Until Justice Be Done: America's First Civil Rights Movement, from the Revolution to Reconstruction* (New York: W. W. Norton, 2021), 97.

105 Susan Zaeske, *Signatures of Citizenship: Petitioning, Antislavery, and Women's Political Identity* (Chapel Hill: University of North Carolina Press, 2003), 1, 2.

106 Corinne T. Field, *The Struggle for Equal Adulthood: Gender, Race, Age, and the Fight for Citizenship in Antebellum America* (Chapel Hill: University of North Carolina Press, 2014). On children and citizenship in early America, see Courtney Weikle-Mills, *Imaginary Citizens: Child Readers and the Limits of American Independence, 1640–1868* (Baltimore: Johns Hopkins University Press, 2013).

107 "Mass. Anti-Slavery Society," *Liberator*, April 7, 1837.

108 "Talk by the Fireside.—No. III."

109 "To the Children of New-Hampshire," *Herald of Freedom*, July 1, 1837. See also "Petitions to Congress," *Slave's Friend* 2, no. 6 (1837): 7–8.

110 "Petitions for Minors," *Liberator*, July 14, 1837.

111 "Twenty-Fourth Congress. Second Session," *Daily National Intelligencer*, January 31, 1837; "Twenty-Fifth Congress. Second Session," *Daily National Intelligencer*, December 30, 1837.

112 Daniel Carpenter, *Democracy by Petition: Popular Politics in Transformation, 1790–1870* (Cambridge, MA: Harvard University Press, 2021), 299.

113 "Children's Petitions," *Liberator*, August 11, 1837.

114 "Children and Youth," *National Anti-Slavery Standard*, November 12, 1840.

115 "Abolition Proceedings," *Boston Quarterly Review*, October 1838, 476.

116 James Henry Hammond, *Remarks of Mr. Hammond, of South Carolina, on the Question of Receiving Petitions for the Abolition of Slavery in the District of Columbia* (Washington, DC: Duff Green, 1836), 6.

117 Lyon G. Tyler, *The Letters and Times of the Tylers*, vol. 1 (Richmond, VA: Whittet and Shepperson, 1884), 578.

118 Lacon, *The Devil in America: A Dramatic Satire* (Philadelphia: J. B. Lippincott, 1860), 139. On *The Devil in America*, see Edward J. Blum and John H. Matsui, *War Is All Hell: The Nature of Evil and the Civil War* (Philadelphia: University of Pennsylvania Press, 2021), 1–3.

119 "Imitation," *Slave's Friend* 2, no. 3 (1837): 7. On Johnston's cartoon, see Elizabeth Kuebler-Wolf, "'Train Up a Child in the Way He Should Go': The Image of Idealized Childhood in the Slavery Debate, 1850–1870," in Marten, *Children and Youth during the Civil War Era*, 30–33.

120 Thomas Jefferson, *Notes on the State of Virginia*, ed. Frank Shuffelton (New York: Penguin, 1999), 168.

121 Charles J. Fox, "Essays on Slavery—No. III," *New York Commercial Advertiser*, January 22, 1820. Fox references Jefferson in a footnote. The essay was reprinted in *Genius of Universal Emancipation*, July 1821, 13–14.

122 Abigail Mott, preface to *Biographical Sketches and Interesting Anecdotes of Persons of Colour* (New York: Mahlon Day, 1826), iii.

123 "Imitation"; "A Talk by the Fireside.—No. I. To Children," *Liberator*, January 28, 1837.

124 Thomas Jefferson, "Degrading Influences of Slavery," in Collins, *Anti-Slavery Picknick*, 45–47.

125 James W. C. Pennington, *The Fugitive Blacksmith; or, Events in the History of James W. C. Pennington*, 2nd ed. (London: Charles Gilpin, 1849), 2, 2–3.

126 "Narrative of James Curry, a Fugitive Slave," *Liberator*, January 10, 1840.

127 Stephanie E. Jones-Rogers, *They Were Her Property: White Women as Slave Owners in the American South* (New Haven, CT: Yale University Press, 2019), 8–9.

128 Ronald J. Zboray, *A Fictive People: Antebellum Economic Development and the American Reading Public* (New York: Oxford University Press, 1993), 196–98.

129 Jones-Rogers, *They Were Her Property*, 13.

130 Connolly, *Slavery in American Children's Literature*, 54, 58.

131 Kuebler-Wolf, "Train Up a Child," 29–30.

CHAPTER 2. "ANTI-SLAVERY PUBLICATIONS ADAPTED TO THE CAPACITY OF CHILDREN"

1 Michaël Roy, *Fugitive Texts: Slave Narratives in Antebellum Print Culture*, trans. Susan Pickford (Madison: University of Wisconsin Press, 2022).

2 De Rosa, *Domestic Abolitionism and Juvenile Literature*; Deborah C. De Rosa, ed., *Into the Mouths of Babes: An Anthology of Children's Abolitionist Literature* (Westport, CT: Praeger, 2005).

3 Anna Mae Duane and Katharine Capshaw, introduction to Capshaw and Duane, *Who Writes for Black Children?*, xvi; De Rosa, *Domestic Abolitionism and Juvenile Literature*, 7.

4 M. O. Grenby, "The Origins of Children's Literature," in *The Cambridge Companion to Children's Literature*, ed. M. O. Grenby and Andrea Immel (Cambridge: Cambridge University Press, 2009), 4–9; Karen Sánchez-Eppler, "Childhood," in *Keywords for Children's Literature*, ed. Philip Nel and Lissa Paul (New York: New York University Press, 2011), 37.

5 J. R. Oldfield, "Anti-Slavery Sentiment in Children's Literature, 1750–1850," *Slavery and Abolition* 10, no. 1 (1989): 44.

6 John Newbery, *Geography Made Familiar and Easy to Young Gentlemen and Ladies* (London: J. Newbery, 1748), 250, 250–51.

7 John Newbery, *The Newtonian System of Philosophy Adapted to the Capacities of Young Gentlemen and Ladies* (London: J. Newbery, 1761), 121. See Oldfield, "Anti-Slavery Sentiment," 46. On Tom Telescope, see James A. Secord, "Newton in the Nursery: Tom Telescope and the Philosophy of Tops and Balls, 1761–1838," *History of Science* 23, no. 2 (1985): 127–51.

8 William Darton, *Little Truths: Containing Information on Divers Subjects, for the Instruction of Children*, vol. 2 (London: William Darton, 1788), 21, 25, 26. Volume 2 has a slightly different title than volume 1.

9 Michèle Cohen, "The Pedagogy of Conversation in the Home: 'Familiar Conversation' as a Pedagogical Tool in Eighteenth and Nineteenth-Century England," *Oxford Review of Education* 41, no. 4 (2015): 447–63.

10 Oldfield, "Anti-Slavery Sentiment," 50.

11 Linda David, *Children's Books Published by William Darton and His Sons* (Bloomington: Lilly Library, Indiana University, 1992), 11.

12 David, 46–49. See also Lawrence Darton, *The Dartons: An Annotated Check-list of Children's Books Issued by Two Publishing Houses, 1787–1876* (London: British Library, 2004).

13 Priscilla Wakefield, *Mental Improvement; or, The Beauties and Wonders of Nature and Art, Conveyed in a Series of Instructive Conversations*, vol. 1 (London: Darton and Harvey, 1794), 161–62, 164, 168, 169. See Johanna M. Smith, "Slavery, Abolition, and the Nation in Priscilla Wakefield's Tour Books for Children," in *Discourses of Slavery and Abolition: Britain and Its Colonies, 1760–1838*, ed. Brycchan Carey, Markman Ellis and Sarah Salih (New York: Palgrave Macmillan, 2004), 178–79; Ruth Graham, "Juvenile Travellers: Priscilla Wakefield's Excursions in Empire," *Journal of Imperial and Commonwealth History* 38, no. 3 (2010): 378; Julie L. Holcomb, *Moral Commerce: Quakers and the Transatlantic Boycott of the Slave Labor Economy* (Ithaca, NY: Cornell University Press, 2016), 116–17.

14 *New and Entertaining Alphabet, for Young Children, Where Some Instruction May Be Gained, and Much Amusement* (London: W. Darton Jr., 1813), 16.

15 Kenneth Morgan, *Slavery and the British Empire: From Africa to America* (Oxford: Oxford University Press, 2007), 173–75.

16 David Brion Davis, *The Problem of Slavery in Western Culture* (New York: Oxford University Press, 1988), 12.

17 *New and Entertaining Alphabet*, 27.

18 Morgan, *Slavery and the British Empire*, 164–66.

19 For a literary analysis of the poem, see Roxanne Eberle, "'Tales of Truth?': Amelia Opie's Antislavery Poetics," in *Romanticism and Women Poets: Opening the Doors of Reception*, ed. Harriet Kramer Linkin and Stephen C. Behrendt (Lexington: University Press of Kentucky, 1999), 77–83.

20 Amelia Opie, introduction to *The Negro Boy's Tale, a Poem, Addressed to Children* (London: Harvey and Darton, 1824), vii.

21 Opie, vi. See Elizabeth Heyrick, *Immediate, Not Gradual Abolition; or, An Inquiry into the Shortest, Safest, and Most Effectual Means of Getting Rid of West Indian Slavery* (London: Hatchard and Son, 1824).

22 William Cowper, *The Negro's Complaint: A Poem* (London: Harvey and Darton, 1826). See also William Cowper, "The Negro's Complaint," in *Amazing Grace: An Anthology of Poems about Slavery, 1660–1810*, ed. James G. Basker (New Haven, CT: Yale University Press, 2002), 300–301.

23 Amelia Opie, *The Black Man's Lament; or, How to Make Sugar* (London: Harvey and Darton, 1826), 2.

24 Opie, 4, 12, 16, 17.

25 Holcomb, *Moral Commerce*, 117.

26 Opie, *Black Man's Lament*, 2.

27 Martha J. Cutter, *The Illustrated Slave: Empathy, Graphic Narrative, and the Visual Culture of the Transatlantic Abolition Movement, 1800–1852* (Athens: University of Georgia Press, 2017), 70, 82, 79. The identity of the illustrator is unknown.

28 Catherine Parr Traill, *Prejudice Reproved; or, The History of the Negro Toy-Seller* (London: Harvey and Darton, 1826), 11–13n, 22n; Mary Anne Hedge, *Radama; or, The Enlightened African* (London: Harvey and Darton, 1824), 176n. On Traill's and Hedge's volumes, see Oldfield, "Anti-Slavery Sentiment," 51–53, 55.

29 Oldfield, "Anti-Slavery Sentiment," 55.

30 "Prospectus of The Liberator," *Liberator*, May 28, 1831.

31 "Editorial Castigation," *Liberator*, January 22, 1831. I have not been able to ascertain the identity of U.I.E.

32 See Basker, *Amazing Grace*, 296–97.

33 "The Family Circle.—No. I," *Liberator*, January 22, 1831; "The Family Circle.—No. IV," *Liberator*, February 19, 1831; "The Family Circle.—No. VI," *Liberator*, April 2, 1831; "The Family Circle.—No. 8," *Liberator*, June 11, 1831; "The Family Circle.—No. 9," *Liberator*, June 25, 1831. "The Family Circle" was later reprinted as part of Aunt Mary, *The Edinburgh Doll and Other Tales for Children* (Boston: John P. Jewett, 1854), a book in the "Juvenile Anti-Slavery Toy Books" series launched by John P. Jewett in 1853. See Sara Lindey, "Sympathy and Science: Representing Girls in Abolitionist Children's Literature," *Journal of the Midwest Modern Language Association* 45, no. 1 (2012): 62–71.

34 Jacqueline S. Reinier, *From Virtue to Character: American Childhood, 1775–1850* (New York: Twayne, 1996), 19.

35 "The Negro Boy's Tale," *Liberator*, August 11, 1832; "What Is a Slave, Mother?," *Liberator*, June 4, 1831; "Letter from an Infant Slave to the Child of Its Mistress—Both Born on the Same Day," *Liberator*, March 12, 1831; "The White Infant's Reply to the Little Slave," *Liberator*, March 26, 1831; "The Two Dolls," *Liberator*, April 9, 1831; "Edward and Mary," *Liberator*, May 21, 1831; "A Slave Market," *Liberator*, March 19, 1831; "The Young Slave," *Liberator*, March 10, 1832; "A Short History," *Liberator*, December 10, 1831; "Family Colloquy," *Liberator*, August 27, 1831.

36 "A Short History," *Liberator*, December 3, 1831; "The Negro Boy's Narrative," *Liberator*, June 9, 1832; Mary Prince, *The History of Mary Prince, a West Indian Slave*, ed. Sara Salih (London: Penguin, 2004), 66; *Liberator*, May 28, 1831; "A Young Orator," *Liberator*, July 9, 1831; "A Word to Afric's Bleeding Sons," *Liberator*, July 9, 1831; "A Good Plan for Colored Boys," *Liberator*, April 26, 1834.

37 "A True Tale for Children," *Liberator*, July 7, 1832; "For the Children Who Read the Liberator," *Liberator*, August 18, 1832; Marie Lindhorst, "Politics in a Box: Sarah Mapps Douglass and the Female Literary Association, 1831–1833," *Pennsylvania History* 65, no. 3 (1998): 272; "A Dialogue between a Mother and Her Children," *Liberator*, September 1, 1832. On Douglass and the Female Literary Association, see also Mary Kelley, "'Talents Committed to Your Care': Reading and Writing Radical Abolitionism in Antebellum America," *New England Quarterly* 88, no. 1 (2015): 37–72; Sinha, *Slave's Cause*, 269–70. Douglass is not mentioned in either De Rosa's *Domestic Abolitionism and Juvenile Literature* or Capshaw and Duane's *Who Writes for Black Children?* For recent discussions of Douglass as an author of children's literature, see Baumgartner, *In Pursuit of Knowledge*, 187–88; Brigitte Fielder, "'Give the Children the Poems and Stories of Their Own People," *New York Times*, March 19, 2022, www.nytimes.com.

38 *Liberator*, December 24, 1831.

39 "A Talk by the Fireside.—No. III. What Can Children Do for the Slaves?," *Liberator*, April 7, 1837.

40 Though 1836 was retrospectively given as the year when the first volume of the *Slave's Friend* was published, the first issue contains material that was reprinted in an August 1835 issue of the *Juvenile Reformer, and Sabbath School Instructor*. Moreover, the *Liberator* announced "the commencement of a new periodical *for children*" as early as March 1835. "The Thankful Child," *Slave's Friend* 1, no. 1 (1836): 12; "The Thankful Child," *Juvenile Reformer, and Sabbath School Instructor*, August 26, 1835; *Liberator*, March 28, 1835.

41 Christopher D. Geist, "The *Slave's Friend*: An Abolitionist Magazine for Children," *American Periodicals* 9 (1999): 28. Geist's is a useful short overview of the *Slave's Friend*, along with John R. Edson, "Slave's Friend," in *Children's Periodicals of the United States*, ed. R. Gordon Kelly (Westport, CT: Greenwood Press, 1984), 408–11.

42 "Circular," *Liberator*, June 20, 1835.

43 Teresa A. Goddu, *Selling Antislavery: Abolition and Mass Media in Antebellum America* (Philadelphia: University of Pennsylvania Press, 2020), 1; Trish Loughran, *The Republic in Print: Print Culture in the Age of U.S. Nation Building, 1770–1870* (New York: Columbia University Press, 2007), 340.

44 "Slave's Friend—No. 3," *Emancipator*, August 1, 1835.

45 Reprinted as "Slavery, Southern Feelings," *Boston Recorder*, August 14, 1835.

46 Reprinted as "The Burnt Papers," *Evening Post*, August 22, 1835. See also "Burning the Slave's Friend," *Slave's Friend* 2, no. 3 (1837): n.p. On the Charleston raid, see Richard R. John, *Spreading the News: The American Postal System from Franklin to Morse* (Cambridge, MA: Harvard University Press, 1995), 257–80.

47 "Anti-Slavery Catechism," *Slave's Friend* 1, no. 5 (1836): 5; "Faith," *Slave's Friend* 1, no. 5 (1836): 5; "The Praying Child," *Slave's Friend* 1, no. 5 (1836): 10; "'Our Father,'" *Slave's Friend* 1, no. 5 (1836): 14–15; "The Butterfly," *Slave's Friend* 1, no. 5 (1836): 9.

48 Spencer D. C. Keralis, "Feeling Animal: Pet-Making and Mastery in the *Slave's Friend*," *American Periodicals* 22, no. 2 (2012): 122, 121. Barbara Hochman concurs that stories of caged animals "reinforce the idea of a slave as a lesser being." Hochman, *"Uncle Tom's Cabin" and the Reading Revolution*, 125. On comparing human and animal suffering more broadly, see Bénédicte Boisseron, *Afro-Dog: Blackness and the Animal Question* (New York: Columbia University Press, 2018).

49 "The Weasel and Chicken," *Slave's Friend* 1, no. 5 (1836): 8.

50 F. Douglass, *Life and Times of Frederick Douglass*, 68.

51 Sinha, *Slave's Cause*, 255.

52 "Charles Ball's Mother," *Slave's Friend* 2, no. 4 (1837): 11–14; "The Mother and Babe," *Slave's Friend* 2, no. 4 (1837): 14–15; "A Slave's Cabin," *Slave's Friend* 2, no. 4 (1837): 15–16; "A Slave's Dream," *Slave's Friend* 2, no. 4 (1837): 16; "Charles Ball's Return," *Slave's Friend* 2, no. 6 (1837): 10–11. The whole January 1838 issue is composed of Thome's letters to children from the West Indies.

53 "Henry Scott," *Slave's Friend* 1, no. 3 (1836): 6–7; "George Thompson," *Slave's Friend* 1, no. 8 (1836): 12–14; "Little Mary," *Slave's Friend* 2, no. 6 (1837): 3–5; "Murder of Mr. Lovejoy," *Slave's Friend* 3, no. 8 (1838): 1–5. On Henry Scott, see chapter 4; on the *Aves* case, see Karen Woods Weierman, *The Case of the Slave-Child, Med: Free Soil in Antislavery Boston* (Amherst: University of Massachusetts Press, 2019).

54 "Texas," *Slave's Friend* 3, no. 3 (1838): 8–9.

55 "The Quakers and Slavery," *Slave's Friend* 3, no. 9 (1838): 16; "Slave-Holder," *Slave's Friend* 1, no. 10 (1836): 2; "Incendiarism," *Slave's Friend* 3, no. 6 (1838): 10n; Nicholas Rinehart, "Reparative Semantics: On Slavery and the Language of History," *Commonplace*, January 2022, http://commonplace.online; "The Good Old Man," *Slave's Friend* 1, no. 6 (1836): 15; "Resolutions," *Slave's Friend* 1, no. 7 (1836): 4–5; "The Word Negro," *Slave's Friend* 3, no. 6 (1838): 13; "The Colored American," *Slave's Friend* 2, no. 11 (1837): 2.

56 Hochman, *"Uncle Tom's Cabin" and the Reading Revolution*, 58.

57 "The Collection Box," *Slave's Friend* 1, no. 1 (1836): 1–3; "A Young Abolitionist," *Slave's Friend* 3, no. 8 (1838): 11; "Interesting Conversation," *Slave's Friend* 1, no. 9

(1836): n.p.; "Slave Products," *Slave's Friend* 2, no. 2 (1837): 6; "New Sugar," *Slave's Friend* 2, no. 2 (1837): 14–16; "Little Tract Distributor," *Slave's Friend* 1, no. 6 (1836): 6; "Reading the Slave's Friend," *Slave's Friend* 2, no. 12 (1837): 13; "Little Sarah," *Slave's Friend* 3, no. 7 (1838): 13–15; "The Emancipated Family," *Slave's Friend* 2, no. 8 (1837): 3; "Is It Right," *Slave's Friend* 3, no. 4 (1838): 14.

58 *Slave's Friend* 1, no. 10 (1836): 16.

59 P. A. Brinsmade, preface to *Abolition of the African Slave-Trade, by the British Parliament*, by Thomas Clarkson, vol. 1 (Augusta, ME: P. A. Brinsmade, 1830), iv.

60 "A Little Orphan Boy," *Slave's Friend* 3, no. 12 (1838): 11; "Fitzhugh Smith," *Slave's Friend* 2, no. 6 (1837): 14–16; "Fitzhugh Smith," *Slave's Friend* 3, no. 8 (1838): 8–9.

61 Lydia Maria Child, *A Lydia Maria Child Reader*, ed. Carolyn L. Karcher (Durham, NC: Duke University Press, 1997), 136.

62 Quoted in Lesley Ginsberg, "Of Babies, Beasts, and Bondage: Slavery and the Question of Citizenship in Antebellum American Children's Literature," in *The American Child: A Cultural Studies Reader*, ed. Caroline F. Levander and Carol J. Singley (New Brunswick, NJ: Rutgers University Press, 2003), 89.

63 Brigitte Fielder, "Black Girls, White Girls, American Girls: Slavery and Racialized Perspectives in Abolitionist and Neoabolitionist Children's Literature," *Tulsa Studies in Women's Literature* 36, no. 2 (2017): 332.

64 "Youth's Cabinet," *Liberator*, May 5, 1837; *Liberator*, November 8, 1839. The *Youth's Cabinet* was also promoted in the *Slave's Friend* 3, no. 3 (1838): n.p.

65 "A Description of the Squirrel," *Colored American*, May 9, 1840; "The Robin and the Squirrel," *Colored American*, April 18, 1840.

66 Nazera Sadiq Wright, "'Our Hope Is in the Rising Generation': Locating African American Children's Literature in the Children's Department of the *Colored American*," in Capshaw and Duane, *Who Writes for Black Children?*, 151, 153. See also N. Wright, *Black Girlhood in the Nineteenth Century*, 54–58.

67 "Thoughts for January, 1841," *Colored American*, January 9, 1841; "The Blood-Hounds," *Colored American*, March 21, 1840.

68 Haywood, "Constructing Childhood," 419. On the *Recorder*, see Eric Gardner, *Black Print Unbound: The "Christian Recorder," African American Literature, and Periodical Culture* (New York: Oxford University Press, 2015). Gardner notes that children's literature in the Black press needs "massive study" (287n16).

69 "Narrative of H. H. Howard," *Youth's Emancipator*, May 1842; "History of a Fugitive Slave," *Youth's Emancipator*, August 1842. On this paper, see Evelyn Schroth, "*The Youth's Emancipator*," in Kelly, *Children's Periodicals of the United States*, 518–22.

70 De Rosa, *Domestic Abolitionism and Juvenile Literature*, 27.

71 "How Shall Children Do Good?," *Child's Friend* 2, no. 4 (July 1844): 111; "Letter II," *Child's Friend* 13, no. 2 (November 1849): 52, 53; "Pic Nic at Dedham," *Child's Friend* 1, no. 1 (October 1843): 21–27; "The Slave Poet," *Child's Friend* 4, no. 6 (September 1845): 255–58. On the recirculation of Horton's poetry in the *Child's Friend*, see Tabitha Lowery, "Early Black Poetry, Social Justice, and Black Children:

Receptions of Child Activism in African American Literary History" (PhD diss., West Virginia University, 2020), 70–76.

72 *Liberator*, June 24, 1853; *Juvenile Instructor*, February 2, 1854; "Solomon Northup," *Juvenile Instructor*, February 16, 1854; *Juvenile Instructor*, November 9, 1854.

73 Stanley Harrold, *The Abolitionists and the South, 1831–1861* (Lexington: University Press of Kentucky, 1995), 68–69.

74 Jonathan Walker, preface to *A Picture of Slavery, for Youth* (Boston: J. Walker and W. R. Bliss, n.d.), 3.

75 J. Walker, 5, 10, 4, 32, 30, 36. On abolitionist support for Native Americans, see Natalie Joy, "The Indian's Cause: Abolitionists and Native American Rights," *Journal of the Civil War Era* 8, no. 2 (2018): 215–42.

76 For instance, "My master . . . endeavoured to soothe her distress by telling her that he would be a good master to me" became "My master . . . tried to sooth[e] her distress by telling her that he would be a good master to me" in the *Slave's Friend*. Charles Ball, *Slavery in the United States: A Narrative of the Life and Adventures of Charles Ball, a Black Man* (New York: John S. Taylor, 1837), 17; "Charles Ball's Mother," 12.

77 "Solomon Northup."

78 Meredith L. McGill, *American Literature and the Culture of Reprinting, 1834–1853* (Philadelphia: University of Pennsylvania Press, 2003). On the circulation of slave narratives across genres and formats, see also Roy, *Fugitive Texts*.

79 Abigail Mott, preface to *The Life and Adventures of Olaudah Equiano; or Gustavus Vassa, the African*, by Olaudah Equiano, abr. Abigail Mott (New York: Samuel Wood and Sons, 1829), iv.

80 See Christopher Densmore, "Quaker Publishing in New York State, 1784–1860," *Quaker History* 74, no. 2 (1985): 39–57; Sarah Wadsworth, "Children's Literature," in Zboray and Zboray, *Oxford History of Popular Print Culture*, 552–53.

81 Mott, *Biographical Sketches and Interesting Anecdotes*, 24.

82 Valentina K. Tikoff, "A Role Model for African American Children: Abigail Field Mott's *Life and Adventures of Olaudah Equiano* and White Northern Abolitionism," in Capshaw and Duane, *Who Writes for Black Children?*, 96; Martha J. Cutter, "The Child's Illustrated Antislavery Talking Book: Abigail Field Mott's Abridgment of Olaudah Equiano's *Interesting Narrative* for African American Children," in Capshaw and Duane, *Who Writes for Black Children?*, 118, 120.

83 Eric D. Lamore, "Olaudah Equiano in the United States: Abigail's Mott 1829 Abridged Edition of the *Interesting Narrative*," in *Reading African American Autobiography: Twenty-First Century Contexts and Criticism*, ed. Eric D. Lamore (Madison: University of Wisconsin Press, 2017), 71. On the 1791 edition, see Akiyo Ito, "Olaudah Equiano and the New York Artisans: The First American Edition of *The Interesting Narrative of the Life of Olaudah Equiano, or Gustavus Vassa, the African*," *Early American Literature* 32, no. 1 (1997): 82–101.

84 Ann Preston, "Henry Box Brown," in *Cousin Ann's Stories for Children* (Philadelphia: J. M. McKim, 1849), 26. On Brown's "early presence" in children's literature,

see Martha J. Cutter, *The Many Resurrections of Henry Box Brown* (Philadelphia: University of Pennsylvania Press, 2022), 255.

85 Beverly Lyon Clark, *Kiddie Lit: The Cultural Construction of Children's Literature in America* (Baltimore: Johns Hopkins University Press, 2003), 48–76.

86 Eric Gardner, "'This Attempt of Their Sister': Harriet Wilson's *Our Nig* from Printer to Readers," *New England Quarterly* 66, no. 2 (1993): 238; Eric Gardner, "Of Bottles and Books: Reconsidering the Readers of Harriet Wilson's *Our Nig*," in *Harriet Wilson's New England: Race, Writing, and Region*, ed. JerriAnne Boggis, Eva Allegra Raimon and Barbara A. White (Durham: University of New Hampshire Press, 2007), 15.

87 "Edward and Mary."

88 "Notices of New Publications," *Christian World*, August 28, 1847; "Frederick Douglass," *Liberator*, May 30, 1845; "More Slave Narratives," *Liberator*, July 6, 1849.

89 James W. C. Pennington, preface to *The Fugitive Blacksmith: or, Events in the History of James W. C. Pennington*, 3rd ed. (London: Charles Gilpin, 1850), xvi.

90 Eric J. Sundquist, *Empire and Slavery in American Literature, 1820–1865* (Jackson: University Press of Mississippi, 2006), 223.

91 James McCune Smith, introduction to F. Douglass, *My Bondage and My Freedom*, 32.

92 E. Ball, *To Live an Antislavery Life*, 59.

93 "A New Book for Sabbath Schools," *Frederick Douglass' Paper*, November 16, 1855.

94 Vincent Y. Bowditch, *Life and Correspondence of Henry Ingersoll Bowditch*, vol. 1 (Boston: Houghton, Mifflin, 1902), 178. References to Hannibal "swearing eternal enmity to Rome" can be found in chapters 3 and 4 of this book. See also "Value of Young Men," *Liberator*, May 26, 1837. Charles T. Torrey is discussed at length in J. Jones, *Young Abolitionists*, 98–102.

95 Henry I. Bowditch, *A Brief Plea for an Ambulance System for the Army of the United States, as Drawn from the Extra Sufferings of the Late Lieut. Bowditch and a Wounded Comrade* (Boston: Ticknor and Fields, 1863), 5. On Henry Ingersoll Bowditch and Nathaniel Bowditch, see John T. Cumbler, "A Family Goes to War: Sacrifice and Honor for an Abolitionist Family," *Massachusetts Historical Review* 10 (2008): 57–83.

96 Thomas Burt, *Thomas Burt, M.P., D.C.L., Pitman and Privy Councillor: An Autobiography* (London: T. Fisher Unwin, 1924), 19. He writes later, "Thus began a keen, lasting interest in the anti-slavery agitation, which afterwards made me familiar with the names and labours of Lloyd Garrison, Wendell Phillips, Theodore Parker, Whittier, Emerson, and other fine spirits, poets, orators, philanthropists, who battled for freedom and righteousness on the other side of the Atlantic" (116).

97 *Radical Abolitionist*, October 1855, 21.

98 Samuel May Jr. to John B. Estlin, September 5, 1848, Anti-Slavery Collection, Boston Public Library. On this translation and its gender dimensions, see Michaël Roy, "'Throwing Pearls Before Swine': The Strange Publication History of *Vie de Frédéric Douglass, esclave américain* (1848)," *Slavery and Abolition* 40, no. 4 (2019): 727–49.

99 "A Letter from a Child," *Frederick Douglass' Paper*, December 7, 1855.

100 See, for instance, "Family Colloquy"; Ohio Anti-Slavery Society, *Proceedings of the Ohio Anti-Slavery Convention* (n.p.: Beaumont and Wallace, 1835), 24; "Interesting Anecdote," *Slave's Friend* 1, no. 11 (1836): 16; "Sugar, and Rice, and Cotton," *Slave's Friend* 2, no. 1 (1837): 6–9; "Boston Juvenile Anti-Slavery Society," *Liberator*, June 16, 1837; J. Jones, *Young Abolitionists*, 20; Hochman, *"Uncle Tom's Cabin" and the Reading Revolution*, 12; Erik A. Stumpf, "Children with a Cause: Training Antebellum Children for the Abolition of Slavery" (PhD diss., Iowa State University, 2018), 91, 169.

101 "Letter from a Child."

CHAPTER 3. "ANTI-SLAVERY SUCCESS TO THE JUNIORS!"

1 Alexis de Tocqueville, *Democracy in America*, trans. and ed. Harvey C. Mansfield and Delba Winthrop (Chicago: University of Chicago Press, 2000), 489 (emphasis added).

2 "Juvenile Sewing Society," *Youth's Companion*, September 8, 1830; "Juvenile Missionary Society, in C—," *Sabbath School Treasury*, August 1832, 190–91; "Juvenile Industry Society," *Family Pioneer and Juvenile Key*, August 31, 1833.

3 Mintz, *Huck's Raft*, 88–89.

4 Quarles, *Black Abolitionists*, 29.

5 Sinha, *Slave's Cause*, 254. The JGIS should not be confused with the Garrison Juvenile Society, a school for African American children opened in 1833. On this school, see Baumgartner, *In Pursuit of Knowledge*, 189–90.

6 Convention for the Improvement of the Free People of Color, *Minutes and Proceedings of the First Annual Convention of the People of Colour* (Philadelphia: Committee of Arrangements, 1831), 5.

7 "Garrison Independent Society," *Liberator*, January 5, 1833; "Notice," *Liberator*, January 5, 1833.

8 E. Ball, *To Live an Antislavery Life*, 13.

9 *Liberator*, March 30, 1833. See Quarles, *Black Abolitionists*, 20–21.

10 "An Address Delivered before the 'Garrison Independent Society,' at Its Second Anniversary, October 16, 1833," *Emancipator*, April 1, 1834.

11 Reprinted in *Liberator*, November 16, 1833.

12 "A Delightful Token of Personal Regard," *Liberator*, April 19, 1834. See also Dorothy B. Porter, "The Organized Educational Activities of Negro Literary Societies, 1828–1846," *Journal of Negro Education* 5, no. 4 (1936): 568–69.

13 "To the Children in New-Hampshire," *Herald of Freedom*, March 25 and April 1, 8, 15, 1837. On the Concord Juvenile Anti-Slavery Society, see American Anti-Slavery Society, *Fourth Annual Report of the American Anti-Slavery Society* (New York: William S. Dorr, 1837), 124.

14 "To the Members of the Concord Juvenile Anti-Slavery Society," *Herald of Freedom*, June 3, 1837; "To the Members of the Concord Juvenile Anti-Slavery Society.—No. 2," *Herald of Freedom*, July 1, 1837; "To the Members of the Concord Juvenile Anti-Slavery Society.—No. 3," *Herald of Freedom*, July 15, 1837; "To the

Members of the Concord Juvenile Anti-Slavery Society.—No. 4," *Herald of Freedom*, July 22, 1837.

15 John W. Lewis to the Executive Committee of the New Hampshire Anti-Slavery Society, December 28, 1840, in *The Black Abolitionist Papers*, vol. 3, *The United States, 1830–1846*, ed. C. Peter Ripley (Chapel Hill: University of North Carolina Press, 1991), 352–55.

16 Goddu, *Selling Antislavery*, 16.

17 "Cent-a-Week Societies," *Slave's Friend* 3, no. 3 (1838): 15.

18 "The Boys of Pittsburgh against the World," *Colored American*, November 23, 1839. See also Quarles, *Black Abolitionists*, 30; David J. Peck and George B. Vashon to Charles B. Ray and Philip A. Bell, November 14, 1839, in Ripley, *Black Abolitionist Papers*, 320–22; Sinha, *Slave's Cause*, 304.

19 Julie Roy Jeffrey, "'No Occurrence in Human History Is More Deserving of Commemoration Than This': Abolitionist Celebrations of Freedom," in *Prophets of Protest: Reconsidering the History of American Abolitionism*, ed. Timothy Patrick McCarthy and John Stauffer (New York: New Press, 2006), 207.

20 "Celebration of the 1st of August in the City of Troy," *Colored American*, September 28, 1838.

21 Olsavsky, *Most Absolute Abolition*, 72.

22 "To the Church and Congregation at T.," *Colored American*, October 20, 1838. On the school, see Annie B. Hantch, "History of the Public Schools of Carlisle," paper read before the Hamilton Library Historical Association, Carlisle, PA, February 19, 1909, 7–8.

23 "A Statistical Review of the Colored School of the Borough of Carlisle," *Colored American*, October 2, 1841.

24 Shirley J. Yee, *Black Women Abolitionists: A Study in Activism, 1828–1860* (Knoxville: University of Tennessee Press, 1992), 87; Sinha, *Slave's Cause*, 269, 275.

25 Salem Female Anti-Slavery Society Record Book, January 10, March 7, December 5, 1838, Phillips Library, Peabody Essex Museum.

26 Stumpf, "Children with a Cause," 82.

27 "Account of Money Received into the Treasury of the Massachusetts A. S. Society," *Liberator*, January 19, 1838, and January 18, 1839; "A Card," *Liberator*, April 5 and July 12, 1839. On Dodge, see Baumgartner, *In Pursuit of Knowledge*, 121.

28 American Anti-Slavery Society, *Fourth Annual Report*, 134.

29 "Communications," *Emancipator*, May 12, 1835; "Items," *Emancipator*, May 5, 1835; New York State Anti-Slavery Society, *Proceedings of the First Annual Meeting of the New-York State Anti-Slavery Society* (Utica: New York State Anti-Slavery Society, 1836), 59.

30 The petition is held in the John Quincy Adams Papers at the Massachusetts Historical Society. For Dorchester's age, see Henry Flagler Rulison, *Genealogy of the Rulison, Rulifson, Ruliffson and Allied Families in America* (Chicago: Printed for private distribution, 1919), 45.

31 American Anti-Slavery Society, *Second Annual Report*, 52–53.

32 Members of the Plymouth, Massachusetts, Juvenile Anti-Slavery Society read aloud from Nathaniel Southard's *Youth's Cabinet* while sewing. Juvenile Anti-Slavery Society Records, Massachusetts Historical Society. For an in-depth look at what these young abolitionists sewed, see Naomi Gardner, "Embroidering Emancipation: Female Abolitionists and Material Culture in Britain and the USA, c. 1780–1865" (PhD diss., Royal Holloway, University of London, 2016), 169–90.

33 "Extract of a Letter Dated Providence, Jan. 29, 1835," *Emancipator*, February 17, 1835; "Juvenile Anti-Slavery Society," *Emancipator*, February 17, 1835; "What Can We Do?," *Slave's Friend* 1, no. 3 (1835): 8–10; "Juvenile Efforts," *Emancipator*, May 12, 1835; "The First Annual Report of the Providence Female Juvenile Anti-Slavery Society," *Liberator*, December 26, 1835; Rhode Island State Anti-Slavery Society, *Proceedings of the Rhode-Island Anti-Slavery Convention* (Providence, RI: H. H. Brown, 1836), 15; Holcomb, *Moral Commerce*, 139–40.

34 "Bangor Juvenile A. S. Society," *Advocate of Freedom*, December 6, 1838.

35 Louis Filler, *The Crusade against Slavery, 1830–1860* (New York: Harper and Row, 1960), 70; Edward Magdol, *The Antislavery Rank and File: A Social Profile of the Abolitionists' Constituency* (Westport, CT: Greenwood Press, 1986); Herbert Aptheker, *Abolitionism: A Revolutionary Movement* (Boston: Twayne, 1989), 41; Sinha, *Slave's Cause*, 253–54.

36 "Pawtucket Juvenile Anti-Slavery Society," *Liberator*, August 20, 1836; "Pawtucket Juvenile Anti-Slavery Society," *National Enquirer, and Constitutional Advocate of Universal Liberty*, August 31, 1836; "Anti-Slavery Meetings," *Liberator*, September 10, 1836; "What Children Can Do," *Slave's Friend* 2, no. 7 (1837): 8–9; "Second Annual Report of the Pawtucket Female Emancipation Society," *Liberator*, October 6, 1837; "Generous Donation," *Liberator*, September 20, 1839; "A Juvenile Pledge," *Liberator*, May 1, 1840; "Letter from C. Lenox Remond," *Colored American*, October 3, 1840; Frances Whipple Green, ed., *The Envoy: From Free Hearts to the Free* (Pawtucket, RI: Juvenile Emancipation Society, 1840), 42–53; Deborah Bingham Van Broekhoven, *The Devotion of These Women: Rhode Island in the Antislavery Network* (Amherst: University of Massachusetts Press, 2002), 119; "Juvenile Fair," *Liberator*, January 8, 1841; "Letter from Abby Kelley," *National Anti-Slavery Standard*, November 4, 1841; "Pawtucket Anti-Slavery Fair," *National Anti-Slavery Standard*, August 1, 1844.

37 "Mansfield and Foxboro' Juvenile Society," *Liberator*, April 19, 1839; "Receipts into the Treasury of the Massachusetts Anti-Slavery Soc.," *Liberator*, May 3, 1839; "Treasurer's Account," *Liberator*, June 5, 1840.

38 Experience Billings to Maria Weston Chapman, August 31, 1840, Anti-Slavery Collection, Boston Public Library.

39 Junior Anti-Slavery Society of Philadelphia constitution and preamble, Pennsylvania Abolition Society Papers, Historical Society of Pennsylvania.

40 Beverly Wilson Palmer, "Biographical Directory," in *Selected Letters of Lucretia Coffin Mott*, ed. Beverly Wilson Palmer (Urbana: University of Illinois Press, 2002), xlvi; Samuel J. Levick, *Life of Samuel J. Levick* (Philadelphia: William H.

Pile's Sons, 1896), 23; Arthur Meredyth Burke, *The Prominent Families of the United States of America*, vol. 1 (London: Sackville Press, 1909), 239; Dennis B. Worthen, "Edward Robinson Squibb (1819–1900): Advocate of Product Standards," *Journal of the American Pharmacists Association* 46, no. 6 (2006): 754; William Penrose Hallowell, *Record of a Branch of the Hallowell Family Including the Longstreth, Penrose, and Norwood Branches* (Philadelphia: Hallowell, 1893), 38–43.

41 "A Young Abolitionist" to Benjamin Lundy, n.d., in *National Enquirer, and Constitutional Advocate of Universal Liberty*, November 12, 1836; "Efforts of the Young," *National Enquirer, and Constitutional Advocate of Universal Liberty*, November 26, 1836; "The Youth of Our Day," *National Enquirer, and Constitutional Advocate of Universal Liberty*, November 12, 1836. Lundy died three years later, at the age of fifty.

42 "House of Representatives," *Liberator*, March 2, 1838; "Annual Report of the Board of Managers of the Junior Anti-Slavery Society," *Pennsylvania Freeman*, January 17, 1839.

43 De Rosa, *Domestic Abolitionism and Juvenile Literature*, 112.

44 *National Enquirer, and Constitutional Advocate of Universal Liberty*, January 14, February 11, and August 10, 1837.

45 Henry Peterson, *Address on American Slavery, Delivered before the Semi-Annual Meeting, of the Junior Anti-Slavery Society, of Philadelphia* (Philadelphia: Merrihew and Gunn, 1838), 3. See also Henry Peterson, *An Address Delivered before the Junior Anti-Slavery Society of the City and County of Philadelphia, December 23, 1836* (Philadelphia: Merrihew and Gunn, 1837). The JASSP also sponsored the publication of William Jackson, *Views of Slavery, in Its Effects on the Wealth, Population, and Character of Nations* (Philadelphia: Junior Anti-Slavery Society, 1838).

46 Levick, *Life of Samuel J. Levick*, 29–30, 31, 33, 34, 36, 39, 76; "Ohio Yearly Meeting of Friends," *National Anti-Slavery Standard*, October 2, 1845; Ira V. Brown, "'Am I Not a Woman and a Sister?': The Anti-Slavery Convention of American Women, 1837–1839," *Pennsylvania History* 50, no. 1 (1983): 14.

47 "Meeting of the Junior Anti-Slavery Society," *Pennsylvania Freeman*, July 11, 1839.

48 Wright's biographer passes quickly over his agency. Lewis Perry, *Childhood, Marriage, and Reform: Henry Clarke Wright, 1797–1870* (Chicago: University of Chicago Press, 1980), 31–32.

49 "Juvenile Anti-Slavery Societies," *New York Evangelist*, December 24, 1836.

50 "Newark Juvenile Anti-Slavery Society," *Emancipator*, January 19, 1837.

51 "Annual Meeting of the New Jersey Anti-Slavery Society," *Liberator*, February 14, 1840; New York Medico-Historical Society, *The Medical Register of New York, New Jersey and Connecticut, for the Year Commencing June 1, 1883* (New York: G. P. Putnam's Sons, 1883), 224–25.

52 American Anti-Slavery Society, *Fourth Annual Report*, 134; B. T. Pierson, *Directory of the City of Newark, for 1841–42* (Newark, NJ: Aaron Guest, 1841), 117; Craig Steven Wilder, *In the Company of Black Men: The African Influence on African American Culture in New York City* (New York: New York University Press, 2001), 83, 161. See also Marion M. Thompson Wright, *The Education of Negroes in New*

Jersey (New York: Teachers College, Columbia University, 1941), 103–4; Charles H. Wesley, "The Negro in the Organization of Abolition," *Phylon* 2, no. 3 (1941): 232.

53 "Newark Juvenile Anti-Slavery Society."

54 "Children of Boston," *Liberator*, April 7, 1837.

55 "Mr. Wright's Preaching to Children," *Slave's Friend* 2, no. 12 (1837): 9.

56 "Children of Boston."

57 "Little Daniel," *Slave's Friend* 2, no. 3 (1837): 10–12.

58 "Children of Boston."

59 "The Proud Girl," *Slave's Friend* 3, no. 11 (1838): 4–5.

60 "Lynn—Nobly Done," *Liberator*, April 7, 1837; "List of Anti-Slavery Societies in Massachusetts," *Liberator*, April 20, 1838; "Boston," *Liberator*, January 11, 1839.

61 "Lynn—Nobly Done."

62 "Money Received from Children," *Slave's Friend* 2, no. 10 (1837): n.p. See also "Money Received from Children," *Slave's Friend* 2, no. 11 (1837): n.p.

63 "For Children. Anti-Slavery Children of Providence," *Friend of Man*, June 28, 1837.

64 Henry Clarke Wright, preface to *A Kiss for a Blow; or, A Collection of Stories for Children Showing Them How to Prevent Quarreling* (Boston: B. B. Mussey, 1842), x. See Sinha, *Slave's Cause*, 255.

65 "For Children."

66 "Children's Anti-Slavery Meeting," *National Enquirer, and Constitutional Advocate of Universal Liberty*, August 24, 1837.

67 "Juvenile Anti-Slavery Agent," *Slave's Friend* 2, no. 8 (1837): 2.

68 William Lloyd Garrison to Elizabeth Pease, July 2, 1842, in *The Letters of William Lloyd Garrison*, vol. 3, *No Union with Slaveholders, 1841–1849*, ed. Walter M. Merrill (Cambridge, MA: Harvard University Press, 1973), 90–91.

69 J. Jones, *Young Abolitionists*, 3, 6–7.

70 "Letter from Henry C. Wright," *Liberator*, March 20, 1857.

71 "The Cause in Essex County," *Liberator*, November 2, 1838.

72 "Mr. Thurston's Journal," *Advocate of Freedom*, April 26, 1838.

73 "Boston Juvenile Anti-Slavery Society," *Liberator*, June 16, 1837. On the story of the African girl, see Hochman, *"Uncle Tom's Cabin" and the Reading Revolution*, 126; on slavery as a cannibalistic institution, see Vincent Woodard, *The Delectable Negro: Human Consumption and Homoeroticism within U.S. Slave Culture* (New York: New York University Press, 2014).

74 Glasgow Ladies' Auxiliary Emancipation Society, *Three Years' Female Anti-Slavery Effort, in Britain and America* (Glasgow: Aird and Russell, 1837), 60.

75 "Abolitionism," *New York Commercial Advertiser*, January 24, 1837.

76 "Anti-Slavery Education," *National Anti-Slavery Standard*, June 3, 1841.

77 "Juvenile Patriotism," *Liberator*, September 26, 1835.

78 "Juvenile Colonization Society," *African Repository and Colonial Journal*, November 1830, 280; "Juvenile Colonization Society," *African Repository and Colonial Journal*, January 1831, 349–50.

79 "A Childish Scheme," *Liberator*, February 19, 1831.

CHAPTER 4. "WE HAVE SEVERAL SCHOOL-MATES WHO HAVE
BEEN SLAVES"

1 "Sarah P. Remond," in *Our Exemplars, Poor and Rich; or, Biographical Sketches of Men and Women Who Have, by an Extraordinary Use of Their Opportunities, Benefited Their Fellow-Creatures*, ed. Matthew Davenport Hill (London: Cassell, Petter, and Galpin, 1861), 279. See Baumgartner, *In Pursuit of Knowledge*, 118–21.

2 "Sarah P. Remond," 280.

3 Holly Keller, "Juvenile Antislavery Narrative and Notions of Childhood," *Children's Literature* 24 (1996): 92.

4 See, for instance, Lillie Chace Wyman, "From Generation to Generation," *Atlantic Monthly* 64 (August 1889): 171.

5 "Reply," *Liberator*, August 13, 1836.

6 Polgar, *Standard-Bearers of Equality*, 45–47.

7 Maurice Jackson, *Let This Voice Be Heard: Anthony Benezet, Father of Atlantic Abolitionism* (Philadelphia: University of Pennsylvania Press, 2010), 22–24.

8 On Forten's education at the African School, see Julie Winch, *A Gentleman of Color: The Life of James Forten* (New York: Oxford University Press, 2002), 25.

9 Quoted in Anna Davis Hallowell, *James and Lucretia Mott: Life and Letters* (Boston: Houghton, Mifflin, 1884), 31.

10 Dorothy Sterling, *Lucretia Mott* (New York: Feminist Press at the City University of New York, 1999), 49; Carol Faulkner, *Lucretia Mott's Heresy: Abolition and Women's Rights in Nineteenth-Century America* (Philadelphia: University of Pennsylvania Press, 2011), 18–19, 29–30.

11 Charles Monaghan and E. Jennifer Monaghan, "Schoolbooks," in *A History of the Book in America*, vol. 2, *An Extensive Republic: Print, Culture, and Society in the New Nation, 1790–1840*, ed. Robert A. Gross and Mary Kelley (Chapel Hill: University of North Carolina Press, 2010), 309. François Furstenberg calls these readers "the hidden bestsellers of early American literature." Furstenberg, *In the Name of the Father*, 151.

12 Lindley Murray, *The English Reader* (New York: Isaac Collins, 1799), 291, 292.

13 Levine-Gronningsater, "Delivering Freedom," 138–44 (quotes at 142).

14 Polgar, *Standard-Bearers of Equality*, 136.

15 American Convention of Abolition Societies, *Minutes of the Adjourned Session of the Twentieth Biennial American Convention for Promoting the Abolition of Slavery, and Improving the Condition of the African Race, Held at Baltimore, Nov. 1828* (Philadelphia: Samuel Parker, 1828), 37.

16 Horton and Horton, *In Hope of Liberty*, 216.

17 New York African Free School Records, vol. 4, New-York Historical Society; Lindley Murray, *The English Reader* (New York: Collins, 1819), 215. Frederick Douglass quoted the same passage in his 1850 address "An Antislavery Tocsin." Frederick Douglass, *Speeches and Writings*, ed. David W. Blight (New York: Library of America, 2022), 147.

18 Sinha, *Slave's Cause*, 100.
19 New York African Free School Records, vol. 3, New-York Historical Society. Scholars who have written on the NYAFS have called Anthony "Joe" or "Joseph," but the records clearly indicate "Ja" for James.
20 Daniel Hack, *Reaping Something New: African American Transformations of Victorian Literature* (Princeton, NJ: Princeton University Press, 2017).
21 American Convention of Abolition Societies, *Minutes of the Adjourned Session*, 32, 63, 67.
22 Quoted in Sinha, *Slave's Cause*, 117.
23 American Convention of Abolition Societies, *Minutes of the Adjourned Session*, 66.
24 Charles C. Andrews, *The History of the New-York African Free-Schools, from Their Establishment in 1787, to the Present Time* (New York: Mahlon Day, 1830), 64.
25 American Convention of Abolition Societies, *Minutes of the Adjourned Session*, 64, 65, 63, 66, 67.
26 Carla L. Peterson, "Black Life in Freedom: Creating an Elite Culture," in *Slavery in New York*, ed. Ira Berlin and Leslie M. Harris (New York: New Press, 2005), 189.
27 Peterson, 189.
28 Levine-Gronningsater, "Delivering Freedom," 181–82.
29 Alexander Crummell, "Eulogium on Henry Highland Garnet, D.D.," in *Africa and America: Addresses and Discourses* (Springfield, MA: Willey, 1891), 300.
30 King, *Stolen Childhood*, 192.
31 "To Our Patrons," *Freedom's Journal*, March 16, 1827.
32 Jacqueline Bacon, "The History of *Freedom's Journal*: A Study in Empowerment and Community," *Journal of African American History* 88, no. 1 (2003): 8.
33 Fielder, "Give the Children the Poems and Stories."
34 Andrews, *History of the New-York African Free-Schools*, 52, 60–68.
35 *Liberator*, May 28, 1831; "Edward and Mary," *Liberator*, May 21, 1831.
36 Isaiah G. De Grasse, *A Sermon on Education* (New York: James Van Norden, 1839), 11.
37 "A Young Orator," *Liberator*, July 9, 1831. On the New Haven college, see Hilary J. Moss, *Schooling Citizens: The Struggle for African American Education in Antebellum America* (Chicago: University of Chicago Press, 2009), 44–62.
38 American Anti-Slavery Society, "The American Anti-Slavery Society Declares Its Sentiments," in *The Antislavery Argument*, ed. William H. Pease and Jane H. Pease (Indianapolis, IN: Bobbs-Merrill, 1965), 66–67.
39 "Young Orator."
40 Address by William Watkins, Jacob M. Moore, and Jacob C. White Sr., November 1836, in Ripley, *Black Abolitionist Papers*, 195–96n13, 198–200n19; Yee, *Black Women Abolitionists*, 108; Sinha, *Slave's Cause*, 271.
41 "Production of Free Labor," *Genius of Universal Emancipation*, February 1833, 57.
42 Joseph Willson, *The Elite of Our People: Joseph Willson's Sketches of Black Upper-Class Life in Antebellum Philadelphia*, ed. Julie Winch (University Park: Penn-

sylvania State University Press, 2000), 115–16; Porter, "Organized Educational Activities," 562.

43 "Young Orator."

44 "A Word to Afric's Bleeding Sons," *Liberator*, July 9, 1831; David Walker, *David Walker's Appeal to the Coloured Citizens of the World*, ed. Peter P. Hinks (University Park: Pennsylvania State University Press, 2000), 5, 4, 22.

45 "What Children Think," *Slave's Friend* 3, no. 6 (1838): 14–16.

46 Ohio Anti-Slavery Society, *Proceedings*, 23–24. The letters were reprinted as "Children's Letters," *Juvenile Reformer, and Sabbath School Instructor*, October 14, 1835; "Children's Letters," *Slave's Friend* 1, no. 4 (1836): 11–13; "Children's Letters," *Morning Star*, December 28, 1836. Scholarly discussions of the letters include King, *Stolen Childhood*, 193–94; Horton and Horton, *In Hope of Liberty*, 216–17.

47 Ohio Anti-Slavery Society, *Proceedings*, 3, 20, 22.

48 Ohio Anti-Slavery Society, 23.

49 Sinha, *Slave's Cause*, 241–42.

50 Ohio Anti-Slavery Society, *Proceedings*, 23.

51 Christopher Hager, *Word by Word: Emancipation and the Act of Writing* (Cambridge, MA: Harvard University Press, 2013), 59.

52 Ohio Anti-Slavery Society, *Proceedings*, 23.

53 Nikki M. Taylor, *Frontiers of Freedom: Cincinnati's Black Community, 1802–1868* (Athens: Ohio University Press, 2005), 164.

54 Lois Brown, "Out of the Mouths of Babes: The Abolitionist Campaign of Susan Paul and the Juvenile Choir of Boston," *New England Quarterly* 75, no. 1 (2002): 52–79 (quote at 72).

55 "Ye Who in Bondage Pine," *Abolitionist*, April 1833, 64.

56 "New-England Anti-Slavery Convention," *Liberator*, May 31, 1834. The *Slave's Friend* version misses a stanza. "Mr. Prejudice," *Slave's Friend* 2, no. 7 (1837): 3–4.

57 Brown, "Out of the Mouths of Babes," 69–70; Pryor, *Colored Travelers*, 72.

58 The first three of these songs, along with author attribution, can be found in William Lloyd Garrison, *A Selection of Anti-Slavery Hymns, for the Use of the Friends of Emancipation* (Boston: Garrison and Knapp, 1834), 6, 19, 36. "The Sugar Plums" is a frequently reprinted poem by Elizabeth Margaret Chandler. See, for instance, Garrison, *Juvenile Poems*, 19–20. "The Petition of the Sugar-Making Slaves" was printed in the *Slave's Friend* 2, no. 1 (1837): 9–10.

59 "Miss Paul's Juvenile Concert," *New York Evangelist*, February 25, 1837.

60 Paul, preface to *Memoir of James Jackson*, 67. There is debate as to whether Paul herself authored the preface.

61 Sinha, *Slave's Cause*, 255. On Paul and the *Memoir*, see also Goodman, *Of One Blood*, 249–52; Lois Brown, introduction to Paul, *Memoir of James Jackson*, 1–63; Sánchez-Eppler, *Dependent States*, 203–5; Baumgartner, *In Pursuit of Knowledge*, 191–94.

62 Paul, *Memoir of James Jackson*, 72, 71, 88–89, 89.

63 "James Jackson," *Liberator*, June 27, 1835.

64 "Correspondence," *Liberator*, August 13, 1836.

65 "Reply."

66 "A Good School," *Slave's Friend* 2, no. 6 (1837): 1, 3.

67 J. Jones, *Young Abolitionists*, 7, 59. The line "hide the outcast" is found in Isaiah 16:3. On its use by abolitionists, see J. Blake Couey and Jeremy Schipper, "Hide the Outcasts: Isaiah 16:3–4 and Fugitive Slave Laws," *Harvard Theological Review* 115, no. 4 (2022): 519–37.

68 Neem, *Democracy's Schools*, 98–102 (quote at 98).

69 M. Jackson, *Let This Voice Be Heard*, 21.

70 "First Annual Meeting of the New-England Non-Resistance Society," *Non-Resistant*, November 16, 1839. On the resonance between the campaign to abolish slavery and the campaign to abolish corporal punishment, see Myra C. Glenn, *Campaigns against Corporal Punishment: Prisoners, Sailors, Women, and Children in Antebellum America* (Albany: State University of New York Press, 1984).

71 Bronson Alcott, preface to *Conversations with Children on the Gospels*, vol. 1 (Boston: James Munroe, 1836), xix. On the Hopedale Home School, see Elizabeth C. Stevens, "'A Symmetrical, Harmonious, Substantial Character': Schools for Abolitionist Children in Mid-Nineteenth-Century New England," in *Schooldays in New England, 1650–1900*, ed. Peter Benes (Dublin, NH: Dublin Seminar for New England Folklife, 2015), 59–72.

72 Larry A. Carlson, "'Those Pure Pages of Yours': Bronson Alcott's *Conversations with Children on the Gospels*," *American Literature* 60, no. 3 (1988): 453. See also Richard Francis, *Fruitlands: The Alcott Family and Their Search for Utopia* (New Haven, CT: Yale University Press, 2010), 17–20.

73 Alcott, preface to *Conversations with Children on the Gospels*, xiv, xv.

74 American Anti-Slavery Society, *First Annual Report of the American Anti-Slavery Society* (New York: Dorr and Butterfield, 1834), 47.

75 Goodman, *Of One Blood*, 51–53; Sinha, *Slave's Cause*, 229–30.

76 "Obituary Notice," *Liberator*, April 2, 1836; Mary E. Bibb to Gerrit Smith, November 8, 1850, in *The Black Abolitionist Papers*, vol. 2, *Canada, 1830–1865*, ed. C. Peter Ripley (Chapel Hill: University of North Carolina Press, 1986), 110–11n3.

77 Baumgartner, *In Pursuit of Knowledge*, 24.

78 "Slavery," *Liberator*, April 6, 1833.

79 "From the Canterbury School," *Religious Intelligencer*, June 15, 1833; "Address, Written by One of Miss Crandall's Scholars," *Liberator*, August 3, 1833.

80 "Obituary Notice."

81 Henry Bibb, *Narrative of the Life and Adventures of Henry Bibb, an American Slave* (New York: Published by the Author, 1849), 190.

82 "Monday Morning in the Millenium [*sic*]," *Liberator*, August 24, 1833.

83 "Boy Stealing!," *Emancipator*, March 25, 1834. See Eric Foner, *Gateway to Freedom: The Hidden History of America's Fugitive Slaves* (Oxford: Oxford University Press, 2015), 61; Jonathan Daniel Wells, *The Kidnapping Club: Wall Street, Slavery, and Resistance on the Eve of the Civil War* (New York: Bold Type Books, 2020), 33–37.

84 "Help from Children," *Emancipator*, April 1, 1834. The name Scimmons also appears in the article as "Scimons."

85 "Little Children, Read This!," *Emancipator*, April 1, 1834. According to most sources, Scott was seven, not six, at the time of his arrest. He was dragged out of school by two men, not three.

86 "Juvenile Composition," *Emancipator*, April 15, 1834.

87 "Little Henry.—More Help," *Emancipator*, April 22, 1834.

88 "Little Henry," *New York Evangelist*, June 14, 1834.

89 Anne M. Boylan, *Sunday School: The Formation of an American Institution, 1790–1880* (New Haven, CT: Yale University Press, 1988), 80–84. The Cincinnati-based American Reform Tract and Book Society was founded in the 1850s in reaction to the ASSU's and other such organizations' silence on slavery. It became a prolific publisher of juvenile antislavery literature in the years preceding the Civil War, with titles such as *The Child's Book on Slavery; or, Slavery Made Plain* (1857). During the same period, New York's Carlton and Porter, a commercial house associated with the Sunday School Union and Tract Society of the Methodist Episcopal Church, also published antislavery literature for children, including a collection of stories by Julia Colman and Matilda G. Thompson titled *The Child's Anti-Slavery Book* (1859). See De Rosa, *Domestic Abolitionism and Juvenile Literature*, 29, 31–37.

90 Brown, introduction to Paul, *Memoir of James Jackson*, 27–30.

91 Boylan, *Sunday School*, 28.

92 "Letter to Uncle Lucius," *Juvenile Instructor*, January 19, 1854.

93 "Worthy of Patronage," *Liberator*, June 6, 1835. Garrison reprinted items from the *Juvenile Reformer, and Sabbath School Instructor* in the *Liberator*. See, for instance, "Slavery—What Is It?," *Liberator*, June 20, 1835; "Injustice," *Liberator*, October 17, 1835.

94 "The Little Blind Boy," *Sabbath School Instructor*, June 18, 1834; "Am I to Blame?," *Sabbath School Instructor*, July 2, 1834; Paul, *Memoir of James Jackson*, 106–10.

95 "A New Book for Sabbath Schools," *Frederick Douglass' Paper*, November 16, 1855.

96 "Jermain W. Loguen's Book," *Weekly Anglo-African*, December 3, 1859.

97 John Pierpont, *The American First Class Book* (Boston: William B. Fowle, 1823), 181–85 (quote at 184). On Montgomery, see Basker, *Amazing Grace*, 611–16.

98 Charles Dexter Cleveland, *The National Orator*, 3rd ed. (New York: N. and J. White, 1832), 40–41, 50–52, 64–68, 168–69, 284–85, 288–90.

99 Monaghan and Monaghan, "Schoolbooks," 318. On the *Eclectic* series, see also Furstenberg, *In the Name of the Father*, 163; Neem, *Democracy's Schools*, 39–46.

100 Samuel Griswold Goodrich, *The First Book of History, for Children and Youth* (Boston: Richardson, Lord and Holbrook, 1831), 81–82 (quote at 82).

101 "Another Peter Fallen," *Philanthropist*, July 2, 1839.

102 Samuel Griswold Goodrich, *The First Book of History, for Children and Youth*, rev. ed. (Boston: Charles J. Hendee, 1840), 81–82. On Goodrich's treatment of slavery in his publications, see Barry Joyce, *The First U.S. History Textbooks: Constructing and Disseminating the American Tale in the Nineteenth Century* (Lanham, MD:

Lexington Books, 2015), 177–78; Donald Yacovone, *Teaching White Supremacy: America's Democratic Ordeal and the Forging of Our National Identity* (New York: Pantheon, 2022), 88–93.

103 Adrian Balbi, *An Abridgement of Universal Geography, Modern and Ancient*, comp. T. G. Bradford (New York: Freeman Hunt, 1835), 113.

104 American Anti-Slavery Society, *Fourth Annual Report*, 35–36.

105 "Celebration in South Scituate," *Liberator*, March 11, 1842.

106 "Speech of Wendell Phillips at the Annual Meeting of the Massachusetts A. S. Society, Thursday Evening, Jan. 27, 1853," *Liberator*, February 18, 1853.

107 Thomas Wentworth Higginson, *Contemporaries* (Boston: Houghton, Mifflin, 1899), 282. See Joe Lockard, "Slavery, Market Censorship and US Antebellum Schoolbook Publishing," *History of Education* 51, no. 2 (2022): 213–14.

108 "Home Education at the South," *De Bow's Review*, May 1855, 660.

109 "Educational Reform at the South," *De Bow's Review*, January 1856, 77, 69.

110 "Education at the South," *De Bow's Review*, December 1856, 651, 650.

111 "Our School Books," *De Bow's Review*, April 1860, 437, 439. On the southern campaign against northern history textbooks, see Joyce, *First U.S. History Textbooks*, 221–65.

112 Samuel Lander, *Our Own School Arithmetic* (Greensboro, NC: Sterling, Campbell and Albright, 1863), 171. On Confederate schoolbooks, see Elson, *Guardians of Tradition*, 98–100; Marten, *Children's Civil War*, 52–61; Connolly, *Slavery in American Children's Literature*, 76–90.

113 Rushmore G. Horton, *A Youth's History of the Great Civil War in the United States, from 1861 to 1865*, 2nd ed. (New York: Van Evrie, Horton, 1866), 48, 51. On Horton's treatment of the Civil War in his textbook, see Yacovone, *Teaching White Supremacy*, 76–81.

CHAPTER 5. "SHE . . . MADE ALL HER CHILDREN ABOLITIONISTS"

1 "The Last Grandchild of President Edwards," *New York Evangelist*, March 6, 1873.

2 Sinha, *Slave's Cause*, 172. On Whiting's children, see Nathaniel Goodwin, *Genealogical Notes; or Contributions to the Family History of Some of the First Settlers of Connecticut and Massachusetts* (Hartford, CT: F. A. Brown, 1856), 343.

3 Sinha, *Slave's Cause*, 545–46.

4 See Mason Whiting Tyler, *Recollections of the Civil War*, ed. William S. Tyler (New York: G. P. Putnam's Sons, 1912).

5 James Oliver Horton, "Generations of Protest: Black Families and Social Reform in Ante-Bellum Boston," *New England Quarterly* 49, no. 2 (1976): 252.

6 The case of the Jay family has recently been explored by David N. Gellman in *Liberty's Chain: Slavery, Abolition, and the Jay Family of New York* (Ithaca, NY: Cornell University Press, 2022).

7 On these memoirs, see Julie Roy Jeffrey, *Abolitionists Remember: Antislavery Autobiographies and the Unfinished Work of Emancipation* (Chapel Hill: University of North Carolina Press, 2008).

8   "Sonnets," *Liberator*, February 20, 1836.

9   William Lloyd Garrison to Helen E. Garrison, March 7, 1836, in *The Letters of William Lloyd Garrison*, vol. 2, *A House Dividing against Itself, 1836–1840*, ed. Louis Ruchames (Cambridge, MA: Harvard University Press, 1971), 60. See Harriet Hyman Alonso, *Growing Up Abolitionist: The Story of the Garrison Children* (Amherst: University of Massachusetts Press, 2002), 51–53; Sinha, *Slave's Cause*, 254.

10 Andrew Jackson, "Seventh Annual Message," December 2, 1835, in *The Addresses and Messages of the Presidents of the United States, from Washington to Harrison* (New York: Edward Walker, 1841), 558.

11 Malcolm Chase, "'Resolved in Defiance of Fool and of Knave'? Chartism, Children and Conflict," in *Conflict and Difference in Nineteenth-Century Literature*, ed. Dinah Birch and Mark Llewellyn (Basingstoke, UK: Palgrave Macmillan, 2010), 126–27.

12 William Lloyd Garrison to Francis Jackson, November 5, 1848, in *Letters of William Lloyd Garrison*, vol. 3, 601.

13 Alonso, *Growing Up Abolitionist*, 83, 98.

14 Villard, *William Lloyd Garrison on Non-Resistance*, 10.

15 Quoted in Alonso, *Growing Up Abolitionist*, 98.

16 Villard, *William Lloyd Garrison on Non-Resistance*, 6.

17 Wendell Phillips Garrison and Francis Jackson Garrison, *William Lloyd Garrison, 1805–1879: The Story of His Life Told by His Children*, vol. 4, *1861–1879* (New York: Century, 1889), 330, 332.

18 William Lloyd Garrison to Francis Jackson Garrison, August 17, 1857, in *The Letters of William Lloyd Garrison*, vol. 4, *From Disunionism to the Brink of War, 1850–1860*, ed. Louis Ruchames (Cambridge, MA: Harvard University Press, 1975), 474. See Alonso, *Growing Up Abolitionist*, 99–100.

19 See Michaël Roy, introduction to *Frederick Douglass in Context*, ed. Michaël Roy (Cambridge: Cambridge University Press, 2021), 1–6.

20 Celeste-Marie Bernier and Andrew Taylor, introduction to *If I Survive: Frederick Douglass and Family in the Walter O. Evans Collection*, ed. Celeste-Marie Bernier and Andrew Taylor (Edinburgh: Edinburgh University Press, 2018), xcvi.

21 Charles Remond Douglass, "Some Incidents of the Home Life of Frederick Douglass," in Bernier and Taylor, *If I Survive*, 669.

22 Rosetta Douglass Sprague, "Anna Murray-Douglass—My Mother as I Recall Her," *Journal of Negro History* 8, no. 1 (1923): 98.

23 Benjamin Fagan, "The Collective Making of *Frederick Douglass' Paper*," *Civil War History* 68, no. 2 (2022): 137–39 (quotes at 138).

24 C. Douglass, "Some Incidents," 670.

25 Sprague, "Anna Murray-Douglass," 97, 98.

26 C. Douglass, "Some Incidents," 673.

27 Lewis Henry Douglass, undated and untitled handwritten statement, ca. 1905, in F. Douglass, *Narrative of the Life of Frederick Douglass*, 271. On the family's Underground Railroad operations, see also Frederic May Holland, *Frederick Douglass:*

The Colored Orator (Toronto: Funk and Wagnalls, 1891), 186; Jesse Olsavsky, "The Underground Railroad," in Roy, *Frederick Douglass in Context*, 284; Leigh Fought, *Women in the World of Frederick Douglass* (New York: Oxford University Press, 2017), 125–26.

28 C. Douglass, "Some Incidents," 670. See David W. Blight, *Frederick Douglass: Prophet of Freedom* (New York: Simon and Schuster, 2018), 296–98.

29 F. Douglass, *Life and Times of Frederick Douglass*, 269.

30 Henry L. Stearns, in *A John Brown Reader: The Story of John Brown in His Own Words, in the Words of Those Who Knew Him, and in the Poetry and Prose of the Literary Heritage*, ed. Louis Ruchames (London: Abelard-Schuman, 1959), 35.

31 John Brown to Henry L. Stearns, July 15, 1857, in Ruchames, *John Brown Reader*, 38. On Brown's relationships with Black children specifically, see Brigitte Fielder, "John Brown, Black History, and Black Childhood: Contextualizing Lorenz Graham's John Brown Books," *Humanities* 11, no. 5 (2022): 2–6. Another Underground Railroad operator, Levi Coffin, wrote in his 1876 memoirs, "I date my conversion to Abolitionism from an incident which occurred when I was about seven years old." Levi Coffin, *Reminiscences of Levi Coffin, the Reputed President of the Underground Railroad* (Cincinnati, OH: Western Tract Society, 1876), 12.

32 Annie Douglass to Frederick Douglass, December 7, 1859, in Frederick Douglass, *Frederick Douglass Papers*, ser. 3, *Correspondence*, vol. 2, *1853–1865*, ed. John R. McKivigan (New Haven, CT: Yale University Press, 2018), 287.

33 "To My British Anti-Slavery Friends," *Douglass' Monthly*, June 1860, 277; "Death of Little Annie Douglass," *Douglass' Monthly*, April 1860, 244. See Fought, *Women in the World of Frederick Douglass*, 172–73; Blight, *Frederick Douglass*, 318–20. Frankie Hutton notes that children in a number of African American communities participated in programs to honor the memory of John Brown and raise money for his widow. "All over the nation," he writes, "black children were made aware of the fate of John Brown and his sacrifices for people of color." Frankie Hutton, *The Early Black Press in America, 1827 to 1860* (Westport, CT: Greenwood Press, 1993), 139.

34 Villard, *William Lloyd Garrison on Non-Resistance*, 2.

35 Hélène Quanquin, *Men in the American Women's Rights Movement, 1830–1890: Cumbersome Allies* (New York: Routledge, 2020), 26; Daina Ramey Berry, "Searching for Anna Douglass in the Archives," *Black Perspectives* (AAIHS), June 6, 2022, www.aaihs.org.

36 Anti-Slavery Convention of American Women, *Proceedings of the Anti-Slavery Convention of American Women* (New York: William S. Dorr, 1837), 12. See Ruth Bogin and Jean Fagan Yellin, introduction to *The Abolitionist Sisterhood: Women's Political Culture in Antebellum America*, ed. Jean Fagan Yellin and John C. Van Horne (Ithaca, NY: Cornell University Press, 1994), 14–15.

37 "Twenty-Fourth Annual Meeting of the American Anti-Slavery Society," *Liberator*, May 22, 1857.

38 J. Jones, *Young Abolitionists*, 20, 21.

39 Steven Mintz, "Why the History of Childhood Matters," *Journal of the History of Childhood and Youth* 5, no. 1 (2012): 23.

40 J. Jones, *Young Abolitionists*, 23. On abolitionist mothers in literature, see De Rosa, *Domestic Abolitionism and Juvenile Literature*, 79–106.

41 Julie Roy Jeffrey, *The Great Silent Army of Abolitionism: Ordinary Women in the Antislavery Movement* (Chapel Hill: University of North Carolina Press, 1998).

42 Aaron M. Powell, *Personal Reminiscences of the Anti-Slavery and Other Reforms and Reformers* (New York: Caulon Press, 1899), 1–2.

43 Powell, 3, 11.

44 "Bond, Mrs. Elizabeth Powell," in *A Woman of the Century: Fourteen Hundred-Seventy Biographical Sketches Accompanied by Portraits of Leading American Women in All Walks of Life*, ed. Frances E. Willard and Mary A. Livermore (Buffalo, NY: Charles Wells Moulton, 1893), 104.

45 Lucy N. Colman, *Reminiscences* (Buffalo, NY: H. L. Green, 1891), 5.

46 Elizabeth C. Stevens, "Elizabeth Buffum Chace and Lillie Chace Wyman: Motherhood as a Subversive Activity in Nineteenth Century Rhode Island," *Quaker History* 84, no. 1 (1995): 38. See also Elizabeth C. Stevens, *Elizabeth Buffum Chace and Lillie Chace Wyman: A Century of Abolitionist, Suffragist and Workers' Rights Activism* (Jefferson, NC: McFarland, 2003).

47 Elizabeth Buffum Chace, *Anti-Slavery Reminiscences* (Central Falls, RI: E. L. Freeman and Son, 1891), 9.

48 Richard S. Newman, *The Transformation of American Abolitionism: Fighting Slavery in the Early Republic* (Chapel Hill: University of North Carolina Press, 2002), 53, 116–17, 119–20.

49 Chace, *Anti-Slavery Reminiscences*, 10.

50 On Quaker opposition to the immediatist abolition campaign, see Ryan P. Jordan, *Slavery and the Meetinghouse: The Quakers and the Abolitionist Dilemma, 1820–1865* (Bloomington: Indiana University Press, 2007).

51 Stevens, "Elizabeth Buffum Chace," 41.

52 Lillie Buffum Chace Wyman and Arthur Crawford Wyman, *Elizabeth Buffum Chace, 1806–1899: Her Life and Its Environment*, vol. 1 (Boston: W. B. Clarke, 1914), 33.

53 Chace, *Anti-Slavery Reminiscences*, 23–24, 23.

54 Stevens, "Elizabeth Buffum Chace," 43.

55 Chace, *Anti-Slavery Reminiscences*, 25.

56 Lillie Chace Wyman, "From Generation to Generation," *Atlantic Monthly*, August 1889, 176, 174.

57 Chace, *Anti-Slavery Reminiscences*, 42.

58 Stevens, "Elizabeth Buffum Chace," 44.

59 Wyman and Wyman, *Elizabeth Buffum Chace*, 141.

60 Chace, *Anti-Slavery Reminiscences*, 36.

61 Wyman, "From Generation to Generation," 167.

62 Chace, *Anti-Slavery Reminiscences*, 40–41.

63 Wyman, "From Generation to Generation," 173.

64 "Questions, Enigmas, Charades, etc.," *Merry's Museum and Parley's Magazine* 32 (1856): 128.

65 "Merry's Monthly Chat with His Friends," *Merry's Museum and Parley's Magazine* 32 (1856): 158; "Letter from Henry C. Wright," *Liberator*, March 20, 1857. See Stevens, "Elizabeth Buffum Chace," 45–46; Stumpf, "Children with a Cause," 219–22.

66 Quoted in Stevens, *Elizabeth Buffum Chace*, 72.

67 There is debate as to whether Remond was born in 1824 or 1826. Her most recent biographer gives 1826 as her year of birth. Sirpa Salenius, *An Abolitionist Abroad: Sarah Parker Remond in Cosmopolitan Europe* (Amherst: University of Massachusetts Press, 2016), 1.

68 Sibyl Ventress Brownlee, "Out of the Abundance of the Heart: Sarah Ann Parker Remond's Quest for Freedom" (PhD diss., University of Massachusetts Amherst, 1997), 53–55 (quote at 55).

69 Brownlee, 62, 69.

70 Maritcha Lyons, in *We Are Your Sisters: Black Women in the Nineteenth Century*, ed. Dorothy Sterling (New York: W. W. Norton, 1984), 97.

71 Salenius, *Abolitionist Abroad*, 31–32.

72 "Sarah P. Remond," in Hill, *Our Exemplars, Poor and Rich*, 284.

73 "Sarah P. Remond," 276, 276–77.

74 E. Ball, *To Live an Antislavery Life*, 100–106.

75 "Sarah P. Remond," 277.

76 Sprague, "Anna Murray-Douglass," 101.

77 Brownlee, "Out of the Abundance of the Heart," 109. See also Yee, *Black Women Abolitionists*, 116–17.

78 Quoted in Quanquin, *Men in the American Women's Rights Movement*, 30. Sarah Parker Remond also credited Abby Kelley Foster as an important influence on her development as an antislavery orator.

79 Brownlee, "Out of the Abundance of the Heart," 109–13.

80 By contrast, the limitations imposed by gender cut short the antislavery career of another young and promising Black abolitionist, Sarah Forten, daughter of James and Charlotte Forten. As Julie Winch has shown, marriage and the birth of eight children "cut her off almost completely from the world she had known [as a child and young adult], the world of international antislavery." Winch, "Sarah Forten's Anti-Slavery Networks," in *Women's Rights and Transatlantic Antislavery in the Era of Emancipation*, ed. Kathryn Kish Sklar and James Brewer Stewart (New Haven, CT: Yale University Press, 2007), 154.

81 Sinha, *Slave's Cause*, 257–59.

82 Kellie Carter Jackson, *Force and Freedom: Black Abolitionists and the Politics of Violence* (Philadelphia: University of Pennsylvania Press, 2019).

83 Alonso, *Growing Up Abolitionist*, 138–39.

84 Wendell Phillips Garrison, who was fourteen at the time, reminisced about the capture of Anthony Burns in Wendell Phillips Garrison, *Parables for School and Home* (New York: Longmans, Green, 1897), 77–78.

85 Alonso, *Growing Up Abolitionist*, 140–63 (quotes at 158 and 159).

86 Quoted in Villard, *William Lloyd Garrison on Non-Resistance*, 20.

87 James M. McPherson, *The Abolitionist Legacy: From Reconstruction to the NAACP* (Princeton, NJ: Princeton University Press, 1975), 37–40 (quotes at 38 and 39).

88 Alonso, *Growing Up Abolitionist*, 3.

89 Rayford W. Logan, *The Negro in American Life and Thought: The Nadir, 1877–1901* (New York: Dial Press, 1954).

90 McPherson, *Abolitionist Legacy*, 159, 157–58, 304, 389 (quote at 389).

91 "The President and His Speeches," *Douglass' Monthly*, September 1862, 707.

92 Blight, *Frederick Douglass*, 370–74; Alonso, *Growing Up Abolitionist*, 144–54.

93 Frederick Douglass to Samuel Clarke Pomeroy, August 27, 1862, in F. Douglass, *Frederick Douglass Papers*, 341–42. The letter suggests that Charles was also considering signing up for the scheme.

94 Blight, *Frederick Douglass*, 385.

95 Ezra Greenspan, "Frederick Bailey Douglass and His People: A Family Biography," unpublished manuscript. Joseph Douglass Jr. published a "family biography" of the Douglasses in 2011, but it is out of print and not readily available. Joseph L. Douglass Jr., *Frederick Douglass: A Family Biography, 1733–1896* (Shelbyville, KY: Winterlight Books, 2011).

96 Bernier and Taylor, introduction to Bernier and Taylor, *If I Survive*, lxxi.

97 M. A. Majors, *Noted Negro Women: Their Triumphs and Activities* (Chicago: Donohue and Henneberry, 1893), 194.

98 Stevens, *Elizabeth Buffum Chace*, 77, 120, 134–46, 154–62 (quotes at 77).

99 Lillie Chace Wyman, "Luke Gardiner's Love," in *Poverty Grass* (Boston: Houghton, Mifflin, 1886), 90.

100 See Hack, *Reaping Something New*, 26.

101 Stevens, *Elizabeth Buffum Chace*, 120–32.

102 Lillie Buffum Chace Wyman, "Girls Together," *Brownies' Book*, April 1921, 109–11 (quote at 110). Diaz appears as "Abigail Morton" in the Juvenile Anti-Slavery Society Records, Massachusetts Historical Society. She discusses her juvenile antislavery activism in Abby Morton Diaz, "Antislavery Times in Plymouth," *New England Magazine*, April 1899, 216–24.

103 Violet J. Harris, "Race Consciousness, Refinement, and Radicalism: Socialization in *The Brownies' Book*," *Children's Literature Association Quarterly* 14, no. 4 (1989): 192.

104 Katharine Capshaw Smith, *Children's Literature of the Harlem Renaissance* (Bloomington: Indiana University Press, 2004), 2.

105 Brigitte Fielder, "'As the Crow Flies': Black Children, Flying Africans, and Fantastic Futures in *The Brownies' Book*," *Journal of the History of Childhood and Youth* 14, no. 3 (2021): 413–14.

106 W. E. B. Du Bois, "The Immortal Child," in *Darkwater: Voices from Within the Veil* (New York: Harcourt, Brace and Howe, 1920), 202, 204, 213.

1 Quoted in Chad Montrie, *The Myth of "Silent Spring": Rethinking the Origins of American Environmentalism* (Oakland: University of California Press, 2018), 1.

2 Teresa A. Goddu, "Climate Activism as the New Abolitionism," *American Literary History*, online forum (2021): e58–e65 (quotes at e58–e59 and e61).

3 "Southern Outrages," *Liberator*, February 22, 1856.

4 Lillie Chace to Anna Elizabeth Dickinson, November 18, 1860, Anna E. Dickinson Papers, Library of Congress.

5 J. Matthew Gallman, *America's Joan of Arc: The Life of Anna Elizabeth Dickinson* (New York: Oxford University Press, 2006), 2–4, 9–11, 16.

6 Jeffrey Kluger, "Kids Just Brought Montana to Court over Climate Change. The Case Could Make Waves beyond the State," *Time*, June 23, 2023, www.time.com.

7 See Michael S. Cummings, *Children's Voices in Politics* (Oxford, UK: Peter Lang, 2020); John Wall, *Give Children the Vote: On Democratizing Democracy* (London: Bloomsbury Academic, 2022); John Wall, ed., *Exploring Children's Suffrage: Interdisciplinary Perspectives on Ageless Voting* (London: Palgrave Macmillan, 2022).

BIBLIOGRAPHY

PRIMARY SOURCES: MANUSCRIPT COLLECTIONS

Adams, John Quincy. Papers. Massachusetts Historical Society.

Anti-Slavery Collection. Boston Public Library.

Connecticut Temperance Society Pledge. Connecticut Historical Society.

Dickinson, Anna E. Papers. Library of Congress.

Juvenile Anti-Slavery Society Records. Massachusetts Historical Society.

New York African Free School Records. New-York Historical Society.

Pennsylvania Abolition Society Papers. Historical Society of Pennsylvania.

Salem Female Anti-Slavery Society Record Book. Phillips Library, Peabody
    Essex Museum.

Wright, Henry Clarke. Letter Book. Cape Ann Museum.

PRIMARY SOURCES: PERIODICALS

Abolitionist

Advocate of Freedom

African Repository and Colonial Journal

Anti-Slavery Bugle

Atlantic Monthly

Boston Commercial Gazette

Boston Quarterly Review

Boston Recorder

Brownies' Book

Child's Friend

Christian Recorder

Christian World

Colored American

Daily National Intelligencer

De Bow's Review

Douglass' Monthly

Emancipator

Evening Post
Family Pioneer and Juvenile Key
Frederick Douglass' Paper
Freedom's Journal
Friend of Man
Genius of Universal Emancipation
Herald of Freedom
Journal of the American Temperance Union
Juvenile Instructor
Juvenile Reformer, and Sabbath School Instructor
Liberator
Merry's Museum and Parley's Magazine
Morning Star
National Anti-Slavery Standard
National Enquirer, and Constitutional Advocate of Universal Liberty
National Era
New England Magazine
New York Commercial Advertiser
New York Evangelist
Non-Resistant
North American Review
North Star
Pennsylvania Freeman
Philanthropist
Radical Abolitionist
Religious Intelligencer
Sabbath School Instructor
Sabbath School Treasury
Slave's Friend
Sunday-School Journal
Weekly Anglo-African
Youth's Cabinet
Youth's Companion
Youth's Emancipator
Youth's Temperance Advocate

PRIMARY SOURCES: BOOKS AND PAMPHLETS

Alcott, Bronson. *Conversations with Children on the Gospels.* Vol. 1. Boston: James Munroe, 1836.

American Anti-Slavery Society. "The American Anti-Slavery Society Declares Its Sentiments." In Pease and Pease, *Antislavery Argument,* 65–71.

———. *First Annual Report of the American Anti-Slavery Society.* New York: Dorr and Butterfield, 1834.

———. *Fourth Annual Report of the American Anti-Slavery Society.* New York: William S. Dorr, 1837.

———. *Second Annual Report of the American Anti-Slavery Society.* New York: William S. Dorr, 1835.

American Convention of Abolition Societies. *Minutes of the Adjourned Session of the Twentieth Biennial American Convention for Promoting the Abolition of Slavery, and Improving the Condition of the African Race, Held at Baltimore, Nov. 1828.* Philadelphia: Samuel Parker, 1828.

Andrews, Charles C. *The History of the New-York African Free-Schools, from Their Establishment in 1787, to the Present Time.* New York: Mahlon Day, 1830.

Anti-Slavery Convention of American Women. *Proceedings of the Anti-Slavery Convention of American Women.* New York: William S. Dorr, 1837.

Aunt Mary. *The Edinburgh Doll and Other Tales for Children.* Boston: John P. Jewett, 1854.

Balbi, Adrian. *An Abridgement of Universal Geography, Modern and Ancient.* Compiled by T. G. Bradford. New York: Freeman Hunt, 1835.

Ball, Charles. *Slavery in the United States: A Narrative of the Life and Adventures of Charles Ball, a Black Man.* New York: John S. Taylor, 1837.

Barber, John W., and Elizabeth G. Barber. *Historical, Poetical and Pictorial American Scenes.* New Haven, CT: J. W. Barber, 1850.

Basker, James G., ed. *Amazing Grace: An Anthology of Poems about Slavery, 1660–1810.* New Haven, CT: Yale University Press, 2002.

———, ed. *American Antislavery Writings: Colonial Beginnings to Emancipation.* New York: Library of America, 2012.

Bernier, Celeste-Marie, and Andrew Taylor, eds. *If I Survive: Frederick Douglass and Family in the Walter O. Evans Collection.* Edinburgh: Edinburgh University Press, 2018.

Bibb, Henry. *Narrative of the Life and Adventures of Henry Bibb, an American Slave.* New York: Published by the Author, 1849.

Bingham, Caleb. *The American Preceptor.* Boston: Manning and Loring, 1794.

———. *The Columbian Orator.* Edited by David W. Blight. New York: New York University Press, 1998.

Bowditch, Henry I. *A Brief Plea for an Ambulance System for the Army of the United States, as Drawn from the Extra Sufferings of the Late Lieut. Bowditch and a Wounded Comrade.* Boston: Ticknor and Fields, 1863.

Bowditch, Vincent Y. *Life and Correspondence of Henry Ingersoll Bowditch*. Vol. 1. Boston: Houghton, Mifflin, 1902.

Brinsmade, P. A. Preface to Clarkson, *Abolition of the African Slave-Trade*, iii–v.

Burke, Arthur Meredyth. *The Prominent Families of the United States of America*. Vol. 1. London: Sackville Press, 1909.

Burt, Thomas. *Thomas Burt, M.P., D.C.L., Pitman and Privy Councillor: An Autobiography*. London: T. Fisher Unwin, 1924.

Chace, Elizabeth Buffum. *Anti-Slavery Reminiscences*. Central Falls, RI: E. L. Freeman and Son, 1891.

Chapman, Maria Weston, ed. *The Liberty Bell*. Boston: Massachusetts Anti-Slavery Fair, 1841.

———, ed. *The Liberty Bell*. Boston: National Anti-Slavery Bazaar, 1848.

———. "Sonnet." In Chapman, *Liberty Bell* (1841), 99–100.

Child, Lydia Maria. *A Lydia Maria Child Reader*. Edited by Carolyn L. Karcher. Durham, NC: Duke University Press, 1997.

Clarkson, Thomas. *Abolition of the African Slave-Trade, by the British Parliament*. Vol. 1. Augusta, ME: P. A. Brinsmade, 1830.

———. *The History of the Rise, Progress, and Accomplishment of the Abolition of the African Slave-Trade by the British Parliament*. Vol. 2. London: Longman, Hurst, Rees and Orme, 1808.

Cleveland, Charles Dexter. *The National Orator*. 3rd ed. New York: N. and J. White, 1832.

Coffin, Levi. *Reminiscences of Levi Coffin, the Reputed President of the Underground Railroad*. Cincinnati, OH: Western Tract Society, 1876.

Collins, John A. *The Anti-Slavery Picknick: A Collection of Speeches, Poems, Dialogues and Songs*. Boston: H. W. Williams, 1842.

Colman, Lucy N. *Reminiscences*. Buffalo, NY: H. L. Green, 1891.

Convention for the Improvement of the Free People of Color. *Minutes and Proceedings of the First Annual Convention of the People of Colour*. Philadelphia: Committee of Arrangements, 1831.

Copley, Esther. *A History of the Slave Trade and Its Abolition*. London: Sunday-School Union, 1836.

Cowper, William. "The Negro's Complaint." In Basker, *Amazing Grace*, 300–301.

———. *The Negro's Complaint: A Poem*. London: Harvey and Darton, 1826.

Crummell, Alexander. *Africa and America: Addresses and Discourses*. Springfield, MA: Willey, 1891.

Darton, William. *Little Truths: Containing Information on Divers Subjects, for the Instruction of Children*. Vol. 2. London: William Darton, 1788.

De Grasse, Isaiah G. *A Sermon on Education*. New York: James Van Norden, 1839.

Douglass, Charles Remond. "Some Incidents of the Home Life of Frederick Douglass." In Bernier and Taylor, *If I Survive*, 669–74.

Douglass, Frederick. *Frederick Douglass Papers*. Ser. 3, *Correspondence*. Vol. 2, *1853–1865*. Edited by John R. McKivigan. New Haven, CT: Yale University Press, 2018.

————. *Life and Times of Frederick Douglass.* Edited by Celeste-Marie Bernier and Andrew Taylor. Oxford: Oxford University Press, 2022.

————. *My Bondage and My Freedom.* Edited by Nick Bromell and R. Blakeslee Gilpin. New York: W. W. Norton, 2021.

————. *Narrative of the Life of Frederick Douglass, an American Slave.* Edited by Celeste-Marie Bernier. Peterborough, ON: Broadview Press, 2018.

————. *Speeches and Writings.* Edited by David W. Blight. New York: Library of America, 2022.

Douglass, Lewis Henry. Undated and untitled handwritten statement (c. 1905). In F. Douglass, *Narrative of the Life of Frederick Douglass,* 270–72.

Du Bois, W. E. B. *Darkwater: Voices from Within the Veil.* New York: Harcourt, Brace and Howe, 1920.

Easton, Hosea. *A Treatise on the Intellectual Character, and Civil and Political Condition of the Colored People of the U. States.* Boston: Isaac Knapp, 1837.

Equiano, Olaudah. *The Life and Adventures of Olaudah Equiano; or Gustavus Vassa, the African.* Abridged by Abigail Mott. New York: Samuel Wood and Sons, 1829.

Follen, Eliza Lee. *The Liberty Cap.* Boston: Leonard C. Bowles, 1846.

————. *The Life of Charles Follen.* Boston: Thomas H. Webb, 1844.

Garrison, Wendell Phillips. *Parables for School and Home.* New York: Longmans, Green, 1897.

Garrison, Wendell Phillips, and Francis Jackson Garrison. *William Lloyd Garrison, 1805–1879: The Story of His Life Told by His Children.* Vol. 1, *1805–1835.* New York: Century, 1885.

————. *William Lloyd Garrison, 1805–1879: The Story of His Life Told by His Children.* Vol. 4, *1861–1879.* New York: Century, 1889.

Garrison, William Lloyd. *Juvenile Poems, for the Use of Free American Children, of Every Complexion.* Boston: Garrison and Knapp, 1835.

————. *The Letters of William Lloyd Garrison.* Vol. 1, *I Will Be Heard! 1822–1835.* Edited by Walter M. Merrill. Cambridge, MA: Harvard University Press, 1971.

————. *The Letters of William Lloyd Garrison.* Vol. 2, *A House Dividing against Itself, 1836–1840.* Edited by Louis Ruchames. Cambridge, MA: Harvard University Press, 1971.

————. *The Letters of William Lloyd Garrison.* Vol. 3, *No Union with Slaveholders, 1841–1849.* Edited by Walter M. Merrill. Cambridge, MA: Harvard University Press, 1973.

————. *The Letters of William Lloyd Garrison.* Vol. 4, *From Disunionism to the Brink of War, 1850–1860.* Edited by Louis Ruchames. Cambridge, MA: Harvard University Press, 1975.

————. *A Selection of Anti-Slavery Hymns, for the Use of the Friends of Emancipation.* Boston: Garrison and Knapp, 1834.

————. *Sonnets and Other Poems.* Boston: Oliver Johnson, 1843.

Glasgow Ladies' Auxiliary Emancipation Society. *Three Years' Female Anti-Slavery Effort, in Britain and America.* Glasgow: Aird and Russell, 1837.

Goodrich, Samuel Griswold. *The First Book of History, for Children and Youth.* Boston: Richardson, Lord and Holbrook, 1831.

———. *The First Book of History, for Children and Youth*. Rev. ed. Boston: Charles J. Hendee, 1840.

Goodwin, Nathaniel. *Genealogical Notes; or Contributions to the Family History of Some of the First Settlers of Connecticut and Massachusetts*. Hartford, CT: F. A. Brown, 1856.

Green, Frances Whipple, ed. *The Envoy: From Free Hearts to the Free*. Pawtucket, RI: Juvenile Emancipation Society, 1840.

Hallowell, Anna Davis. *James and Lucretia Mott: Life and Letters*. Boston: Houghton, Mifflin, 1884.

Hallowell, William Penrose. *Record of a Branch of the Hallowell Family Including the Longstreth, Penrose, and Norwood Branches*. Philadelphia: Hallowell, 1893.

Hamilton, William. *An Oration Delivered in the African Zion Church, on the Fourth of July, 1827, in Commemoration of the Abolition of Domestic Slavery in this State*. New York: Gray and Bunce, 1827.

Hammond, James Henry. *Remarks of Mr. Hammond, of South Carolina, on the Question of Receiving Petitions for the Abolition of Slavery in the District of Columbia*. Washington, DC: Duff Green, 1836.

Hedge, Mary Anne. *Radama; or, The Enlightened African*. London: Harvey and Darton, 1824.

Heyrick, Elizabeth. *Immediate, Not Gradual Abolition; or, An Inquiry into the Shortest, Safest, and Most Effectual Means of Getting Rid of West Indian Slavery*. London: Hatchard and Son, 1824.

Higginson, Thomas Wentworth. *Contemporaries*. Boston: Houghton, Mifflin, 1899.

Hill, Matthew Davenport, ed. *Our Exemplars, Poor and Rich; or, Biographical Sketches of Men and Women Who Have, by an Extraordinary Use of Their Opportunities, Benefited Their Fellow-Creatures*. London: Cassell, Petter, and Galpin, 1861.

Holland, Frederic May. *Frederick Douglass: The Colored Orator*. Toronto: Funk and Wagnalls, 1891.

Horton, Rushmore G. *A Youth's History of the Great Civil War in the United States, from 1861 to 1865*. 2nd ed. New York: Van Evrie, Horton, 1866.

Hunt, Thomas P. *The Cold Water Army*. Boston: Whipple and Damrell, 1840.

———. *Life and Thoughts of Rev. Thomas P. Hunt: An Autobiography*. Wilkes-Barre, PA: Robert Baur and Son, 1901.

Jackson, Andrew. "Seventh Annual Message." December 2, 1835. In *The Addresses and Messages of the Presidents of the United States, from Washington to Harrison*, 534–60. New York: Edward Walker, 1841.

Jackson, William. *Views of Slavery, in Its Effects on the Wealth, Population, and Character of Nations*. Philadelphia: Junior Anti-Slavery Society, 1838.

Jefferson, Thomas. "Degrading Influences of Slavery." In Collins, *Anti-Slavery Picknick*, 45–47.

———. *Notes on the State of Virginia*. Edited by Frank Shuffelton. New York: Penguin, 1999.

Jewett, Charles. *The Temperance Toy*. Boston: Whipple and Damrell, 1840.

———. *The Youth's Temperance Lecturer*. Boston: Whipple and Damrell, 1841.

Jones, Absalom, and Richard Allen. *A Narrative of the Proceedings of the Black People, during the Late Awful Calamity in Philadelphia, in the Year 1793*. Philadelphia: William W. Woodward, 1794.

Jones, Jane Elizabeth. *The Young Abolitionists; or, Conversations on Slavery*. Boston: Anti-Slavery Office, 1848.

Lacon. *The Devil in America: A Dramatic Satire*. Philadelphia: J. B. Lippincott, 1860.

Lander, Samuel. *Our Own School Arithmetic*. Greensboro, NC: Sterling, Campbell and Albright, 1863.

Levick Samuel J. *Life of Samuel J. Levick*. Philadelphia: William·H. Pile's Sons, 1896.

Majors, M. A. *Noted Negro Women: Their Triumphs and Activities*. Chicago: Donohue and Henneberry, 1893.

Marsh, John. *Temperance Recollections: Labors, Defeats, Triumphs. An Autobiography*. New York: Charles Scribner, 1866.

Morse, Jedidiah. *The American Geography*. Elizabethtown, NJ: Shepard Kollock, 1789.

Mott, Abigail. *Biographical Sketches and Interesting Anecdotes of Persons of Colour*. New York: Mahlon Day, 1826.

———. Preface to Equiano, *Life and Adventures of Olaudah Equiano*, iv.

Murray, Lindley. *The English Reader*. New York: Isaac Collins, 1799.

———. *The English Reader*. New York: Collins, 1819.

National Convention of Colored Citizens. *Minutes of the National Convention of Colored Citizens*. New York: Piercy and Reed, 1843.

New and Entertaining Alphabet, for Young Children, Where Some Instruction May Be Gained, and Much Amusement, A. London: W. Darton Jr., 1813.

Newbery, John. *Geography Made Familiar and Easy to Young Gentlemen and Ladies*. London: J. Newbery, 1748.

———. *The Newtonian System of Philosophy Adapted to the Capacities of Young Gentlemen and Ladies*. London: J. Newbery, 1761.

New York Medico-Historical Society. *The Medical Register of New York, New Jersey and Connecticut, for the Year Commencing June 1, 1883*. New York: G. P. Putnam's Sons, 1883.

New York State Anti-Slavery Society. *Proceedings of the First Annual Meeting of the New-York State Anti-Slavery Society*. Utica: New York State Anti-Slavery Society, 1836.

Ohio Anti-Slavery Society. *Proceedings of the Ohio Anti-Slavery Convention*. N.p.: Beaumont and Wallace, 1835.

Opie, Amelia. *The Black Man's Lament; or, How to Make Sugar*. London: Harvey and Darton, 1826.

———. *The Negro Boy's Tale, a Poem, Addressed to Children*. London: Harvey and Darton, 1824.

Palmer, Beverly Wilson. "Biographical Directory." In *Selected Letters of Lucretia Coffin Mott*, xlv–li. Edited by Beverly Wilson Palmer. Urbana: University of Illinois Press, 2002.

Paul, Susan. *Memoir of James Jackson, the Attentive and Obedient Scholar, Who Died in Boston, October 31, 1833, Aged Six Years and Eleven Months.* Edited by Lois Brown. Cambridge, MA: Harvard University Press, 2000.

Pease, William H., and Jane H. Pease, eds. *The Antislavery Argument.* Indianapolis, IN: Bobbs-Merrill, 1965.

Pennington, James W. C. *The Fugitive Blacksmith; or, Events in the History of James W. C. Pennington.* 2nd ed. London: Charles Gilpin, 1849.

———. *The Fugitive Blacksmith; or, Events in the History of James W. C. Pennington.* 3rd ed. London: Charles Gilpin, 1850.

Peterson, Henry. *An Address Delivered before the Junior Anti-Slavery Society of the City and County of Philadelphia, December 23, 1836.* Philadelphia: Merrihew and Gunn, 1837.

———. *Address on American Slavery, Delivered before the Semi-Annual Meeting, of the Junior Anti-Slavery Society, of Philadelphia.* Philadelphia: Merrihew and Gunn, 1838.

Pierpont, John. *The American First Class Book.* Boston: William B. Fowle, 1823.

Pierson, B. T. *Directory of the City of Newark, for 1841–42.* Newark, NJ: Aaron Guest, 1841.

Powell, Aaron M. *Personal Reminiscences of the Anti-Slavery and Other Reforms and Reformers.* New York: Caulon Press, 1899.

Preston, Ann. *Cousin Ann's Stories for Children.* Philadelphia: J. M. McKim, 1849.

Prince, Mary. *The History of Mary Prince, a West Indian Slave.* Edited by Sara Salih. London: Penguin, 2004.

Remond, Sarah Parker. "Sarah P. Remond." In Hill, *Our Exemplars, Poor and Rich,* 276–86.

Rhode Island State Anti-Slavery Society. *Proceedings of the Rhode-Island Anti-Slavery Convention.* Providence, RI: H. H. Brown, 1836.

Ripley, C. Peter, ed. *The Black Abolitionist Papers.* Vol. 2, *Canada, 1830–1865.* Chapel Hill: University of North Carolina Press, 1986.

———, ed. *The Black Abolitionist Papers.* Vol. 3, *The United States, 1830–1846.* Chapel Hill: University of North Carolina Press, 1991.

Robinson, Robert. *Slavery Inconsistent with the Spirit of Christianity: A Sermon Preached at Cambridge, on Sunday, Feb. 10, 1788.* Cambridge, UK: J. Archdeacon, 1788.

Rowson, Susanna. *An Abridgment of Universal Geography.* Boston: John West, 1806.

Ruchames, Louis, ed. *A John Brown Reader: The Story of John Brown in His Own Words, in the Words of Those Who Knew Him, and in the Poetry and Prose of the Literary Heritage.* London: Abelard-Schuman, 1959.

Rulison, Henry Flagler. *Genealogy of the Rulison, Rulifson, Ruliffson and Allied Families in America.* Chicago: Printed for private distribution, 1919.

Smith, James McCune. Introduction to F. Douglass, *My Bondage and My Freedom,* 19–33.

Sprague, Rosetta Douglass. "Anna Murray-Douglass—My Mother as I Recall Her." *Journal of Negro History* 8, no. 1 (1923): 93–101.

Sterling, Dorothy, ed. *We Are Your Sisters: Black Women in the Nineteenth Century.* New York: W. W. Norton, 1984.

Tocqueville, Alexis de. *Democracy in America.* Translated and edited by Harvey C. Mansfield and Delba Winthrop. Chicago: University of Chicago Press, 2000.

Townsend, Hannah, and Mary Townsend. *The Anti-Slavery Alphabet.* Philadelphia: Printed for the Anti-Slavery Fair, 1846.

Traill, Catherine Parr. *Prejudice Reproved; or, The History of the Negro Toy-Seller.* London: Harvey and Darton, 1826.

Tribute to the Memory of Fitzhugh Smith, the Son of Gerrit Smith, A. New York: Wiley and Putnam, 1840.

Tyler, Lyon G. *The Letters and Times of the Tylers.* Vol. 1. Richmond, VA: Whittet and Shepperson, 1884.

Tyler, Mason Whiting. *Recollections of the Civil War.* Edited by William S. Tyler. New York: G. P. Putnam's Sons, 1912.

Villard, Fanny Garrison. *William Lloyd Garrison on Non-Resistance.* New York: Nation, 1924.

Wakefield, Priscilla. *Mental Improvement; or, The Beauties and Wonders of Nature and Art, Conveyed in a Series of Instructive Conversations.* Vol. 1. London: Darton and Harvey, 1794.

Walker, David. *David Walker's Appeal to the Coloured Citizens of the World.* Edited by Peter P. Hinks. University Park: Pennsylvania State University Press, 2000.

Walker, Jonathan. *A Picture of Slavery, for Youth.* Boston: J. Walker and W. R. Bliss, n.d.

Warren, Charles J. *The Cold Water Army.* New Haven, CT: Hitchcock and Stafford, 1842.

Webster, Noah, Jr. *The Little Reader's Assistant.* Hartford, CT: Elisha Babcock, 1790.

———. *The Little Reader's Assistant.* 4th ed. Northampton, MA: William Butler, 1798.

Willard, Frances E., and Mary A. Livermore, eds. *A Woman of the Century: Fourteen Hundred-Seventy Biographical Sketches Accompanied by Portraits of Leading American Women in All Walks of Life.* Buffalo, NY: Charles Wells Moulton, 1893.

Willson, Joseph. *The Elite of Our People: Joseph Willson's Sketches of Black Upper-Class Life in Antebellum Philadelphia.* Edited by Julie Winch. University Park: Pennsylvania State University Press, 2000.

Wright, Henry Clarke. *A Kiss for a Blow; or, A Collection of Stories for Children Showing Them How to Prevent Quarreling.* Boston: B. B. Mussey, 1842.

———. *Marriage and Parentage; or, The Reproductive Element in Man, as a Means to His Elevation and Happiness.* Boston: Bela Marsh, 1866.

———. "Reminiscences: My First Acquaintance with Garrison and Anti-Slavery." In Chapman, *Liberty Bell* (1848), 148–58.

Wyman, Lillie Chace. *Poverty Grass.* Boston: Houghton, Mifflin, 1886.

Wyman, Lillie Chace, and Arthur Crawford Wyman. *Elizabeth Buffum Chace, 1806–1899: Her Life and Its Environment.* Vol. 1. Boston: W. B. Clarke, 1914.

SECONDARY SOURCES

Alonso, Harriet Hyman. *Growing Up Abolitionist: The Story of the Garrison Children*. Amherst: University of Massachusetts Press, 2002.

Aptheker, Herbert. *Abolitionism: A Revolutionary Movement*. Boston: Twayne, 1989.

Bacon, Jacqueline. "The History of *Freedom's Journal*: A Study in Empowerment and Community." *Journal of African American History* 88, no. 1 (2003): 1–20.

Baker, Anne. *Heartless Immensity: Literature, Culture, and Geography in Antebellum America*. Ann Arbor: University of Michigan Press, 2006.

Ball, Erica L. *To Live an Antislavery Life: Personal Politics and the Antebellum Middle Class*. Athens: University of Georgia Press, 2012.

Basker, James G. Introduction to Basker, *American Antislavery Writings*, xxvii–xli.

Baumgartner, Kabria. *In Pursuit of Knowledge: Black Women and Educational Activism in Antebellum America*. New York: New York University Press, 2019.

Benes, Peter, ed. *Schooldays in New England, 1650–1900*. Dublin, NH: Dublin Seminar for New England Folklife, 2015.

Berlin, Ira, and Leslie M. Harris, eds. *Slavery in New York*. New York: New Press, 2005.

Bernier, Celeste-Marie, and Andrew Taylor. Introduction to Bernier and Taylor, *If I Survive*, lvii–xcvi.

Bernstein, Robin. *Racial Innocence: Performing American Childhood from Slavery to Civil Rights*. New York: New York University Press, 2011.

Berry, Daina Ramey. "Searching for Anna Douglass in the Archives." *Black Perspectives* (AAIHS), June 6, 2022. www.aaihs.org.

Birch, Dinah, and Mark Llewellyn, eds. *Conflict and Difference in Nineteenth-Century Literature*. Basingstoke, UK: Palgrave Macmillan, 2010.

Blight, David W. *Frederick Douglass: Prophet of Freedom*. New York: Simon and Schuster, 2018.

Blum, Edward J., and John H. Matsui. *War Is All Hell: The Nature of Evil and the Civil War*. Philadelphia: University of Pennsylvania Press, 2021.

Boggis, JerriAnne, Eva Allegra Raimon, and Barbara A. White, eds. *Harriet Wilson's New England: Race, Writing, and Region*. Durham: University of New Hampshire Press, 2007.

Bogin, Ruth, and Jean Fagan Yellin. Introduction to Yellin and Van Horne, *Abolitionist Sisterhood*, 1–19.

Boisseron, Bénédicte. *Afro-Dog: Blackness and the Animal Question*. New York: Columbia University Press, 2018.

Boylan, Anne M. *Sunday School: The Formation of an American Institution, 1790–1880*. New Haven, CT: Yale University Press, 1988.

Brown, Ira V. "'Am I Not a Woman and a Sister?': The Anti-Slavery Convention of American Women, 1837–1839." *Pennsylvania History* 50, no. 1 (1983): 1–19.

Brown, Lois. Introduction to Paul, *Memoir of James Jackson*, 1–63.

———. "Out of the Mouths of Babes: The Abolitionist Campaign of Susan Paul and the Juvenile Choir of Boston." *New England Quarterly* 75, no. 1 (2002): 52–79.

Brownlee, Sibyl Ventress. "Out of the Abundance of the Heart: Sarah Ann Parker Remond's Quest for Freedom." PhD diss., University of Massachusetts Amherst, 1997.

Buccola, Nicholas. *The Political Thought of Frederick Douglass: In Pursuit of American
Liberty*. New York: New York University Press, 2012.

Byrd, Brandon R., Leslie M. Alexander, and Russell Rickford. Introduction to *Ideas
in Unexpected Places: Reimagining Black Intellectual History*, edited by Brandon R.
Byrd, Leslie M. Alexander, and Russell Rickford, 3–12. Evanston, IL: Northwestern
University Press, 2022.

Capshaw, Katharine, and Anna Mae Duane, eds. *Who Writes for Black Children?
African American Children's Literature before 1900*. Minneapolis: University of Minnesota Press, 2017.

Carey, Brycchan, Markman Ellis, and Sarah Salih, eds. *Discourses of Slavery and Abolition: Britain and Its Colonies, 1760–1838*. New York: Palgrave Macmillan, 2004.

Carlson, Larry A. "'Those Pure Pages of Yours': Bronson Alcott's *Conversations with
Children on the Gospels*." *American Literature* 60, no. 3 (1988): 451–60.

Carpenter, Daniel. *Democracy by Petition: Popular Politics in Transformation, 1790–
1870*. Cambridge, MA: Harvard University Press, 2021.

Carrere, Marissa. "'Little Conversations': Child Communities and Political Agency in
the Writing of Frederick Douglass." In Moruzi and Smith, *Literary Cultures and
Nineteenth-Century Childhoods*, 139–56.

Carretta, Vincent. *Equiano, the African: Biography of a Self-Made Man*. Athens: University of Georgia Press, 2005.

Casey, Jim. "'We Need a Press—a Press of Our Own': The Black Press beyond Abolition." *Civil War History* 68, no. 2 (2022): 117–30.

Chase, Malcolm. "'Resolved in Defiance of Fool and of Knave'? Chartism, Children
and Conflict." In Birch and Llewellyn, *Conflict and Difference*, 126–40.

Clark, Beverly Lyon. *Kiddie Lit: The Cultural Construction of Children's Literature in
America*. Baltimore: Johns Hopkins University Press, 2003.

Cohen, Michèle. "The Pedagogy of Conversation in the Home: 'Familiar Conversation'
as a Pedagogical Tool in Eighteenth and Nineteenth-Century England." *Oxford
Review of Education* 41, no. 4 (2015): 447–63.

Connolly, Paula T. *Slavery in American Children's Literature, 1790–2010*. Iowa City:
University of Iowa Press, 2013.

Couey, J. Blake, and Jeremy Schipper. "Hide the Outcasts: Isaiah 16:3–4 and Fugitive
Slave Laws." *Harvard Theological Review* 115, no. 4 (2022): 519–37.

Crandall, John C. "Patriotism and Humanitarian Reform in Children's Literature, 1825–
1860." *American Quarterly* 21, no. 1 (1969): 3–22.

Cumbler, John T. "A Family Goes to War: Sacrifice and Honor for an Abolitionist Family." *Massachusetts Historical Review* 10 (2008): 57–83.

Cummings, Michael S. *Children's Voices in Politics*. Oxford, UK: Peter Lang, 2020.

Cutter, Martha J. "The Child's Illustrated Antislavery Talking Book: Abigail Field Mott's
Abridgment of Olaudah Equiano's *Interesting Narrative* for African American Children." In Capshaw and Duane, *Who Writes for Black Children?*, 117–44.

———. *The Illustrated Slave: Empathy, Graphic Narrative, and the Visual Culture of the Transatlantic Abolition Movement, 1800–1852*. Athens: University of Georgia Press, 2017.

———. *The Many Resurrections of Henry Box Brown*. Philadelphia: University of Pennsylvania Press, 2022.

Dain, Bruce. *A Hideous Monster of the Mind: American Race Theory in the Early Republic*. Cambridge, MA: Harvard University Press, 2002.

Darton, Lawrence. *The Dartons: An Annotated Check-list of Children's Books Issued by Two Publishing Houses, 1787–1876*. London: British Library, 2004.

David, Linda. *Children's Books Published by William Darton and His Sons*. Bloomington: Lilly Library, Indiana University, 1992.

Davis, David Brion. *The Problem of Slavery in Western Culture*. New York: Oxford University Press, 1988.

Densmore, Christopher. "Quaker Publishing in New York State, 1784–1860." *Quaker History* 74, no. 2 (1985): 39–57.

De Rosa, Deborah C. *Domestic Abolitionism and Juvenile Literature, 1830–1865*. Albany: State University of New York Press, 2003.

———, ed. *Into the Mouths of Babes: An Anthology of Children's Abolitionist Literature*. Westport, CT: Praeger, 2005.

de Schweinitz, Rebecca. *If We Could Change the World: Young People and America's Long Struggle for Racial Equality*. Chapel Hill: University of North Carolina Press, 2009.

———. "'Waked Up to Feel': Defining Childhood, Debating Slavery in Antebellum America." In Marten, *Children and Youth during the Civil War Era*, 13–28.

Douglass, Joseph L., Jr. *Frederick Douglass: A Family Biography, 1733–1896*. Shelbyville, KY: Winterlight Books, 2011.

Drescher, Seymour. *Abolition: A History of Slavery and Antislavery*. Cambridge: Cambridge University Press, 2009.

Duane, Anna Mae. *Educated for Freedom: The Incredible Story of Two Fugitive Schoolboys Who Grew Up to Change a Nation*. New York: New York University Press, 2020.

Duane, Anna Mae, and Katharine Capshaw. Introduction to Capshaw and Duane, *Who Writes for Black Children?*, ix–xxvii.

Eberle, Roxanne. "'Tales of Truth?': Amelia Opie's Antislavery Poetics." In Linkin and Behrendt, *Romanticism and Women Poets*, 71–98.

Edson, John R. "*Slave's Friend*." In Kelly, *Children's Periodicals of the United States*, 408–11.

Elbert, Monika, ed. *Enterprising Youth: Social Values and Acculturation in Nineteenth-Century American Children's Literature*. New York: Routledge, 2008.

Elson, Ruth Miller. *Guardians of Tradition: American Schoolbooks in the Nineteenth Century*. Lincoln: University of Nebraska Press, 1964.

Escott, Margaret. "Corbett, Panton." In *The House of Commons, 1820–1832*, vol. 4, edited by D. R. Fisher, 748–52. Cambridge: Cambridge University Press, 2009.

Fagan, Benjamin. "The Collective Making of *Frederick Douglass' Paper*." *Civil War History* 68, no. 2 (2022): 131–46.

Faulkner, Carol. *Lucretia Mott's Heresy: Abolition and Women's Rights in Nineteenth-Century America*. Philadelphia: University of Pennsylvania Press, 2011.

Field, Corinne T. *The Struggle for Equal Adulthood: Gender, Race, Age, and the Fight for Citizenship in Antebellum America*. Chapel Hill: University of North Carolina Press, 2014.

———. "Why Little Thinkers Are a Big Deal: The Relevance of Childhood Studies to Intellectual History." *Modern Intellectual History* 14, no. 1 (2017): 269–80.

Field, Corinne T., and Nicholas L. Syrett. Introduction to *Age in America: The Colonial Era to the Present*, edited by Corinne T. Field and Nicholas L. Syrett, 1–20. New York: New York University Press, 2015.

———. Introduction to "Chronological Age: A Useful Category of Historical Analysis." *American Historical Review* 125, no. 2 (2020): 371–84.

Fielder, Brigitte. "'As the Crow Flies': Black Children, Flying Africans, and Fantastic Futures in *The Brownies' Book*." *Journal of the History of Childhood and Youth* 14, no. 3 (2021): 413–36.

———. "Black Girls, White Girls, American Girls: Slavery and Racialized Perspectives in Abolitionist and Neoabolitionist Children's Literature." *Tulsa Studies in Women's Literature* 36, no. 2 (2017): 323–52.

———. "Frederick Douglass's Narrative of Childhood." *Black Perspectives* (AAIHS), April 23, 2019. www.aaihs.org.

———. "'Give the Children the Poems and Stories of Their Own People.'" *New York Times*, March 19, 2022. www.nytimes.com.

———. "John Brown, Black History, and Black Childhood: Contextualizing Lorenz Graham's John Brown Books." *Humanities* 11, no. 5 (2022): 1–18.

Filler, Louis. *The Crusade against Slavery, 1830–1860*. New York: Harper and Row, 1960.

Foner, Eric. *Gateway to Freedom: The Hidden History of America's Fugitive Slaves*. Oxford: Oxford University Press, 2015.

Fought, Leigh. *Women in the World of Frederick Douglass*. New York: Oxford University Press, 2017.

Francis, Richard. *Fruitlands: The Alcott Family and Their Search for Utopia*. New Haven, CT: Yale University Press, 2010.

Franklin, V. P. *The Young Crusaders: The Untold Story of the Children and Teenagers Who Galvanized the Civil Rights Movement*. Boston: Beacon, 2021.

Frick, John W. *Theatre, Culture and Temperance Reform in Nineteenth-Century America*. Cambridge: Cambridge University Press, 2003.

Furstenberg, François. *In the Name of the Father: Washington's Legacy, Slavery, and the Making of a Nation*. New York: Penguin, 2006.

Gallman, J. Matthew. *America's Joan of Arc: The Life of Anna Elizabeth Dickinson*. New York: Oxford University Press, 2006.

Gardner, Eric. *Black Print Unbound: The "Christian Recorder," African American Literature, and Periodical Culture*. New York: Oxford University Press, 2015.

———. "Of Bottles and Books: Reconsidering the Readers of Harriet Wilson's *Our Nig*." In Boggis, Raimon, and White, *Harriet Wilson's New England*, 3–26.

———. "'This Attempt of Their Sister': Harriet Wilson's *Our Nig* from Printer to Readers." *New England Quarterly* 66, no. 2 (1993): 226–46.

———. "Two Texts on Children and Christian Education." *PMLA* 123, no. 1 (2008): 156–65.

Gardner, Naomi. "Embroidering Emancipation: Female Abolitionists and Material Culture in Britain and the USA, c. 1780–1865." PhD diss., Royal Holloway, University of London, 2016.

Geist, Christopher D. "The *Slave's Friend*: An Abolitionist Magazine for Children." *American Periodicals* 9 (1999): 27–35.

Gellman, David N. *Liberty's Chain: Slavery, Abolition, and the Jay Family of New York.* Ithaca, NY: Cornell University Press, 2022.

Ginsberg, Lesley. "Of Babies, Beasts, and Bondage: Slavery and the Question of Citizenship in Antebellum American Children's Literature." In Levander and Singley, *American Child*, 85–105.

Gleadle, Kathryn, and Ryan Hanley. "Children against Slavery: Juvenile Agency and the Sugar Boycotts in Britain." *Transactions of the Royal Historical Society* 30 (2020): 97–117.

Glenn, Myra C. *Campaigns against Corporal Punishment: Prisoners, Sailors, Women, and Children in Antebellum America.* Albany: State University of New York Press, 1984.

Goddu, Teresa A. "Climate Activism as the New Abolitionism." *American Literary History*, online forum (2021): e58–e65.

———. "Reform." In Zboray and Zboray, *Oxford History of Popular Print Culture*, 597–610.

———. *Selling Antislavery: Abolition and Mass Media in Antebellum America.* Philadelphia: University of Pennsylvania Press, 2020.

Goodman, Paul. *Of One Blood: Abolitionism and the Origins of Racial Equality.* Berkeley: University of California Press, 1998.

Graham, Ruth. "Juvenile Travellers: Priscilla Wakefield's Excursions in Empire." *Journal of Imperial and Commonwealth History* 38, no. 3 (2010): 373–93.

Greenspan, Ezra. "Frederick Bailey Douglass and His People: A Family Biography." Unpublished manuscript.

Grenby, M. O. "The Origins of Children's Literature." In Grenby and Immel, *Cambridge Companion to Children's Literature*, 3–18.

Grenby, M. O., and Andrea Immel, eds. *The Cambridge Companion to Children's Literature.* Cambridge: Cambridge University Press, 2009.

Grinspan, Jon. *The Virgin Vote: How Young Americans Made Democracy Social, Politics Personal, and Voting Popular in the Nineteenth Century.* Chapel Hill: University of North Carolina Press, 2016.

Gross, Robert A., and Mary Kelley, eds. *A History of the Book in America.* Vol. 2, *An Extensive Republic: Print, Culture, and Society in the New Nation, 1790–1840.* Chapel Hill: University of North Carolina Press, 2010.

Hack, Daniel. *Reaping Something New: African American Transformations of Victorian Literature.* Princeton, NJ: Princeton University Press, 2017.

Hager, Christopher. *Word by Word: Emancipation and the Act of Writing*. Cambridge, MA: Harvard University Press, 2013.

Hale, Jon N. *A New Kind of Youth: Historically Black High Schools and Southern Student Activism, 1920–1975*. Chapel Hill: University of North Carolina Press, 2022.

Hantch, Annie B. "History of the Public Schools of Carlisle." Paper read before the Hamilton Library Historical Association, Carlisle, PA, February 19, 1909.

Harris, Leslie M. *In the Shadow of Slavery: African Americans in New York City, 1626–1863*. Chicago: University of Chicago Press, 2003.

Harris, Violet J. "Race Consciousness, Refinement, and Radicalism: Socialization in *The Brownies' Book*." *Children's Literature Association Quarterly* 14, no. 4 (1989): 192–96.

Harrold, Stanley. *The Abolitionists and the South, 1831–1861*. Lexington: University Press of Kentucky, 1995.

Haywood, Chanta M. "Constructing Childhood: The *Christian Recorder* and Literature for Black Children, 1854–1865." *African American Review* 36, no. 3 (2002): 417–28.

Heywood, Colin. *A History of Childhood: Children and Childhood in the West from Medieval to Modern Times*. Cambridge, UK: Polity, 2001.

Hines, Michael. "Learning Freedom: Education, Elevation, and New York's African-American Community, 1827–1829." *History of Education Quarterly* 56, no. 4 (2016): 618–45.

Hochman, Barbara. *"Uncle Tom's Cabin" and the Reading Revolution: Race, Literacy, Childhood, and Fiction, 1851–1911*. Amherst: University of Massachusetts Press, 2011.

Holcomb, Julie L. *Moral Commerce: Quakers and the Transatlantic Boycott of the Slave Labor Economy*. Ithaca, NY: Cornell University Press, 2016.

Holden, Vanessa M. "Generation, Resistance, and Survival: African-American Children and the Southampton Rebellion of 1831." *Slavery and Abolition* 38, no. 4 (2017): 673–96.

Horton, James Oliver. "Generations of Protest: Black Families and Social Reform in Ante-Bellum Boston." *New England Quarterly* 49, no. 2 (1976): 242–56.

Horton, James Oliver, and Lois E. Horton. *In Hope of Liberty: Culture, Community and Protest among Northern Free Blacks, 1700–1860*. New York: Oxford University Press, 1997.

Hutton, Frankie. *The Early Black Press in America, 1827 to 1860*. Westport, CT: Greenwood Press, 1993.

Ito, Akiyo. "Olaudah Equiano and the New York Artisans: The First American Edition of *The Interesting Narrative of the Life of Olaudah Equiano, or Gustavus Vassa, the African*." *Early American Literature* 32, no. 1 (1997): 82–101.

Jackson, Debra. "A Black Journalist in Civil War Virginia: Robert Hamilton and the *Anglo-African*." *Virginia Magazine of History and Biography* 116, no. 1 (2008): 42–72.

Jackson, Kellie Carter. *Force and Freedom: Black Abolitionists and the Politics of Violence*. Philadelphia: University of Pennsylvania Press, 2019.

Jackson, Maurice. *Let This Voice Be Heard: Anthony Benezet, Father of Atlantic Abolitionism*. Philadelphia: University of Pennsylvania Press, 2010.

Jeffrey, Julie Roy. *Abolitionists Remember: Antislavery Autobiographies and the Unfinished Work of Emancipation.* Chapel Hill: University of North Carolina Press, 2008.

———. *The Great Silent Army of Abolitionism: Ordinary Women in the Antislavery Movement.* Chapel Hill: University of North Carolina Press, 1998.

———. "'No Occurrence in Human History Is More Deserving of Commemoration than This': Abolitionist Celebrations of Freedom." In McCarthy and Stauffer, *Prophets of Protest,* 200–219.

Jirik, Michael E. "Abolition and Academe: Struggles for Freedom and Equality at British and American Colleges, 1742–1855." PhD diss., University of Massachusetts Amherst, 2019.

John, Richard R. *Spreading the News: The American Postal System from Franklin to Morse.* Cambridge, MA: Harvard University Press, 1995.

Jones, Martha S. *All Bound Up Together: The Woman Question in African American Public Culture, 1830–1900.* Chapel Hill: University of North Carolina Press, 2007.

Jones-Rogers, Stephanie E. *They Were Her Property: White Women as Slave Owners in the American South.* New Haven, CT: Yale University Press, 2019.

Jordan, Ryan P. *Slavery and the Meetinghouse: The Quakers and the Abolitionist Dilemma, 1820–1865.* Bloomington: Indiana University Press, 2007.

Joy, Natalie. "The Indian's Cause: Abolitionists and Native American Rights." *Journal of the Civil War Era* 8, no. 2 (2018): 215–42.

Joyce, Barry. *The First U.S. History Textbooks: Constructing and Disseminating the American Tale in the Nineteenth Century.* Lanham, MD: Lexington Books, 2015.

Keller, Holly. "Juvenile Antislavery Narrative and Notions of Childhood." *Children's Literature* 24 (1996): 86–100.

Kelley, Mary. "'Talents Committed to Your Care': Reading and Writing Radical Abolitionism in Antebellum America." *New England Quarterly* 88, no. 1 (2015): 37–72.

Kelly, R. Gordon, ed. *Children's Periodicals of the United States.* Westport, CT: Greenwood Press, 1984.

Keralis, Spencer D. C. "Feeling Animal: Pet-Making and Mastery in the *Slave's Friend.*" *American Periodicals* 22, no. 2 (2012): 121–38.

Kerr-Ritchie, J. R. *Rites of August First: Emancipation Day in the Black Atlantic World.* Baton Rouge: Louisiana State University Press, 2007.

King, Wilma. *Stolen Childhood: Slave Youth in Nineteenth-Century America.* 2nd ed. Bloomington: Indiana University Press, 2011.

Kluger, Jeffrey. "Kids Just Brought Montana to Court over Climate Change: The Case Could Make Waves beyond the State." *Time,* June 23, 2023. www.time.com.

Kuebler-Wolf, Elizabeth. "'Train Up a Child in the Way He Should Go': The Image of Idealized Childhood in the Slavery Debate, 1850–1870." In Marten, *Children and Youth during the Civil War Era,* 29–45.

Lamore, Eric D. "Olaudah Equiano in the United States: Abigail's Mott 1829 Abridged Edition of the *Interesting Narrative.*" In Lamore, *Reading African American Autobiography,* 66–88.

————, ed. *Reading African American Autobiography: Twenty-First Century Contexts and Criticism*. Madison: University of Wisconsin Press, 2017.

Levander, Caroline F., and Carol J. Singley, eds. *The American Child: A Cultural Studies Reader*. New Brunswick, NJ: Rutgers University Press, 2003.

Levine-Gronningsater, Sarah. "Delivering Freedom: Gradual Emancipation, Black Legal Culture, and the Origins of Sectional Crisis in New York, 1759–1870." PhD diss., University of Chicago, 2014.

Lindey, Sara. "Sympathy and Science: Representing Girls in Abolitionist Children's Literature." *Journal of the Midwest Modern Language Association* 45, no. 1 (2012): 62–71.

Lindhorst, Marie. "Politics in a Box: Sarah Mapps Douglass and the Female Literary Association, 1831–1833." *Pennsylvania History* 65, no. 3 (1998): 263–78.

Linkin, Harriet Kramer, and Stephen C. Behrendt, eds. *Romanticism and Women Poets: Opening the Doors of Reception*. Lexington: University Press of Kentucky, 1999.

Lockard, Joe. "Slavery, Market Censorship and US Antebellum Schoolbook Publishing." *History of Education* 51, no. 2 (2022): 207–23.

Logan, Rayford W. *The Negro in American Life and Thought: The Nadir, 1877–1901*. New York: Dial Press, 1954.

Loughran, Trish. *The Republic in Print: Print Culture in the Age of U.S. Nation Building, 1770–1870*. New York: Columbia University Press, 2007.

Lowery, Tabitha. "Early Black Poetry, Social Justice, and Black Children: Receptions of Child Activism in African American Literary History." PhD diss., West Virginia University, 2020.

MacCann, Donnarae. *White Supremacy in Children's Literature: Characterizations of African Americans, 1830–1900*. New York: Routledge, 1998.

MacLeod, Anne Scott. *A Moral Tale: Children's Fiction and American Culture, 1820–1860*. Hamden, CT: Archon Books, 1975.

Magdol, Edward. *The Antislavery Rank and File: A Social Profile of the Abolitionists' Constituency*. Westport, CT: Greenwood Press, 1986.

Marten, James, ed. *Children and Youth during the Civil War Era*. New York: New York University Press, 2012.

————. *The Children's Civil War*. Chapel Hill: University of North Carolina Press, 1998.

Masur, Kate. *Until Justice Be Done: America's First Civil Rights Movement, from the Revolution to Reconstruction*. New York: W. W. Norton, 2021.

Mayer, Henry. *All on Fire: William Lloyd Garrison and the Abolition of Slavery*. New York: St. Martin's Press, 1998.

McCarthy, Timothy Patrick, and John Stauffer, eds. *Prophets of Protest: Reconsidering the History of American Abolitionism*. New York: New Press, 2006.

McDaniel, W. Caleb. "The Fourth and the First: Abolitionist Holidays, Respectability, and Radical Interracial Reform." *American Quarterly* 57, no. 1 (2005): 129–51.

McGill, Meredith L. *American Literature and the Culture of Reprinting, 1834–1853*. Philadelphia: University of Pennsylvania Press, 2003.

McPherson, James M. *The Abolitionist Legacy: From Reconstruction to the NAACP.* Princeton, NJ: Princeton University Press, 1975.

Midgley, Clare. *Women against Slavery: The British Campaigns, 1780–1870.* London: Routledge, 1992.

Mintz, Steven. *Huck's Raft: A History of American Childhood.* Cambridge, MA: Harvard University Press, 2004.

———. "Why the History of Childhood Matters." *Journal of the History of Childhood and Youth* 5, no. 1 (2012): 15–28.

Monaghan, Charles, and E. Jennifer Monaghan. "Schoolbooks." In Gross and Kelley, *History of the Book in America*, 304–18.

Montrie, Chad. *The Myth of "Silent Spring": Rethinking the Origins of American Environmentalism.* Oakland: University of California Press, 2018.

Morgan, Kenneth. *Slavery and the British Empire: From Africa to America.* Oxford: Oxford University Press, 2007.

Moruzi, Kristine, and Michelle J. Smith, eds. *Literary Cultures and Nineteenth-Century Childhoods.* Cham, Switzerland: Palgrave Macmillan, 2023.

Moss, Hilary J. *Schooling Citizens: The Struggle for African American Education in Antebellum America.* Chicago: University of Chicago Press, 2009.

Neem, Johann N. *Democracy's Schools: The Rise of Public Education in America.* Baltimore: Johns Hopkins University Press, 2017.

Nel, Philip, and Lissa Paul, eds. *Keywords for Children's Literature.* New York: New York University Press, 2011.

Newman, Richard S. *The Transformation of American Abolitionism: Fighting Slavery in the Early Republic.* Chapel Hill: University of North Carolina Press, 2002.

Oldfield, J. R. "Anti-Slavery Sentiment in Children's Literature, 1750–1850." *Slavery and Abolition* 10, no. 1 (1989): 44–59.

———. *Popular Politics and British Anti-Slavery: The Mobilisation of Public Opinion against the Slave Trade, 1787–1807.* London: Routledge, 1998.

Olsavsky, Jesse. *The Most Absolute Abolition: Runaways, Vigilance Committees, and the Rise of Revolutionary Abolitionism, 1835–1861.* Baton Rouge: Louisiana State University Press, 2022.

———. "The Underground Railroad." In Roy, *Frederick Douglass in Context*, 281–92.

Perry, Lewis. *Childhood, Marriage, and Reform: Henry Clarke Wright, 1797–1870.* Chicago: University of Chicago Press, 1980.

Peterson, Carla L. "Black Life in Freedom: Creating an Elite Culture." In Berlin and Harris, *Slavery in New York*, 181–214.

Polgar, Paul J. *Standard-Bearers of Equality: America's First Abolition Movement.* Chapel Hill: University of North Carolina Press, 2019.

Porter, Dorothy B. "The Organized Educational Activities of Negro Literary Societies, 1828–1846." *Journal of Negro Education* 5, no. 4 (1936): 555–76.

Pryor, Elizabeth Stordeur. *Colored Travelers: Mobility and the Fight for Citizenship before the Civil War.* Chapel Hill: University of North Carolina Press, 2016.

Quanquin, Hélène. *Men in the American Women's Rights Movement, 1830–1890: Cumbersome Allies*. New York: Routledge, 2020.

Quarles, Benjamin. *Black Abolitionists*. New York: Oxford University Press, 1969.

Rael, Patrick. *Black Identity and Black Protest in the Antebellum North*. Chapel Hill: University of North Carolina Press, 2002.

———. *Eighty-Eight Years: The Long Death of Slavery in the United States, 1777–1865*. Athens: University of Georgia Press, 2015.

Reinier, Jacqueline S. *From Virtue to Character: American Childhood, 1775–1850*. New York: Twayne, 1996.

Rinehart, Nicholas. "Reparative Semantics: On Slavery and the Language of History." *Commonplace*, January 2022. http://commonplace.online.

Roy, Michaël, ed. *Frederick Douglass in Context*. Cambridge: Cambridge University Press, 2021.

———. *Fugitive Texts: Slave Narratives in Antebellum Print Culture*. Translated by Susan Pickford. Madison: University of Wisconsin Press, 2022.

———. Introduction to Roy, *Frederick Douglass in Context*, 1–6.

———. "'Throwing Pearls before Swine': The Strange Publication History of *Vie de Frédéric Douglass, esclave américain* (1848)." *Slavery and Abolition* 40, no. 4 (2019): 727–49.

Salenius, Sirpa. *An Abolitionist Abroad: Sarah Parker Remond in Cosmopolitan Europe*. Amherst: University of Massachusetts Press, 2016.

Sánchez-Eppler, Karen. "Childhood." In Nel and Paul, *Keywords for Children's Literature*, 35–41.

———. *Dependent States: The Child's Part in Nineteenth-Century American Culture*. Chicago: University of Chicago Press, 2005.

Schroth, Evelyn. "*The Youth's Emancipator*." In Kelly, *Children's Periodicals of the United States*, 518–22.

Secord, James A. "Newton in the Nursery: Tom Telescope and the Philosophy of Tops and Balls, 1761–1838." *History of Science* 23, no. 2 (1985): 127–51.

Sinha, Manisha. *The Slave's Cause: A History of Abolition*. New Haven, CT: Yale University Press, 2016.

Sklar, Kathryn Kish, and James Brewer Stewart, eds. *Women's Rights and Transatlantic Antislavery in the Era of Emancipation*. New Haven, CT: Yale University Press, 2007.

Sledge, Martha L. "'A Is an Abolitionist': The *Anti-Slavery Alphabet* and the Politics of Literacy." In Elbert, *Enterprising Youth*, 69–82.

Smith, Johanna M. "Slavery, Abolition, and the Nation in Priscilla Wakefield's Tour Books for Children." In Carey, Ellis, and Salih, *Discourses of Slavery and Abolition*, 175–93.

Smith, Katharine Capshaw. *Children's Literature of the Harlem Renaissance*. Bloomington: Indiana University Press, 2004.

Stabell, Ivy Linton. "Innocence in Ann Plato's and Susan Paul's Black Children Biographies." In Capshaw and Duane, *Who Writes for Black Children?*, 75–93.

Sterling, Dorothy. *Lucretia Mott*. New York: Feminist Press at the City University of New York, 1999.

Stevens, Elizabeth C. *Elizabeth Buffum Chace and Lillie Chace Wyman: A Century of Abolitionist, Suffragist and Workers' Rights Activism.* Jefferson, NC: McFarland, 2003.
———. "Elizabeth Buffum Chace and Lillie Chace Wyman: Motherhood as a Subversive Activity in Nineteenth Century Rhode Island." *Quaker History* 84, no. 1 (1995): 37–58.
———. "'A Symmetrical, Harmonious, Substantial Character': Schools for Abolitionist Children in Mid-Nineteenth-Century New England." In Benes, *Schooldays in New England,* 59–72.
Strickland, Charles. "A Transcendentalist Father: The Child-Rearing Practices of Bronson Alcott." *History of Childhood Quarterly* 1, no. 1 (1973): 4–51.
Stumpf, Erik A. "Children with a Cause: Training Antebellum Children for the Abolition of Slavery." PhD diss., Iowa State University, 2018.
Sundquist, Eric J. *Empire and Slavery in American Literature, 1820–1865.* Jackson: University Press of Mississippi, 2006.
Taylor, Nikki M. *Frontiers of Freedom: Cincinnati's Black Community, 1802–1868.* Athens: Ohio University Press, 2005.
Tikoff, Valentina K. "A Role Model for African American Children: Abigail Field Mott's *Life and Adventures of Olaudah Equiano* and White Northern Abolitionism." In Capshaw and Duane, *Who Writes for Black Children?,* 94–116.
Turley, David. *The Culture of English Antislavery, 1780–1860.* London: Routledge, 1991.
Van Broekhoven, Deborah Bingham. *The Devotion of These Women: Rhode Island in the Antislavery Network.* Amherst: University of Massachusetts Press, 2002.
Wadsworth, Sarah. "Children's Literature." In Zboray and Zboray, *Oxford History of Popular Print Culture,* 549–63.
Wall, John, ed. *Exploring Children's Suffrage: Interdisciplinary Perspectives on Ageless Voting.* London: Palgrave Macmillan, 2022.
———. *Give Children the Vote: On Democratizing Democracy.* London: Bloomsbury Academic, 2022.
Webster, Crystal Lynn. *Beyond the Boundaries of Childhood: African American Children in the Antebellum North.* Chapel Hill: University of North Carolina Press, 2021.
Weierman, Karen Woods. *The Case of the Slave-Child, Med: Free Soil in Antislavery Boston.* Amherst: University of Massachusetts Press, 2019.
Weikle-Mills, Courtney. *Imaginary Citizens: Child Readers and the Limits of American Independence, 1640–1868.* Baltimore: Johns Hopkins University Press, 2013.
Wells, Jonathan Daniel. *The Kidnapping Club: Wall Street, Slavery, and Resistance on the Eve of the Civil War.* New York: Bold Type Books, 2020.
Wesley, Charles H. "The Negro in the Organization of Abolition." *Phylon* 2, no. 3 (1941): 223–35.
White, William P. "A Historic Nineteenth Century Character." *Journal of the Presbyterian Historical Society* 10, no. 5 (1920): 161–74.
Wilder, Craig Steven. *In the Company of Black Men: The African Influence on African American Culture in New York City.* New York: New York University Press, 2001.
Winch, Julie. *A Gentleman of Color: The Life of James Forten.* New York: Oxford University Press, 2002.

———. "Sarah Forten's Anti-Slavery Networks." In Sklar and Stewart, *Women's Rights and Transatlantic Antislavery in the Era of Emancipation*, 143–57.

Wirzbicki, Peter. *Fighting for the Higher Law: Black and White Transcendentalists against Slavery*. Philadelphia: University of Pennsylvania Press, 2021.

Woodard, Vincent. *The Delectable Negro: Human Consumption and Homoeroticism within U.S. Slave Culture*. New York: New York University Press, 2014.

Worthen, Dennis B. "Edward Robinson Squibb (1819–1900): Advocate of Product Standards." *Journal of the American Pharmacists Association* 46, no. 6 (2006): 754–58.

Wright, Marion M. Thompson. *The Education of Negroes in New Jersey*. New York: Teachers College, Columbia University, 1941.

Wright, Nazera Sadiq. *Black Girlhood in the Nineteenth Century*. Urbana: University of Illinois Press, 2016.

———. "'Our Hope Is in the Rising Generation': Locating African American Children's Literature in the Children's Department of the *Colored American*." In Capshaw and Duane, *Who Writes for Black Children?*, 147–63.

Yacovone, Donald. *Teaching White Supremacy: America's Democratic Ordeal and the Forging of Our National Identity*. New York: Pantheon, 2022.

———. "The Transformation of the Black Temperance Movement, 1827–1854: An Interpretation." *Journal of the Early Republic* 8, no. 3 (1988): 281–97.

Yee, Shirley J. *Black Women Abolitionists: A Study in Activism, 1828–1860*. Knoxville: University of Tennessee Press, 1992.

Yellin, Jean Fagan, and John C. Van Horne, eds. *The Abolitionist Sisterhood: Women's Political Culture in Antebellum America*. Ithaca, NY: Cornell University Press, 1994.

Zaeske, Susan. *Signatures of Citizenship: Petitioning, Antislavery, and Women's Political Identity*. Chapel Hill: University of North Carolina Press, 2003.

Zboray, Ronald J. *A Fictive People: Antebellum Economic Development and the American Reading Public*. New York: Oxford University Press, 1993.

Zboray, Ronald J., and Mary Saracino Zboray, eds. *The Oxford History of Popular Print Culture*. Vol. 5, *US Popular Print Culture to 1860*. Oxford: Oxford University Press, 2019.

INDEX

Page numbers in italics indicate Figures

ABOUT THE AUTHOR

MICHAËL ROY is Associate Professor of American Studies at Université Paris Nanterre and a Fellow of the Institut Universitaire de France. He is the author of *Fugitive Texts: Slave Narratives in Antebellum Print Culture* and the editor of *Frederick Douglass in Context* and *Escapes from Cayenne: A Story of Socialism and Slavery in an Age of Revolution and Reaction.*